WITHDRAWN

# Allen Klein

## BOOKS BY FRED GOODMAN

*Fortune's Fool*

*The Secret City*

*The Mansion on the Hill*

# ALLEN KLEIN

## THE MAN WHO BAILED OUT
## THE BEATLES, MADE
## THE STONES,
## AND TRANSFORMED
## ROCK & ROLL

## FRED GOODMAN

AN EAMON DOLAN BOOK • HOUGHTON MIFFLIN HARCOURT
BOSTON NEW YORK 2015

For information about permission to reproduce selections from this book,
write to Permissions, Houghton Mifflin Harcourt Publishing Company,
215 Park Avenue South, New York, New York 10003.

www.hmhco.com

*Library of Congress Cataloging-in-Publication Data*
Goodman, Fred.
Allen Klein : the man who bailed out the Beatles, made the Stones,
and transformed rock & roll / Fred Goodman.
pages  cm
"An Eamon Dolan Book."
Includes bibliographical references and index.
ISBN 978-0-547-89686-1 (hardcover) — ISBN 978-0-547-89689-2 (ebook)
1. Klein, Allen, 1931–2009. 2. Sound recording executives and producers
— Biography. 3. Rolling Stones. 4. Beatles. I. Title.
ML429.K58G66 2015
781.66092 — dc23
[B]
2015007138

Book design by Brian Moore

Printed in the United States of America
DOC 10 9 8 7 6 5 4 3 2 1

*For Jeffrey Ressner and Eddie Karp*

# CONTENTS

The devil is a spirit that is neither good nor evil; he is considered to be the guardian of most of the secrets that are accessible to human beings and to have strength and power over material things. Since he is a fallen angel, he is identified with the human race, and he is always ready to make deals and exchange favors.

—PAULO COELHO, *THE PILGRIMAGE*


*Now he worships at an altar of a stagnant pool*
*And when he sees his reflection, he's fulfilled*
*For man is opposed to fair play*
*He wants it all and he wants it his way.*

—BOB DYLAN, "LICENSE TO KILL"

# PROLOGUE: LONDON, AUGUST 1969

EVERYONE IN THE WORLD wants to be a Beatle. Everyone, perhaps, except the Beatles.

Their musical and cultural impact is nearly unimaginable and unlikely to be duplicated soon. Not merely famous and successful, the Beatles have transcended music and caused listeners around the world to take a fresh look at their own possibilities and expectations. For that they are adored — not in the manner of pop or film stars but as saints, the fathers of nations, or any unspoiled signs of hope and possibility are adored. But while they may be a light to the world, the Beatles are also a deeply troubled business partnership. They have complicated problems they are unequipped to handle, many as broad and unique as their success. When no road maps exist, who will drive the car?

Until two years ago the driver was Brian Epstein, their manager. But he died at thirty-two of an accidental drug overdose. A gifted impresario and earnest advocate, Epstein had recognized the diamond in the rough, overseen its cutting and buffing. But he was nowhere near as visionary in business. His deals for the band were consistently substandard — not just for the biggest and most influential group in the world, but for any group. Still, he had helped the Beatles to become stars, which was as much as they'd dreamed of at the start, and they had trusted him. Though shocked by the unexpected tragedy of

Brian's death, John Lennon instantly foresaw a second calamity. "We've fuckin' had it," he told himself.

Since then, the group's finances have grown increasingly precarious. Attempting to run their own affairs, the Beatles formed Apple Corps, a move that now looms as a disaster. Conceived in a burst of optimism and largesse as a new kind of creative company for a new kind of world, Apple is wide ranging, ill conceived, and out of control. Caught in a vise of Epstein's inferior and poorly paid contracts on one side and the folly of their own making that is Apple on the other, Lennon saw bankruptcy ahead. But now — finally! — after years of not knowing where to turn, Lennon has found his man in Allen Klein.

Blunt-featured and barrel-chested with a full head of dramatically dark, pomaded hair, Klein doesn't share his clients' flair for fashion. He prefers sneakers and sweatshirts to paisleys and Nehru jackets. But while Klein doesn't look like the most powerful and controversial player in the music business, he is in fact a ruthless and brilliant businessman given to bold talk, bolder strategies, and a confrontational style that ranges from brusque to insulting.

Klein has been making regular forays to London, selling himself to producers and artists and battling the business practices of record companies, music publishers, and booking agents when no one else would. He is more interested in results than rules. "Don't talk to me about ethics," Klein says dismissively. "Every man makes his own. It's like a war. You choose your side early and from then on, you're being shot at. The man you beat is likely to call you unethical. So what?" He is an obsessive chess master who keeps opponents on the back foot with a painstakingly constructed game of seemingly endless litigation, negotiation, and obfuscation. To the hidebound, class-conscious record executives and press of 1960s Britain, he embodies every cliché of ill breeding and grotesquerie that can be conjured by the phrase *New York Jew*, and they detest him. Yet what most upsets the establishment is that he is right.

For more than a decade, Klein has been arguing — vociferously and alone — that rock and pop artists are grossly underpaid, that the industry infantilizes them in order to cheat them. Though a brawler by temperament, he is an accountant by training, a gimlet-eyed skeptic decoding the record industry's rules and ledgers and rewriting them in the artists' favor. Because of Klein, his clients — most notably Sam Cooke and the Rolling Stones — have taken once-unthinkable giant steps, reaping bonanzas and gaining creative control over their work and careers. In 1965, when the Beatles were still receiving a royalty of a penny a record — split four ways — Klein negotiated record deals for the Stones worth over two and a half million dollars. This did not escape the notice of either Lennon or his partner Paul McCartney. Lennon is a big fan of Klein, but McCartney doesn't like him; he finds Klein abrasive, and he knows that Klein demands an outsize share and habitually finds creative ways to cut himself a piece of an artist's holdings and career.

John, otherwise suspicious of businessmen, has a special bond with the up-from-the-streets Klein. He loves that he comes on like gangbusters. Allen doesn't confine himself to beating up adversaries; an adviser in a business lousy with professional handholders and toadies, he's the pistol-packing, face-slapping tough guy from an old movie. Lennon is ready to give Klein carte blanche; Allen will be the answer, the bulwark and savior — the gunslinger they so desperately need. George Harrison and Ringo Starr agree, and in the spring of 1969, Allen Klein becomes the Beatles' business manager.

For Klein, who has yearned, strategized, and schemed for years to manage the Beatles, it's more than sweet. It's validation. Like everyone else in the world, Klein wants to be a Beatle — just not for the same reasons. Now he is the undisputed master of the music business, managing the affairs of the Beatles *and* the Rolling Stones. He may be more powerful and transformative than anyone before or after him in the music industry. For him, money alone has never been proof of that — he likes it, wants it, and spends it lustily, but doesn't use it to keep score. It is the work, the groundbreaking deals that only he can conjure, that tells the tale.

He certainly has his work cut out for him now. The Beatles' affairs are a mess, an unwieldy, seaweed-slippery anchor chain that defies movement let alone unwinding. Management contracts, publishing and record deals — everything is twisted together and problematic. Just dismantling and restructuring Apple could keep him busy for a year. It has already kept him away from his Broadway office and in London for months. And he *still* has to find the Beatles' money — it shocked him to see how little they actually had — if he wants to make this work and prove himself peerless. Who could fail to appreciate that?

Keith Richards, for one. It's a busy and challenging time for Richards and his fellow Rolling Stones. They have a new producer, Jimmy Miller, and a new lead guitarist, Mick Taylor, to replace the undependable and drugged-out Brian Jones. For Jones, it proved the end; just a few weeks after Taylor took over, Jones was discovered drowned in his pool. But the Rolling Stones have found another gear. Their first album with Miller, *Beggars Banquet,* is at least as good as anything they've ever done and a great deal more ambitious and professional than their previous work. Their first session with Taylor resulted in the single "Honky Tonk Women," an enormous hit on its way to topping sales charts around the world. The Stones are rolling like never before.

Andrew Loog Oldham, the Stones' original co-manager and image guru, brought Klein onboard in 1965 to renegotiate the band's contracts and help put them over the top in America. When Oldham and the Stones later parted, Klein reached an understanding with singer Mick Jagger: Allen, who steers clear of the band's creative decisions, oversees business in the States; the Stones — meaning Jagger — handle the creative and business ends in London.

Mick is becoming increasingly sophisticated and hands-on regarding the Stones' business, and though he will later characterize Klein as "very much ahead of his time," he and Allen are growing wary of each other. But Richards is another story; he is the only member of the band whom Klein feels genuine affection for. For his part, the guitarist considers Oldham's hiring of Klein to be his savviest move, and he credits Allen with helping the band understand and conquer America, turning the Stones into a global attraction. If there's a Klein stalwart in the band, it's Keith. But not today.

The band, having recently played an enormous free concert in Hyde

Park for 250,000 fans, is planning an American tour, its first in three years. "Honky Tonk Women" is climbing the charts, and the Stones are completing a new album, *Let It Bleed,* for Christmas. The band, with a transfusion of new blood from Taylor and Miller, sounds fantastic. It's time for the Stones to get back out there, back on the road in the States. America is Klein's responsibility, and the group needs him.

It's impossible for him to take on that responsibility, he tells them. Can't Keith understand that he's up to his neck in Beatles business?

Richards couldn't care less what happens to the Beatles, who had stopped touring years earlier — and Klein should know it.

"Allen," he says, "only one of us is a working band."

Klein reddens. It's a rare moment of embarrassment. Richards has a right to expect him to deliver, a right to believe in himself and his band over everything. But having come this far, achieved his prize, Klein is too intent on the Beatles to be of any use to the Rolling Stones.

But he'll make it up to them later. There isn't a situation he can't get out of, a deal he can't rewrite, a judgment he can't reverse, a client or a woman he can't bring around.

That's who he is; that's what he does.

# ALLEN KLEIN

# 1

## A FOUNDLING'S TALE

IT MAY HAVE BEEN the dramatic grounds; he may have been impressed that George C. Scott and Colleen Dewhurst were renting it. Whatever the reason, Allen Klein wanted the house.

Practically, buying it made more sense than moving back to New Jersey; if he wasn't in London, Allen was either in his midtown office or out with clients late into the night, and he was unlikely to ever find his way home if it meant crossing the George Washington Bridge. He could certainly afford it now—although his not having money rarely kept him from getting what he wanted. The year was 1966 and the price was a stratospheric one hundred and fifty thousand dollars.

It was a regal house—a rich man's house—on a wooded, meandering estate road in the exclusive and surprisingly bucolic Riverdale section of the Bronx. Set back from a cliff, stone walls rose behind tall, weathered stockade fences hiding a front lawn as long and green as a fairway and a view from the property's western edge that is more than picturesque; it is violent and indomitable as only nature can be, and to a degree one rarely associates with New York City: two hundred feet below, the wide and seething Hudson River floods in and out with the tides, while a mile across, on the Jersey side, the towering red wall of the Palisades climbs forbiddingly skyward.

To the surprise of everyone, not least the in-laws who had been propping him up financially, Allen has become wildly successful. Allen Klein and Associates, his small accounting and business-management firm, rocketed into profitability two years earlier, first with Sam Cooke and Bobby Vinton and then with a string of British rock acts that included the Dave Clark Five, the Animals, Herman's Hermits, Donovan, Lulu, and the Kinks and culminated in the Rolling Stones. Later, when Allen manages the Beatles, the front doorbell will chime the chorus of "All You Need Is Love." But if Klein is feeling mischievous, as he often is, he will call his home "the house that Jagger built."

And build it they did. Allen and his wife, Betty, immediately made many improvements: terraced garden, back patio, swimming pool. And, of course, the bathrooms. There had been three when they bought the house; now there were eleven, including two in the new pool cabana and one for each of the six bedrooms. It was a subject of some ribbing from friends and guests—"Jesus, Allen, what the hell have you been eating?"—yet the bathrooms and their privacy were the most important part of the house for Allen.

The earliest homes Allen could remember were with his grandparents. When Allen was born, in December 1931—the youngest of four children and the only son—his mother, Rose, brought him home to the Newark apartment of her in-laws on Springfield Avenue. The Jewish Newark of the thirties revolved around two south-side neighborhoods: Weequahic and the working-class Clinton Hill, where the Kleins lived. "Weequahic was mainly the upper-class Jews," said Allen's sister Naomi Henkle. "Weequahic High was the Jew school. If you were Jewish and had fifty cents in your pocket, you went there. It was upper crust." The Kleins weren't upper crust. Allen's father, Philip, was a butcher.

Taciturn and distant, Philip Klein was a perplexing man whose most lasting impact on Allen was to make him feel unloved. Family legend had it that Philip was playing cards when Allen was born. "You have a king to go with your three queens," the doctor dryly informed him. It was Allen's paternal grandfather, Sam, a rabbi and *mashgiach,* or kosherer, who took an interest in him and became a substitute father figure.

"I really loved my grandfather," Klein recalled. "He was a different sort of a guy. He didn't speak much — and only Hungarian and Yiddish. But he was so good. He worked six and a half days a week, dressed in a black suit with a top hat, and would bless the meat and check to see the way that they killed the animals. He worked until he was eighty-one. That was one thing he taught me: he gave me a work ethic. He walked home one day, said he wasn't feeling well, and went to lie down. He never got up again. He was also learned and he took no shit from my grandmother. She was a *farbissineh"*— Yiddish for an embittered, sullen person —"and never smiled." Allen remembered his grandparents' apartment. It was around the corner from a cemetery and next door to a four-lane bowling alley operated by the Moose Lodge. What he didn't remember was his mother.

Allen's parents, Philip and Rose, lived a hard and precarious life. Sent to America at the age of thirteen, Philip had risen to the occasion, earning enough money to bring over his sisters and his parents. He gained his American citizenship by serving as an MP during the First World War. But it was Rose, who'd arrived in America as an infant, who taught Philip to read and write English. She bore him four children and was his partner and coworker in a butcher shop. "I think she really carried her weight," Allen said. Ill during her final pregnancy, Rose died of cancer at thirty-two, when Allen was nine months old. Her passing was a blow to the family and sent Allen's life careening in unforeseen directions. When the butcher shop succumbed to the one-two punch of the Depression and the loss of Rose's help, the Kleins could no longer afford their own apartment. After her death, Philip worked at Reinfeld's, a market in Spring Valley, New York, owned by a cousin. But a full-time job and four children was more than he could handle. He relied on his two older teenage daughters, Esther and Anna, to keep an eye on three-year-old Naomi, but Allen was problematic. Barely a year old, he was sent to live with his maternal grandparents, Joe and Anita Brown, and their daughter, Helen, in their apartment on

Newark's South Nineteenth Street. Delighted to care for Rose's baby, they doted on Allen.

That didn't please his paternal grandparents, who, unlike Joe and Anita, were deeply religious. They knew the Browns loved Allen, but they abhorred the thought of having their grandson brought up by nonobservant Jews. *The woman can't go to shul or the mikvah*—the ritual bath used by Orthodox Jews—*but she can play cards?* It wasn't right.

Everything changed in the summer of 1935 when Philip received an urgent phone call at work. It was the hospital. Seven-year-old Naomi had fallen from a moving car.

"My sister Esther was working and Anna was supposed to be the watchdog," Naomi said. "She took me on one of her safari rides one day with a bunch of wild Indians. I fell out of a rumble seat and my father had to come get me in the hospital. Anna was always a wild child. She had, what, five husbands?" Clearly, the girls needed more supervision—and Philip's parents were still carping about their grandson being raised like a goy at the Browns'. That August, Philip solved all his problems by having Anna, Naomi, and four-year-old Allen placed in Newark's Hebrew Orphanage and Sheltering Home.

Though he didn't know what was happening, Allen remembered the day vividly. "It was very strange," he recalled. "My grandmother was dressing me and crying. I was standing on a chair and crying because she was crying. And I got put into a station wagon with two of my sisters."

The home, a looming stone Victorian with a circular driveway, was across town on Lincoln Avenue in Newark's north side. It was a quiet residential area and a world away from the bustling Jewish south side. Virtually none of the thirty-odd children living there at any given moment were actually orphans; in almost every case they, like the Kleins, were Jewish children from Depression-battered families that couldn't care for them. The home took children only up until the age of sixteen, and Allen's eldest sister, Anna, aged out after just a few weeks. But the four-year-old Allen was the youngest child they had ever accepted.

"We were dropped off at this three-story house and when I turned around, everybody was gone," said Allen. "I needed to go to the bathroom and I walked around this house but I couldn't find it. I went back outside; they had a big backyard with swings and stuff. I was upset because I really had to use the bathroom. There were bushes and I went in and I took a crap in the bushes. And I remember, you know, later, walking around there and seeing the flies . . . the horseflies. And being embarrassed and saying, 'It's not mine. *That's not mine.*'"

Allen and Naomi slept in separate dormitory rooms but were otherwise together every day and attended the nearby Bergen Street public school. Small, Allen was friendly but shy and felt apart from the other kids, who nicknamed him Weasel. (The name stuck. Thirty years later, his nephews and nieces knew him as Uncle Weasel.) "We walked to school every day in line," he said. "We were the home kids; 'Those are the kids from the home.' I tried to straggle behind. I think I just ignored everything."

Life at the institution was far from cruel. There were chores but there was also time to be a child. "There was a playground," said Naomi. "Allen fell off a swing and broke his arm, and you had to learn how to climb over the fence if you wanted to get out to get candy and stuff. This wasn't a jail. It wasn't great, but it wasn't jail." During the summer there were two weeks at the YMHA camp in Milford, Pennsylvania, and day trips to a beach on Staten Island.

Weekends were the worst. On Sundays, families could take their children out for the day. Worried that Allen looked frail, his grandmother brought groceries to the home on Sundays and convinced the nurse that he needed a special breakfast of soft-boiled eggs, butter, and bread. But as his grandmother's health failed, her visits became less and less frequent.

Philip came to the home just once, to take the children on a brief summer trip to visit relatives in Wheeling, West Virginia. The driver from Reinfeld's, where Philip worked, picked up Naomi and Allen one or two Saturdays a year so they could spend a night at the apartment Philip shared with Anna and Esther or at the one their aunt Helen lived in with her husband, Lenny. Another aunt, Bell, occasionally visited and once even drove them to a Howard Johnson's for ice cream.

But those were rare occasions. Almost every Sunday, Allen and Naomi hung on the orphanage's gate watching as other children boarded the number 27 bus with their families and headed downtown for Chinese food. "Sundays were bad," Naomi said. "We used to weep a lot."

And that was how they passed five years. With a new Hebrew orphanage under construction nearby, Allen looked forward to a time when he wouldn't have to sleep in a bunk bed and had his own clothes closet. Now, when clothes came back from the laundry, everything was dumped in the middle of the room and it was a mad scrum to dig for what was yours. He hated retrieving his clothes almost as much as he hated the way his old socks, darned at the heels, chafed his feet. Life would be better at the new orphanage.

October 5, 1941, was a legendary day in New York sports. In the bottom of the ninth of Game 4 of the World Series, a game-ending third strike was called on Yankee batter Tommy Henrich. That should have given the Brooklyn Dodgers a victory and tied the series at two games each, but the ball skipped past Brooklyn catcher Mickey Owen, allowing Henrich to reach base and the Yankees to rally to win the game (and, ultimately, the series). Ten-year-old Allen, listening raptly to the radio at the orphanage, didn't realize it was a big day in his life too. All he knew was that George, his sister Esther's husband, was coming to get Naomi and him and that the blue wool suit with knickers that he had to wear was itching like crazy.

After a stop at George and Esther's apartment on Stuyvesant Avenue, the children were driven to a three-story, six-apartment building on Tillinghast Street in Weequahic.

"We walked upstairs and opened the door and there on the left was a brown Philco radio and a color picture of my father sitting on it," said Allen. "So something lit up in my head." Indeed, his father was there — as were his grandmother, his aunt Helen, and a woman he didn't know.

"This is your new home," Philip announced. "You'll never have to go back to the Hebrew orphanage home." The stranger was introduced to Allen and Naomi as Lillian Drucks, their new mother.

Allen was thrilled. "Somebody wants to be my mother?" he recalled years later. "*Anybody!* You want to be my mother? I'm ready!"

Several years older than Philip, she had been married with grown children when she met and became smitten with the butcher. "He was the man about town and Lilly followed him all around," said Naomi. When Philip said he'd marry her if she'd make a home for his children, she divorced her husband. Though Philip didn't explain it to the kids then, he and Lillian had married that morning.

Allen and Naomi were ecstatic as they ran through the apartment, hugging each other when they reached their new bedroom at the other end. "We couldn't believe this was happening," said Naomi. Allen was most stunned by what he saw in the kitchen. "There's no lock on the refrigerator!" he whispered to Naomi. "Do you think we could get a drink?"

Allen now had the run of the neighborhood, and it was liberating. The schoolyard and ball fields around the corner at the Hawthorne Avenue School were the center of his new world—"Allen was Mr. Playground," said Naomi—and he came to love his stepmother. "I really had no relationship with my father," he said, "but Lillian was great."

Saturdays and summers he spent working with Lillian's two grown sons, who operated a small painting and wallpapering business. Allen was their dollar-a-day helper, cleaning the paintbrushes, wrapping them in newspaper, and folding the tarps. "Then I graduated to painting behind the radiators and in the closets." Sundays and Jewish holidays were reserved for trips to the Hebrew cemetery on South Orange Avenue. Allen loathed them. Confused and frightened, he wasn't even sure what death was, and the passing of his maternal grandmother just six months after he came home from the orphanage did nothing to lessen the mystery and fear. Allen told an aunt that he wanted to become a doctor and bring his mother back to life; he listened to the weekly show *Mr. Keen, Tracer of Lost Persons* with a mixture of terror and hope that the popular radio detective would find her. "I hated going to the cemetery," he said. "I was afraid to go. I was afraid of dead people."

An indifferent student, Allen coasted through school on the strengths of a quick mind and an exceptional memory. At Weequahic High School he was the loud ringleader of a small group of neighborhood boys who shuttled between the movie theaters and the playgrounds. Still, he wasn't otherwise popular or socially successful and he craved companionship. "I'll tell you what I got from my father and from being in the home," he said. "I knew what it was like to be on my own." His high-school yearbook was signed by just one classmate: Philip Roth, the neighborhood's future chronicler and literary light. They were not friends, and Roth has no recollection of Klein. Perhaps Allen simply envied or longed to know the gifted classmate who, even then, seemed most likely to succeed.

Work was a different story than school; he embraced it completely. At fourteen Allen began working for a next-door neighbor, Melvin Stein, who was a few years older. Already out of school, Stein had purchased a newspaper route in nearby Short Hills, and he hired Allen to help. "He was a hard-working guy," Klein said, "and I looked up to him. He was like an older brother I never had."

At first Allen hoped his new friend and mentor would help him figure out a way to win his father's affection. "I would talk about my father and he would say, 'Your father will just keep breaking your heart. Don't think about it.'" Indeed, Philip Klein seemed incapable of seeing good in his son or taking his part in any argument.

"I got into a fight in front of our house and this guy was bigger than me and I finally got on top of him," Allen recalled. "My father came and held my hands while this guy hit me. Because *I* had to be wrong." In high school, Allen got into a spat with a girlfriend who threw a glass at him, necessitating stitches. "I didn't say anything—I told them it was an accident—but the girl's mother found out and she called my father and Lillian." When the mother blamed Allen and threatened to take action, Philip was apologetic. It was Lillian who stood up for him. "She said, 'You people talk too much. It takes two to tango.'"

His friend Melvin encouraged Allen to focus on work. Within the year, the two were also employees of a Newark newspaper and magazine distribution company, Essex County News, which dealt with eight hundred accounts, largely candy stores and newsstands. Every month, shipments to each account had to be tallied and billed, after which Essex paid publishers for what had been sold and returned the banners and covers of unsold newspapers and magazines for credit. Allen, who was already demonstrating an affinity for numbers, could add up a bill in his head as rapidly as the boss or the billing clerk could figure it out on an adding machine. He was a quick success at Essex.

Though just a teenager, Klein got an eyeful of some seamy if common business practices, watching as people created false accounts, cheated suppliers, and padded bills. Not only did items "fall off the truck" as van drivers pulled magazines from orders and sold them elsewhere, but the company purposely inverted numbers on invoices to its advantage, hoping that stores wouldn't notice if they were billed, say, $32.17 when they should have been charged $23.17. If anyone caught the "mistake," a credit and a quick apology were issued, but often no one did. Allen discovered that outdated and unsold magazines — which Essex was supposed to scrap after returning the front covers for credit — were being sold coverless in the New York subway for a dime each. Despite being repulsed by some of these practices, particularly Essex's ripping off mom-and-pop candy stores, Allen enjoyed work more than school and he fantasized about having his own business.

In January 1951, Klein graduated high school, six months late, and talked his friend Henry Newfield into enlisting in the army with him. He had two reasons for joining up: first, Allen wanted to go to college and knew his father couldn't or wouldn't send him, so he would need the financial assistance provided by the GI Bill; second, and more urgent, the Korean War was under way and he was sure to be drafted. By volunteering, he hoped to gain more control over his training and his chances of remaining stateside. "I figured they were going to get me anyway," he said. "And that's what got me interested in going to school."

Klein's strategy worked. After basic training at Fort Dix in New Jersey, he was shipped to Fort Benjamin Harrison in Indiana for eighteen weeks of further training; there, he opted to learn shorthand and typing in the hope that office skills would land him a safe assignment. With the exception of West Virginia and Florida, where he had been taken to visit relatives, Indiana was Allen's first exposure to the world beyond cloistered Jewish Newark. The culture shock was lessened by the discovery of a nearby Jewish country club, Broadmoor, which had an open-door policy for Jewish servicemen.

There, Klein learned to play both golf and tennis, and the latter became a lifelong passion at which he both excelled and cheated. Singer Bobby Vinton, a Klein client in the early sixties who remained friendly with Allen, recalled a doubles match in which they opposed each other. "My partner asked, 'Who is this guy?'" said Vinton, "and I said, 'My accountant.' He says, 'Well, if he does your books like he keeps score, he's screwing you bad.'" Klein's plan for avoiding Korea worked out better than he could have hoped. When his father, Philip, developed fainting spells, the Klein family physician requested that Allen be stationed as close to home as possible, and he became a clerk for a general on Governors Island in New York Harbor. The most lasting impact of Klein's army hitch, however, came from serving with soldiers who were better educated and worldlier than he. Henry, the friend with whom he'd enlisted, was two years older than Allen and had already spent some time in college, and now Allen found himself serving with young doctors drafted from medical schools.

"The people who were being drafted were all college guys and I would hear them talk and feel embarrassed by my lack of knowledge," he said. "They read philosophy — I would hear them talking about Nietzsche — and I didn't know shit. I was really fucking embarrassed."

It wasn't just about books; even when he'd been stationed in Indiana, Klein had felt like a bumpkin. What was wrong with him, he wondered, that he didn't share the tastes of the men he was meeting? It didn't matter whether the topic was champagne or olives, history or opera, it ate at him that others seemed at home in a world he knew nothing about. "Some of it was petty, but it bothered me."

In search of answers, Klein became an autodidact. "I spent an enormous amount of my time in the army in the library." Along with developing a love of opera, he became a voracious reader. Novels with exotic settings were a favorite, and he was particularly devoted to Graham Greene and Somerset Maugham, but his biggest influence was Upton Sinclair's Lanny Budd novels.

Now rarely read, the then-popular eleven-book romans-fleuves recounted the life and international adventures of Budd, the socialist son of an American munitions manufacturer. Published between 1940 and 1953, the series included the Pulitzer Prize–winning *Dragon's Teeth*, a fictionalized account of the rise of Nazism, and painted an epic, left-leaning chronicle of world events and politics from the outbreak of World War I through the aftermath of World War II. "I read every one of those books," Klein said. "I learned about the war from Upton Sinclair."

After his years in the orphanage, the death of his mother, and the indifference of his father, Allen could see himself only as an outsider, as less than everyone else and undeserving of affection. But his crash course in self-improvement brought the reassuring epiphany that doubt and the struggle for self-worth were common threads woven through the human experience. Reading had given him a life-altering revelation, lifting an enormous weight. "It was an amazing thing to realize that I'm not the only screwed-up guy," he said.

Around the same time, Klein made another intriguing discovery, one that would have an equally profound and lifelong impact. Though he'd carried a chip on his shoulder as an orphanage kid, his story actually had a good deal of romantic cachet. The men he met in the army, even the doctors and the Ivy Leaguers, were intrigued to hear the tales from his institutional childhood. However painful his past, he wasn't a loser or an outcast — he was a Dickensian exotic.

One thing Allen could not overcome was his fear of death. Though he loved his stepmother, Lillian, and was deeply grateful for the way she had always stuck up for him, when she suddenly died, he couldn't face going home for her funeral. That fearfulness extended to his relationship with her sons; although he liked them and had enjoyed assisting in their wallpapering business, after her death, he never spoke to them again.

·  ·  ·

Upon his discharge from the army in the spring of 1953, Allen returned to Newark, where his father had quickly remarried. Whether by coincidence or because Philip saw no reason to buck a winning formula, his third wife's name was also Lillian — and she immediately became known within the family as "Lilly the second." Allen moved in with them, but his hopes of going to school full-time were short-lived. Philip insisted Allen earn his keep.

"My father said, 'You have to work,'" he recalled. "So I went out and I got a job at the Sherwood Paint Company doing inventory. I didn't know what the fuck I was doing. And I hated it. I hated the smell of the paint."

Fortunately, it was only for the summer. In the fall, Klein enrolled at Upsala College in nearby East Orange, attending classes in the morning and working afternoons and weekends at his old job with the Essex County News. He picked up a second job with Brainen and Company, a father-and-son accounting firm. His idea was to clerk for them with an eye toward becoming an accountant.

Allen enjoyed Upsala and his courses; a required class on comparative religious ethics offered at the Lutheran college left a lasting impression. But he wasn't there to expand his mind or continue the rigorous self-examination he'd experienced in the army. A child of the Depression and the only son of a working-class family, Klein was at Upsala to learn accounting and acquire a profession; there was no romance to it. As a soldier, he'd recognized that the army needed clerks and that mastering office skills would earn him a secure berth. He viewed accounting in the same way: there was a demand for it, and he had a gift for numbers.

Money, though never far from his mind, was not an end in itself. Allen didn't dream of being rich; he dreamed of being a success. And what was success? For Allen, it always came down to having the things he'd missed as a child: companionship, a sense of worth, and power over his own life.

Philip Klein added insult to all the injuries by not attending Allen's college graduation in June 1957. "My father was the pride of the street and the sorrow of the home," Allen said. He and a friend, Lenny Kantzel, opted to celebrate on their own a few months later by driving to Miami in the car Allen had bought with his earnings as a waiter at a hotel in the Catskills the previous summer.

Hanging around the hotels on the beach, they swam, ate, lolled about, and trolled for girls. On their final afternoon in Miami, Allen noticed a young and exceptionally pretty girl swimming in the pool at the Surfcomber Hotel. He tried to strike up a conversation with her but she gave him the brushoff.

Betty Rosenblum was a seventeen-year-old Hunter College student who worked part-time in her uncle's New York real estate firm, and, like Klein, she was on her first vacation with a friend. Guys had been hitting on them steadily. "I was tired and couldn't be bothered," she said. "When this man started to talk to me, I made him wait until I came out of the pool and got a drink of water. Then I said, 'What do you want?'" Trying to keep Allen at arm's length proved a poor strategy. Angered by the perceived insult, he yelled at her. "I really should have stopped talking to him," Betty said. "But he wound up asking me out — *and* he had a car. That was a big deal; my parents didn't have a car. What more can I say?"

The date was a flop. She was flabbergasted when Allen had the nerve to announce that he was going to marry her. "I thought, *This is going to be somebody's father? You gotta be joking.*"

Though the evening went poorly, Allen wasn't ready to quit. As he was leaving Miami, he convinced his sister Anna, with whom he'd stayed in Miami, to call the Surfcomber and track Betty down. By the time Allen got back to Newark, Anna was able to pass along Betty's phone number and the name of a camp in Connecticut where she'd be working that summer. "I was very young," said Betty. "He was seven years older and very persistent."

Klein was far more than persistent; the lasting legacy of his childhood was his all-consuming fear of abandonment. He detested being alone and would do anything to avoid it — anything. Now, through equal measures of intelligence, hunger, and fear, Allen was becoming extraordinarily adept at reading people in order to keep them close, developing an almost unfailing knack for identifying their needs and desires. It wasn't altruistic; it was as necessary to him as eating and breathing. Generous and ingratiating when he wished to be, Allen overwhelmed his quarry with the force of his personality and intelligence. It wasn't a conversation so much as a riveting performance crossed with an out-and-out assault; he told you what you needed and how he was going to get it for you, and you agreed. What started as a personal tool for battling loneliness would soon become his great calling card in business.

"Allen would have been a great psychologist and an even better trial lawyer," said Alan Steckler, creative director for ABKCO, Klein's company. Steckler had never seen anything like Klein's unique ability to identify what someone wanted or needed and then deliver it. "He could really *hear;* he was able to sort out people, their weaknesses and their needs. He could figure out what they needed and then give it to them. That's why he was so successful with artists and with women. He was charming. And he was ruthless." Said his friend and attorney Leonard Leibman, "Women were a pushover for Allen. He would tell them about the orphanage and have them eating out of his hand." "Klein could recognize a vacuum," said Harold Seider, who was Allen's neighbor and the in-house attorney for ABKCO. "Call it leadership or whatever. And he was a terrific salesman — he was essentially a salesman." The boy once spurned by the world was now ready to conquer it.

"When Allen wants something," said Betty Klein, "he sucks the blood out of you."

## 2

# ALLEN KLEIN AND COMPANY

KLEIN CONTINUED WORKING Saturdays for Brainen and Company in New Jersey and landed his first full-time accounting job with a Manhattan firm, Joseph Fenton and Company. The precursor to Prager and Fenton, a leading specialist in music- and film-industry accounting, the company already had a thriving practice among music publishers when Klein joined in 1957.

In the years since World War II, the record industry had been growing in rapid and dramatic fashion. The 45 rpm single, introduced by RCA in 1949, and the arrival of rock 'n' roll just a few years later ushered in both a change in the culture and a new market, one that was initially ignored by established major record companies like Columbia, RCA, and Capitol. This provided an opening for small independents like Sun Records in Memphis, Chess in Chicago, Atlantic in New York, and Specialty in Los Angeles to launch the careers of Elvis Presley, Chuck Berry, Ray Charles, and Little Richard, respectively. By the second half of the decade, the big labels saw the error of their ways. Even if they couldn't wholeheartedly embrace rhythm and blues and rock 'n' roll ("It smells but it sells" was a favorite old-guard witticism), the majors moved to secure a piece of the market. In October 1955, RCA purchased Presley's contract from Sun for the then-exorbitant sum of thirty-five thousand dollars; the following year, Warner Brothers Films decided to start its own record company. The business was booming.

If the record industry was getting a fashion makeover and hitting the town, music publishing was the sister who stayed home. Regardless of changes in trends and tastes, its business remained essentially the same: to copyright and exploit songs. The rock 'n' roll record business was for wildcatters, a chance for the more daring independent artists, producers, and manufacturers to strike it rich; music publishing was the backroom, penny-counting, administrative equivalent of traditional banking: staid and comparatively boring, but steady and lucrative if you had the right songs.

Klein's first big assignment was to fly to California and assist Joe Fenton in an audit on behalf of a key music publishers' organization, the Harry Fox Agency. Founded by music publishers in 1927, the agency grants and tracks mechanical licenses, the legal agreements permitting copyrighted songs to be recorded. The agency also collects royalties due and distributes them to the publishers, who then split that with the songwriters.

The spur for the Fenton audit was the pending sale of Dot Records to Paramount Pictures. The Fox Agency, as the representative for music publishers whose songs had been recorded by artists on Dot, had to check Dot's sales figures before agreeing to let Paramount assume liability. Allen found Los Angeles exciting. Staying at the Hollywood Roosevelt Hotel, he couldn't help but notice that the other guests included Presley, Sidney Poitier, and Claude Rains. He had no one to hang out with, but that didn't deter him from taking the measure of the town and lunching alone at the Brown Derby.

Yet the trip's most lasting impression came from the work, which also involved separate audits of several other record companies, including Liberty and Monarch. Allen hadn't forgotten the tricks he'd seen at Essex County News, but he was nonetheless surprised to discover that each audit turned up widespread underpayment to publishers and writers. It got him thinking: If that was the situation for the music publishers—a group with the professional organization, money, and wherewithal to police record-company payments—how bad was it for the performers? They certainly didn't have anything like the Harry Fox Agency representing them. "I said, 'Holy shit! If there's money here for the publishers, there's got to be money for the artists.'"

His suspicions were confirmed a few months later by a chance meeting. On his way home one day after visiting Betty at her parents' apartment in Washington Heights, Allen was waiting at a stoplight when he heard his name called and saw someone waving from the corner of 187th Street and Fort Washington Avenue. Though the two hadn't been friends in school, Klein recognized a former Upsala student, Don Kirshner. "Hey, bub!" Kirshner said. "Let me buy you an egg cream!"

Best known on campus as a baseball player, Kirshner had taken a job as a seventy-dollar-a-week song plugger for Vanderbilt Music, a small publisher at 1650 Broadway. His job was to convince record producers to pair Vanderbilt's songs with their recording artists. The company was owned by Al Lewis, an old-time Tin Pan Alley lyricist who'd scored hits with Eddie Cantor and Rudy Vallee in the twenties and thirties and written such Depression-era classics as "Now's the Time to Fall in Love" and "You Gotta Be a Football Hero." Lewis's career got its second wind in 1956 when a song he wrote in the forties, "Blueberry Hill," was covered by Fats Domino and became a huge hit. He eagerly climbed on the R&B train. Kirshner paired Lewis—whom Klein remembered as "an old, diabetic Jew"—with Sylvester Bradford, a blind African American songwriter. The unlikely duo soon scored another modest success with Domino on "I'm Ready" and then hit pay dirt with "Tears on My Pillow," a huge hit for the doo-wop group Little Anthony and the Imperials.

When Kirshner heard that Klein had been auditing labels for music publishers and was now thinking about offering similar services to individual performers and songwriters, he not only agreed that there was a need for it but offered to introduce him to likely clients.

"Don said, 'I'm gonna make you a star,'" Allen recalled with a laugh. "I don't know what he wanted, but he was a guy who would say, 'I'm gonna make you a millionaire.'" The two struck up a friendship—"I used to drive him to work and he would chip in with me for park-

ing"— and before long, Kirshner came through with several key introductions.

"Man, he had all these contacts," Klein said. "Bobby Darin was his
buddy. He knew Connie Francis, Steve Lawrence and Eydie Gormé.
He was a real good schmoozer, a good listener."

Kirshner's abilities as both a publisher and a dealmaker would soon
become apparent. In 1958 he left Vanderbilt to partner with Al Nevins,
and their publishing company, Aldon Music, became a quick success.
With a stable of top-notch young songwriters including Carole King
and Gerry Goffin, Barry Mann and Cynthia Weil, Paul Simon, Neil
Sedaka, and Howard Greenfield, Aldon cranked out hits and became
closely associated with rock and pop's Brill Building period, the late fifties and early sixties. The New York sound was a commercial marriage
between singers and songwriters presided over by producers. Kirshner
was the matchmaker.

"In the beginning, it was Don Kirshner who had a lot to do with our
early successes," said Gerry Goffin, who, in partnership with his wife at
the time, Carole King, wrote and published numerous big hits through
Aldon, including "Will You Love Me Tomorrow," "The Loco-Motion,"
and "Take Good Care of My Baby." "He would say, 'Write a song for
the Shirelles,' and we did. He was a very good publisher. He would say,
'I got these kids and they know what's happening. Give me the artist,
and I'll give you the song.' And he was right most of the time." Like
Kirshner, Klein was good at the work and intrigued by the opportunities inherent in the expanding music business. "I liked the action," he
said. But his tenure with Fenton and Company proved brief; he was
fired after just four months.

"Allen couldn't keep a job," said Betty. "He couldn't get in on time.
He didn't mind working until two or three in the morning, but he
could not get in on time. And for an accountant, you can't work your
own hours." The parting was so bitter that the company wrote to the
State of New Jersey, where Allen was to take the examination to become a certified public accountant, and strongly urged officials not to
certify him. Klein opted not to sit for the exam and never became a

CPA. He made a halfhearted stab at law school but couldn't square his work habits with evening classes.

Cut adrift, Allen had an abundance of energy and ideas but few solid prospects. He scraped by on day work with a midtown accountant and the occasional referral from Kirshner, who was an usher at Allen and Betty's June 1958 wedding. The entertainment at the reception was provided by Klein's first music-business client, Ersel Hickey. A rockabilly performer and songwriter from upstate New York, Hickey had just scored a modest hit on Epic Records with "Bluebirds over the Mountain." Surprisingly, Allen's label audit on his behalf failed to turn up any money.

That gave Klein pause. After the record-company audits he'd conducted for Fenton, Allen assumed that looking for underpayments on behalf of artists would be a ripe area to explore, and he'd been hatching a scheme to set himself up in a watchdog role similar to Harry Fox's. He had even picked a name: RAPA, for the Recording Artists Protective Association. The idea was to sign up performers and conduct audits in return for a percentage of whatever he found. But the situation now looked less promising — and perhaps more nefarious — than he'd thought. The record companies didn't have to doctor their books to avoid paying artists; they were already stacking the deck against them in the recording contracts.

"I learned a lesson," he said. "The artists never had any money. They were always paid with an advance, which they would spend, and then the session costs [also] came off their money. So they were always in the hole. And they were frequently represented by someone who didn't want someone else to come in and show them what they hadn't been doing right."

After a ten-day whirlwind Caribbean honeymoon with stops in Cuba, Puerto Rico, and Haiti, the newlyweds settled into a $185-a-month one-bedroom apartment on 190th Street in Washington Heights, near Betty's parents. Getting an irresistible deal on pink wall-to-wall carpeting, they painted the walls to match; Allen's desk doubled as the dining-room table. "Because of the pink walls, the apartment always looked warmer than any other when you looked up from the street," said Betty. "We had my teenage bedroom set and a cot that we put a throw over and used as a couch. And that was it. And love."

What they didn't have was money. Betty was still attending Hunter and working part-time in her uncle's real estate office, and Allen was making $135 a month, which didn't even cover their rent. Inexplicably, Allen insisted on taking a cab when he went to work in midtown, despite owning a car and living just a few blocks from the subway. But it was often difficult to tell what Allen was thinking or how his hectic mind arrived at a particular decision. He was a man of surprises.

The day after they returned from their honeymoon, Allen didn't come home from work. Frantic, Betty spent an interminable night thinking she'd become a widow in record time. It was after nine the next morning when Allen telephoned with the news that he was in jail. The car he never drove to work or, apparently, moved for alternate-side-of-the-street parking days had collected 110 tickets. Klein, who had been paying a neighborhood beat cop to take care of it and thought he didn't have to worry, was surprised to discover he was one of New York's biggest scofflaws. Betty's father, Abe Rosenblum, bailed him out.

After Allen's father, his in-laws were manna from heaven. And as perplexing as their intense and unpredictable new son-in-law was, they embraced him. "My parents were very good to us," said Betty, "and Allen loved my parents. My mother understood him. She said, 'You can't change the spots on a leopard.' My father just wanted to be part of his life."

As co-owner of a health club in Manhattan, the Luxor Baths, Abe was the kind of even-keeled businessman that Allen, who could spin out ideas at an alarming rate and seemed to work best by making up the rules as he went along, would never be. Yet the elder man freely gave him respect and trust. Even more than that, when Allen concluded just prior to getting married that he would make it only if he worked for himself and that he needed to start his own accounting company, Abe agreed to provide the sizable twenty-five-thousand-dollar stake. "My father-in-law never understood how I could do this because he's such a conservative guy," Klein said. "He didn't own a car, worked all the time. Yet he never, ever, *ever* asked me what I thought I was doing. He was just terrific."

Allen didn't have the necessary CPA license to start the business, but it wasn't difficult to find someone who did—his old school friend and army buddy Henry Newfield. Henry and another CPA, Marty Weinberg, already had a scuffling startup practice in Lakewood, New Jersey. They agreed to work two days a week in midtown Manhattan for the new Allen Klein and Company, which subcontracted its midtown office space from S. T. Seidman, a small advertising company. Seidman was also, at $125 a month, Klein and Company's biggest account. Along with a paint store in Washington Heights, Allen was counting on having two more clients: his father-in-law's health club and his friend Don Kirshner's publishing company, Aldon Music. As disappointing as the Hickey audit had been, Allen still believed his future was in the music business, and he was hustling like mad to meet people. His most important new contact was an attorney, Marty Machat.

The Brooklyn-born Machat was, like Klein and Kirshner, a hungry, self-invented hustler. A stylish man, he favored the thin cigars of a grandee, the tailor-made suits of a dandy, and the company of young beautiful women. According to attorney and music executive Eric Kronfeld, who began his career working for him, Machat told him his original last name was Moskowitz and that he'd changed it to Machat because it sounded classy, although that story is disputed by Machat's son Steven. Regardless, *Machat* proved a somewhat unfortunate name; as Marty's practice grew and he conducted more and more business in Europe, he was frequently greeted by raised eyebrows when he introduced himself (*Machat* is pronounced like the French slang phrase *mon chat,* "my pussy").

What isn't disputed is that Machat started his career as a negligence lawyer. Only chance, in the form of a phone call from a former high-school classmate who'd just had an accident while driving the boxer Sugar Ray Robinson in his cab, led Marty into the entertainment business. Machat began representing Robinson, who was friendly with many performers and musicians, and soon had a thriving music-business practice. In the coming years, his clients would include the Four Seasons, James Brown, Phil Spector, and Leonard Cohen. But no one would be more important to his career than Allen Klein.

The two most likely met in 1957 when they worked together on behalf of the film composer Dimitri Tiomkin on a grievance hearing before ASCAP, the American rights organization for songwriters and composers to which Tiomkin belonged. "Marty knew nothing about economics and math, and I'm pretty sure he retained Allen to be his expert in an arbitration hearing," said Kronfeld. "In fact, Marty was a pretty lousy lawyer and I didn't think he really knew the law that well."

Klein didn't care if Machat thought writs were crackers. "He was a good contact for me," Allen said, and he launched a charm offensive. Just before Allen's wedding, he and Marty discussed teaming up to conduct audits on behalf of two of Machat's clients, the singer Brook Benton and the record producer Morty Craft. Figuring he had a couple of potentially juicy jobs lined up for when he returned home from his honeymoon, Allen was confident about getting his company off the ground. He phoned Machat as soon as he returned to New York. "Oh," Klein recalled Machat saying, "that's not happening."

Annoyed, Allen then learned that two of the clients he'd been counting on, Aldon and his father-in-law's health club, wouldn't be signing on with Allen Klein and Company after all. In both cases, the partners feared favoritism and were uncomfortable with having their books handled by someone the business's owner was so close with. The only good news was that Kirshner could at least hook Allen up with the singers Steve Lawrence and Eydie Gormé and a pair of Texan musicians and songwriters, Buddy Knox and Jimmy Bowen.

Under Knox's name and as Jimmy Bowen with the Rhythm Aces, Buddy and Jimmy had written and recorded several rockabilly hits, including 1957's million-selling "Party Doll" and "I'm Sticking with You." But their record company, Roulette, was slow to pay them. Klein, eager to prove his mettle, demanded an audit.

Roulette's owner, Morris Levy, didn't receive many demands for anything. On the contrary; Levy was widely regarded as the music industry's toughest operator, a man both respected and feared. His route into the business had been through the hat-check concessions in nightclubs, enterprises notoriously susceptible to Mob influence, and Levy offered no apologies for his friendship with gangsters. He went on to own several famous Manhattan music clubs, notably Birdland, the Downbeat, the Embers, and the Peppermint Lounge. Levy's connections included a silent partnership with the all-important rock disk jockey Alan Freed, and he also owned a chain of record stores and operated as a lender and collector of last resort for other record labels. He was, as they say in those quarters, someone you just don't fuck with, and there was nothing unusual in the particulars of Bowen and Knox's case; it was Levy's habit to pay performers as little as he could get away with. But as tough as Levy was, Klein found him straightforward and amenable to a settlement — as long as Levy could dictate the terms. The two hit it off.

"He had a charming way — he really did," Klein said. "I came in to do the audit and he didn't mind. He had a bookkeeper named Fischer who was a nice guy." Yet when the audit showed that Bowen and Knox were owed money, Levy was unperturbed. He proposed to pay them what he owed over four years. When Klein said that wasn't acceptable, Levy shrugged and invited Klein to sue him. Morris wouldn't deny that he owed the money, he said — he'd simply tell the court he didn't have it. "I'll tell the judge I'm a little tight but that I'll pay it out to you," he told Klein.

Allen knew he'd been outmaneuvered, and he wasn't going to pay a lawyer to chase Levy through court for a year when he was unlikely to get anything better than the schedule he was being offered now. Instead, he went back to Bowen and Knox and convinced them to take the drawn-out settlement. For Klein, it was an important lesson: it was better to get what was possible than hold out for the impossible. "I got them money and I bought myself a car," he said. As for Levy and Klein, the affinity they felt for each other was real, and they became friends, with Levy occasionally throwing him work. Over the years, Allen visited Morris several times at his horse farm in upstate New York; twenty years after they met, when Klein's son, Jody, celebrated his bar mitz-vah, the biggest gift — an Israeli bond — came from Levy.

Still, dealing with Levy convinced Allen that he couldn't go to war without a loaded gun. Klein's audit deal for artists was simple: anything he found, they split fifty-fifty. He now offered to split his 50 percent with Machat whenever he needed a lawyer to sue — or at least threaten to sue — a publisher or label.

It was a natural match. "Marty was one of the only lawyers in New York engaged in the music business," said Kronfeld, adding that Klein probably would not have found a receptive ear with a more strait-laced industry attorney like Walter Hofer or Paul Marshall. "The others sim-ply would not have tolerated Allen — nor Allen them."

It was the first of many agreements between the two. Eager to es-tablish himself as a force, Allen needed Machat's assistance and busi-ness. "We wooed him," said Betty Klein. "We used to go out to dinner [with Machat] every Friday night." For his part, Marty started steering his clients, like producer and label owner Morty Craft and disk jockey Jocko Henderson, to Klein. But before long the parameters would shift. "The relationship with Marty was unequal, then equal," recalled Betty. "Then Allen became dominant." This would become the standard pat-tern in Klein's relationships. Allen's ability to make rapid, hardheaded reads of people and craft unique strategies and solutions coupled with his voracious personality and overweening desire to succeed made him formidable. Seemingly devoid of self-doubt, he was headstrong and needed to be in charge. When Allen's associates Henry Newfield and Marty Weinberg found that the days working in Manhattan for Klein exacted a heavy toll on their New Jersey practice, they proposed a merger. The resulting firm, Allen Klein, Newfield, and Weinberg, was 85 percent owned by Allen and an almost instantaneous failure. When the new company hit a cash shortfall, Allen shrugged and wrote checks the business couldn't cover. Horrified, Weinberg was sure he'd made a terrible mistake throwing his lot in with Klein. What kind of accounting firm wrote rubber checks? "Henry Newfield was a very easygoing guy and friendly with Allen," said accountant Joel Silver, who'd joined the company in 1960 when he was still a student at NYU and stayed his entire career. "But Marty Weinberg was a no-nonsense guy. When a check bounced, Marty went bonkers. It didn't bother Allen that much," he said with a laugh. "Allen did not do partnerships well." After just three months, the firm was once again named Allen Klein and Company, with Newfield staying on as an employee and Weinberg departing, eventually becoming an FBI agent.

Dealing with Allen could be rough, even if you were a friend or client. "We were somewhat friendly—he was at my wedding," said Marvin Schlachter, a partner in Scepter Records, for which Klein did some accounting. Still, Schlachter found him hard to take: "He was a sharp, bullying sort of an individual." Klein made no apologies. Indeed, he could sound more like a gunfighter than an accountant. "I'd go over the books and I'd find that the companies were always short. Whenever I caught them at it, I'd take 50% of whatever I found for the artists. Which was fine with the artist—but I was making the record companies look like crooks even if it was an honest mistake on their part. They hated my guts. Said I was an unethical bastard. I don't know if what I did was ethical or not; it was just my hustle. A way to get into the business." Others felt gratitude, loyalty, and admiration for him. Lloyd Price, the singer, songwriter, and bandleader, came to Klein as a client in 1961 and became a lifelong friend and fan. "I was signed to ABC/Paramount and Allen found me sixty thousand dollars," he said. "After that, we just had a great relationship." Price said they shared "innumerable lunches" over the next four decades.

Many of Klein's employees were equally devoted to him, finding him an unusual and engagingly idiosyncratic boss. Over the years, the company developed a rhythm and style tailored to the boss's habits; most employees were in by ten, but little was done until Allen arrived a few hours later, and then the day began in earnest and often lasted late into the evening. No one complained about the long hours, and everybody's meals—first from the best delis Allen could find and later from Zabar's—were delivered and covered. Indeed, the typical lines between the professional and the personal were blurred from the very beginning. In its aspirations, ethics, style, and practices, the company was in every way an extension of Allen Klein. Though Allen Klein and

Company's corporate successor, ABKCO Industries, would rapidly become a music-industry powerhouse and ultimately the manager of the Beatles and the Rolling Stones, it would never stop being what it was at its core: a Jewish family business.

Adrienne Zanghi Faillace was eighteen when she became the secretary and first employee at Allen Klein and Company. She didn't mind that, along with the predictable duties of typing audit spreadsheets and answering the phones, her job also quickly came to include fixing Allen breakfast (he liked her to mix his soft-boiled eggs with bread and butter, just the way the nurse had made it for him in the orphanage) and going to his house on Saturdays to babysit for Allen and Betty's infant daughter, Robin, while they worked. "He was very good to me, even though I didn't make a lot of money," she said. "I can't remember if I got paid when I came in on a Saturday. I would take the subway to his house on Cabrini Boulevard, bring them crumb buns and bagels for breakfast. As a boss, we all liked him. People didn't leave." Indeed, Ken Salinsky, who interviewed for his initial job as office boy only because he'd won the appointment the night before in a poker game, stayed over fifty years.

Just as enamored with Klein's intelligence and business acumen, Faillace remembered nothing underhanded or untoward in his practices and dismissed most of his critics. Rather, she recalled a nascent and competitive business made up of strivers and schemers who were trying to invent a hustle as they went along—and she believed Klein's biggest crime was being the cleverest in the crowd.

"He was a great manipulator," she said. "Everyone in the business—that was their goal. Don Kirshner, Clive Davis; it was a cutthroat business and everyone was hungry and greedy. They were poor boys who saw they could make a lot of money. And Allen was really the brains behind a lot of this stuff, and not just the audits. He had a way about him that people believed in him, okay? It was a personality thing and in this business it's all about personality and who you know. Allen was very aggressive and he was very smart. I'm not saying Allen was a saint. But as far as I'm concerned, anything bad that was said about Allen was not accurate. The people who said it were mad and angry that he audited the books of these record companies that were stealing from the artists. They resented that he blew the top off it — they were furious! When you're the first to do anything, you make a lot of enemies."

Though his firm did regular accounting for music clients like Scepter Records and the singer/songwriter Neil Sedaka, audits had become Klein's calling card. In the earliest days, when he was scuffling along on his own, Allen would round up virtually everyone he could find — his wife, his sister, and even his mother-in-law — and introduce them as his team of auditors. Whether or not they provided anything beyond window dressing, it was Allen's ability to blow away the financial smoke and crack the accounting mirrors employed by record companies and music publishers that cemented his reputation.

Taking a cue from his years in the newspaper-and-magazine-distribution business, Klein wouldn't accept the figures proffered by a record company. Instead, he wanted to see the raw-goods orders. Knowing he was unlikely to get much in the way of cooperation or straight answers, he always asked the kind of questions that shook company employees up and, hopefully, made them reveal things he could use against them. How many record sleeves did they order, and how many were still on hand? How many shipping boxes? How much vinyl? Masters and mothers (the parts needed to manufacture a specific single or album) had limited lives; how many were made or purchased for a particular record? How many hours did the machines run? Where were the bills of lading? The customer invoices? Allen didn't come in to look at the books — he came in to rewrite them.

Keenly aware that pressing a hit record was analogous to printing money and that a dishonest record company could cheat an artist simply by having additional records manufactured at an unacknowledged plant, he started with the assumption that every label's accounting was likely bogus, and it was his job to come away with *something*. Usually that wasn't difficult. And when it was, Allen took it as a special challenge.

The estate of filmmaker Mike Todd hired Klein to audit the manufacturer of the soundtrack to the film *Around the World in 80 Days,* and the job proved unusually problematic. Though the album was on Decca Records, its pressing was subcontracted to an independent operation in Swarthmore, Pennsylvania, owned by a savvy music-business veteran named Dave Miller. The producer of one of the first rock 'n' roll hits, "Crazy Man, Crazy," by Bill Haley and His Comets, Miller actually made his mark with a schlocky but popular easy-listening series, 101 Strings, a budget-priced collection aimed at casual music fans that featured titles like *East of Suez, "Exodus" and Other Great Movie Themes, I Love Paris,* and *The Emotion of 101 Strings at Gypsy Campfires.* Miller had the albums recorded on the cheap in Germany using a radio orchestra and handled everything else himself, including manufacturing the covers and pressing the records at his own factory. When Klein came in to audit, he found that Miller had done much the same for *Around the World in 80 Days* and had all the answers — and receipts. With nothing to challenge, Klein began grasping at straws. "He could manufacture the records," recalled Klein. "He could create the paper. He would buy the plaster compound and so you wouldn't know how many [masters] he made. He had his own presses. So I'm there and, oh God, what do you do? I'm looking and I'm looking and I'm looking." Finally, Klein discovered that while Miller had purchased the necessary mechanical license for monaural albums, he'd neglected to buy a separate one for stereo albums. Though it wasn't much of an error, it was enough to coerce a payment. Klein had his scalp.

Aggressive about getting results, Allen was maniacal when it came to selling himself. An invitation to Don Kirshner's wedding was more than a happy occasion; it was a blessed business opportunity. After the groom introduced singer Bobby Darin to his good friend and genius accountant Allen Klein, Allen didn't bother with chitchat. When the singer stuck out his hand, Allen said, "I can get you a hundred thousand dollars."

This story became part of Klein's legend, quite possibly because he told it frequently. But how well he delivered on his pitch is unclear. Klein found some money for Darin via a publishing company he co-owned with the songwriter Woody Harris, whom Klein also represented, and he later intimated that he'd discovered Kirshner was short-changing Darin in their overseas publishing agreements. But an audit of Atlantic Records, to which Darin was then signed, turned up almost nothing, and their relationship was brief.

That didn't prevent Allen from using the connection to attract other clients. To woo singer Bobby Vinton away from his then-manager, Klein and Machat promised one million dollars paid over twenty years, and Allen used Darin as his entrée. "I didn't know much about Allen," said Vinton. "I said, 'What did you do, Allen?' and he said, 'I was an accountant for Bobby Darin.' So when I saw Darin on the street, I said, 'Bobby, what do you think of Allen Klein?' And he said, 'You live and you learn.' And that's all he had to say! I kept saying to Allen, 'What does he mean by that? You live and you learn?' He said, 'Ehh ehh ehh . . .'"

Steve Blauner, an agent who became Darin's manager, groaned at the mention of Klein.

"The only [underpayment] he found was ten thousand copies of 'Splish Splash,' a single on Atlantic," Blauner said, adding that Darin's low royalty rate—a 5 percent payment on 90 percent of all records sold—meant it wasn't much of a victory. "We're talking pennies. That's what he found, period." Worse, Blauner suggested Klein tried to swindle him.

"He then got me to buy stock in a Canadian company—maybe Seven Arts, I'm not sure. My father had been on Wall Street and wiped out in the crash. He told me if I ever bought stock, make sure I have the certificates, don't let the brokerage hold on to them. I called and called and called Klein and I couldn't get the stock certificates. Finally, I said, 'You've got twenty-four hours before I report you to the authorities—and before I send someone over there who's going to break an arm or a leg.' I finally got the stock certificates. Allen Klein was a thief."

Klein did have a tenuous connection to Seven Arts. A film company founded by producers Eliot Hyman and Ray Stark, it also held valuable syndication and television rights to cartoons and older movies, and Hyman and Stark would, a few years later, parlay that into a brief ownership of Warner Brothers before selling the combined company to Steve Ross's Kinney Corporation. Seven Arts's holdings included United Telefilms, a Canadian company begun by Lou Chesler, a Toronto wheeler-dealer and gambler who'd relocated to Miami and was reputed to have Mob connections. It was in Miami that Chesler met record producer Morty Craft and agreed to back his company, Warwick Records, for which Allen Klein and Company did the books. Craft was a key client, paying Allen $125 a month.

With his accounting business slow, Klein hit on the idea of setting up racks in supermarkets to sell hit singles. Dubbing the operation Top Twenty, he made a deal with a New Jersey supermarket chain and tried to raise his profit margins by trading Craft's records, which he got at a discount, to record wholesalers in exchange for the hits he needed. Unfortunately, Warwick didn't produce enough hits of its own to sustain the scheme.

More promising, Craft took a shine to Klein and introduced him to potential music and film clients. When singer Eddie Fisher started his own label, Ramrod Records — Ramrod was Fisher's pet name for his wife at the time, Elizabeth Taylor — it was administered by Warwick. Hoping to get Ramrod as an account, Allen volunteered to deliver legal papers to Fisher and even bought a new tie in case he ran into Taylor. He didn't meet the actress or land the label, and Ramrod, which released just one record, had an even shorter life than the Fisher-Taylor marriage. But Allen was developing a keen interest and appreciation for the way an emerging group of independent film producers did deals.

Ever networking, Klein had moved his offices to 729 Seventh Avenue, just north of Times Square. The building was known for its street-level club, the Metropole, where drummer Gene Krupa had been the featured performer before it devolved into a strip club, and the upper floors at 729 were a bustle of film-related businesses. Allen Klein and Company's new offices were shared with Bernie Kamber, a press agent and Runyonesque Broadway habitué who liked and took an interest in Klein. "Bernie wasn't a client but he was like a father to Allen," said Adrienne Faillace. Kamber's clients and friends included George Burns and Joe DiMaggio but at that moment his hot client was actor Burt Lancaster and Lancaster's cutting-edge company, Hecht-Hill-Lancaster Productions.

In the early fifties, Lancaster and Harold Hecht, his agent, teamed first with Warner Brothers and then with United Artists in what would prove to be groundbreaking artist-production deals. Unlike the other major motion-picture companies, United Artists was not a studio; it did not make films, only financed and distributed them. That meant backing wasn't tied to an agreement to use UA's soundstages and other facilities, spelling greater autonomy — and potential profits — for independent producers. To top it off, the producer maintained ownership. If a producer could line up the stars, the director, the editor, and the writer, it was the best deal in town, as Hecht-Hill-Lancaster demonstrated in 1955 when their UA-distributed film *Marty* — made for $330,000 and grossing $4 million — won numerous Academy Awards, including Best Picture. It spelled a sea change in Hollywood; according to film historian Tino Balio, Hecht-Hill-Lancaster opened a floodgate and washed away the final remnants of the already antiquated studio system. By the following year, many of Hollywood's top actors, including Frank Sinatra, Kirk Douglas, Gregory Peck, and Robert Mitchum, had followed Lancaster's lead into production deals with UA. The ripples from Hecht-Hill-Lancaster's big splash were felt even in the shallows. In 1961, when Klein took a job for a few weeks as the accountant on a low-budget independent film being shot in Miami, *Force of Impulse,* he'd already digested the lessons of independent production espoused by Kamber: If you could make the product yourself, all you needed was a distributor — *and you didn't bargain away any rights beyond that!* It seemed a straightforward formula, and Allen was eager to try his hand at it.

With *Force of Impulse,* Klein believed he'd found a team that could make the product for him. Directed by Saul Swimmer, the film was coproduced by Peter Gayle, whose financing came from a family business in New York's garment district, and Tony Anthony, one of the film's stars. The following year, Klein produced his first film. Originally shot in Florida as *Pity Me Not* but released as *Without Each Other,* it starred Anthony and was directed by Swimmer. Despite Allen's best efforts — he took the film to Cannes, screened it at his own expense, and then placed an ad in *Variety* claiming it had been selected as the Best American Film at Cannes, a nonexistent honor — the movie never found a distributor and was a nearly total loss. But the relationships it led to proved lifelong, with Allen producing several films, from romantic comedies to spaghetti Westerns, that starred Anthony, and Swimmer getting the nod to direct both the forgettable *Mrs. Brown, You've Got a Lovely Daughter* starring Herman's Hermits and the historic documentary film for *The Concert for Bangladesh.*

The failure of *Without Each Other* didn't dampen Allen's belief in Hecht-Hill-Lancaster's independent model; it simply brought home the fact that to make money, you had to sell something worth buying. He would shortly take the lessons he'd learned from the movies and apply them to the music business in ways no one else had.

# 3

## SAM COOKE

NEW YEAR'S DAY 1963 found Allen Klein with little to celebrate. Despite Klein's growing reputation in the music industry as the man to hire if you wanted to uncover hidden money or give your record company agita, his own balance sheet was far from impressive; the company desperately needed more clients, and *Without Each Other* was a never-to-be-recouped stinker. Nor was that film his only expensive lesson.

For years, Klein had hoped to land work from Betty's uncle Marvin Kratter, the real estate executive. Kratter, a CPA and an attorney, was just the kind of high roller Klein aspired to be; his large home in Riverdale, complete with swimming pool, was very much like the one Allen would eventually own. Kratter was also a scrapper. Following an early failure—Kratter went bankrupt in the forties with an Arizona dude ranch—he returned to New York and grew wealthy nearly overnight organizing real estate syndicates. He owned, at various times, Knickerbocker Beer, the Boston Celtics, New York's St. Regis Hotel, and a pharmaceutical company. But nothing in the way of work trickled down to Allen. Five years after forming Allen Klein and Company, Klein was still on the outside with his nose pressed up against the candy-store window; Kratter wouldn't use him. The real estate magnate did, however, have a little inside dope for him.

Recalled Klein: "He came to me and said, 'Allen, I got this stock tip for you. Crescent Petroleum.' I said, 'Really? What is it?' 'Don't worry, buy it.' I said, 'I don't have the money.' 'I'll loan it to you.'"

Thus encouraged, with Kratter's loan, Klein bought twenty-five thousand dollars' worth of the Canadian company's stock — and then watched it die. "As soon as I bought the stock it went into the toilet," he said, adding that he subsequently came to believe he was buying shares that Kratter was dumping. "And he started bugging me for the money. It was incredible pressure."

Mortified, Klein confessed his problems to his in-laws. His mother-in-law called Kratter in high dudgeon, but in the end, his father-in-law paid the debt. It was an indication of how much Klein wanted a big score and of how poorly he was doing. He had a young daughter, Robin, and a second child on the way, and he was feeling the pressure to succeed even more acutely. He didn't know where that success would come from — only that he had to have more clients. When one of them, R&B disk jockey Douglas "Jocko" Henderson, dropped by a few days into the new year with a business proposal, Allen was all ears.

Henderson, with daily shows in both New York and Philadelphia, was one of the most influential and successful radio personalities, black or white, in the business. Unlike Klein, the immigrant butcher's son, Henderson grew up in a solid family of Talented Tenth professionals. Both his parents were educators in Baltimore, and Jocko's decision to go into radio rather than teaching had been a sore point. But Henderson certainly didn't lack initiative; after a year on Baltimore radio, he moved to Philadelphia and became a star with *Jocko's Rocket Ship Show*, first on R&B station WHAT and then every weekday afternoon on WDAS. The records he played and his own trademark rhyming patter —"Eee-tiddly-ock, this is the Jock. And I'm back on the scene with the record machine, saying ooh-pop-a-doo, how do you do?"— became the city's soundtrack and transformed its host into the emcee of the streets and an early influence on the first generation of rappers. In the late fifties, Jocko added a New York show. Both shows were broadcast live, which necessitated daily train trips between Philadelphia and New York. Whatever the strain, though, it made Jocko a key player in two of the country's biggest radio and record markets. He was savvy enough to seize his opportunities.

With few exceptions, radio stations didn't pay lavish salaries to their deejays, and certainly nothing commensurate with the profiles of many of the medium's stars. But that notoriety and the disk jockey's role as tastemaker were fungible commodities. Payola—bribes given to deejays by record companies in exchange for airplay of their songs—was widespread until 1959, when Congress held hearings condemning the practice in general and scapegoating pioneering rock jock Alan Freed in particular. Freed ultimately pleaded guilty to two counts of commercial bribery, yet when he died just five years later—an industry pariah and a broken man at forty-three—payola was still alive and well.

Disk jockeys remained hugely important to record labels and artists, and there were still many ways for an enterprising radio star to capitalize on his position. Good fees might be earned emceeing concerts; it wasn't unusual for a disk jockey to be paid as much or more than a performer for some appearances. Jocko, with a popular daily broadcast and a big following, frequently hosted shows with top R&B artists at Harlem's Apollo Theater, where he made a dramatic entrance riding a rocket hung from wires. Record companies had other ways of showing their gratitude as well. Wand, Scepter Records' sister label, which boasted the Shirelles, Dionne Warwick, and the Isley Brothers, packaged its greatest hits into albums for the disk jockey as *Jocko's Show Stoppers* and *Jocko's Rocket to the Stars*. Henderson also received publishing interests in some of the label's biggest hits, including "Baby, It's You" and "Will You Love Me Tomorrow." Following the lead of another Philadelphia disk jockey, Dick Clark, who avoided Freed's fate by unloading his holdings in a variety of music-publishing and record-manufacturing interests, Jocko eventually sold his Scepter songs. The subsequent and current owner of those rights is Betalbin Music, the first music-publishing company started and owned by Allen Klein.

They came from different worlds, but each man recognized a kindred soul and admired the other's savvy and hustle. Henderson respected Klein's quick, aggressive thinking and nonpareil ability to ferret out funds, and Klein appreciated Henderson's intelligence, ambition, wit, and taste, and their mutual admiration ultimately blossomed into real friendship. For his part, Allen knew he wasn't in Jocko's class; the disk jockey and his wife, a teacher, were bright, sophisticated, and urbane. On one occasion, Allen and Betty, along with her parents, stopped by the Hendersons' West Philadelphia home, and a surprise snowstorm forced them to spend the night. "Jocko was so elegant," said Klein. "He was a great tennis player, a great golfer. He had built a brand-new house that was really nice, and their furnishings and cutlery were all better than ours. Jocko's house was whiter than mine."

The pitch Jocko now brought to Klein was intriguing. While Henderson had his Apollo shows in New York, he had nothing going in Philadelphia. Indeed, a rival disk jockey, Georgie Woods, was mounting successful R&B shows in Philly at the Uptown Theater. Jocko, eager to plant a flag in his home market, had heard that the State Theater, at Fifty-Second and Chestnut, was available but needed work. Would Klein be his partner?

Though America continued to be defined by de facto segregation, partnerships between blacks and whites were not unusual in the music business; cultures and commercial interests overlapped as much or more than in any other industries, and the field was certainly ahead of the country as a whole. Klein, who had black clients throughout his career, never indicated that it was an issue, nor that he was particularly progressive, although he became a regular supporter of the United Negro College Fund. His behavior simply reflected the business; it didn't matter whether you were from the North or the South or if you were black or white — you limited your opportunities if you had a problem dealing across racial lines.

To Allen's way of thinking, the value of Jocko's offer wasn't the theater or ticket sales — it was the chance the shows would provide him to meet and woo artists for Allen Klein and Company. And considering how eager many of them were to make Jocko happy, it certainly wouldn't hurt his prospects to be introduced as Jocko's partner. Allen quickly agreed to the deal. Repairs to the State proved costly (after coughing up money for a new water tower, Jocko started to refer to the theater as Big Mouth), but the two were ready by March with a ten-day run featuring several Scepter acts: Dionne Warwick, the Shirelles, Chuck Jackson, and Tommy Hunt. Also on the show was a New York girl group, the Crystals, as well as the Valentinos, a family band from Cleveland. Initially a gospel group dubbed the Womack Brothers, the Valentinos had only recently scored their first pop hit, "Looking for a Love." They were signed to SAR Records, a California label owned by the singer Sam Cooke, and one of the band's members, Bobby Womack, played guitar in Sam's touring band. It was Cooke who would be headlining the State's debut show.

The singer and the disk jockey had known each other for some time — and Cooke owed Jocko. Originally a gospel star with the Soul Stirrers, Cooke and his then-producer Bumps Blackwell had reached out to Henderson in the fall of 1957, when the singer was looking to cross over to the pop world. According to Jocko, they rang his doorbell unexpectedly — at four a.m. That prompted Jocko to answer the door with a gun tucked in his bathrobe. "I said to myself, what the hell is this?"

"You don't know me," said Cooke, "but we think we have a hit." The record they played for him, "You Send Me," was an obvious smash, and you didn't have to be Jocko Henderson to realize its potential. Though recorded for the small Keen label, it would become Sam's first pop hit and his only one to reach number one on the *Billboard* Hot 100 singles chart. Three weeks after knocking on Jocko's door, Sam was performing in one of the disk jockey's Apollo shows.

Since then, Cooke had remained a fixture on both the pop and R&B charts. He was hard-working and earnestly interested in success; during an appearance on the popular television music show *American Bandstand*, when host Dick Clark asked Cooke what caused him to switch from gospel to pop, he smiled and gave a direct answer: "My economic situation." At that point, the performer whose career Sam most hoped to emulate was Harry Belafonte. Though best known for Calypso-flavored pop hits like "Day-O (the Banana Boat Song)," Belafonte was comfortable singing just about anything and never hesitated to perform folk, show tunes, blues, or standards, achieving a level of success and critical acclaim rarely enjoyed by black artists to this day. For Cooke, who had broken out of gospel, the idea of being limited to R&B — or any slice of the pop market — was anathema. He'd learned a lot in his still-young career, about both the business and his craft, and he consciously sought to succeed simultaneously in the black, white, and teen markets. But Cooke was more than simply savvy and seasoned; he was easily as much of an artist as Belafonte, wholly convincing whether he was singing about God in heaven or Cokes in the icebox. He was capable of conveying a wide range of emotions, and he was a commanding performer whose feel for a song — usually one he'd written — was as true and unquestionable as a heartbeat.

None of which Allen Klein knew. Yes, he had an inkling of Cooke's career and certainly didn't question Jocko's choice of him as their first headliner. But it wasn't until rehearsals that Allen, parked in the State's otherwise-empty upper balcony with his pregnant wife and young daughter, was able to connect the man to the music.

"I heard the voice, and I said, 'Oh, I know that! I *know* that!' His voice was incredible. And I watched him the entire week. I was impressed as hell."

When Jocko later introduced the singer to Klein, Allen was atypically bashful; he was intrigued by Sam and more than a little in awe of him. The man had it all: brains, talent, taste, good looks, and a breezy confidence that Klein took as charisma. Whatever else motivated Allen Klein, he was earnestly smitten with Sam Cooke, captivated by his presence.

"I looked up to Sam Cooke," he said. "I was amazed. He was a little older than me, like a year. But he knew so much more than I did. It was easy to believe in someone. I would believe in him."

Loyal to his partner, Jocko was not shy in singing Allen's praises to Sam. "I don't know what Jocko said but he certainly talked me up pretty good," Klein recalled. It wasn't the first Cooke was hearing of him; Lloyd Price had already told Sam about his accountant in New

York who had a special talent for putting the fear of God in record companies and for finding money. Cooke had been eager to meet him.

For perhaps the only time in his life, Klein undersold himself. Indeed, he largely stayed out of Sam's way, talking instead to the singer's road manager through most of the first week's engagement. "I was very reserved. I certainly was not pushy, just trying to get a fix on his ambitions and attitude." But at the end of the run, Cooke came to talk with Klein, complaining about the way he was treated as an artist and a man.

At first blush, most of Cooke's concerns appeared to be with his record company, RCA. He did not believe the executives were giving him a straight accounting. "I've been calling and calling and calling and I never get a call back," he told Klein. Allen urged him to keep at it — he found it hard to believe the label would ignore an important artist — and to think specifically about what he wanted from Klein. They agreed to speak again the next month.

In April, Klein contacted Cooke, and the singer was on tour but eager to see him. The two met in Tampa, and Sam said he still couldn't get RCA's head of A&R, Bob Yorke, to return his calls. Allen urged him to give it one more shot, and he did, but that, too, proved futile. "Well, what do you think?" Cooke asked. Replied Klein: "I think they're treating you like a nigger, and that's terrible, and you shouldn't let them do it." Years later, Klein would tell Cooke biographer Peter Guralnick that he hadn't intended to speak so plainly. "Sometimes, you know, you just say things — I didn't plan that, I just spit it out."

Of course, the same thought had already occurred to Cooke. "You're right," he said. "I want you to go after them."

Whatever frustrations Cooke was having with RCA, his years in gospel and then pop had produced a healthy respect for business, and he took an ambitious and informed approach to his career. Though employing a variety of managers, associates, and administrators, Sam was firmly in control and calling many of the creative shots. While personally signed to RCA, Cooke had established a record company, SAR, to find and record other artists, and he ran his own music-publishing company, Kags. In an effort to sidestep publishing agreements he had signed earlier in his career, Sam gave the songwriting credit on many of his biggest hits to his wife, Barbara Campbell.

Klein quickly discovered that although Sam was far thinking, he was nonetheless cash poor. SAR was eating up a good deal of Cooke's income, and whatever money he made on the road went out about as quickly as it came in. Though he lived comfortably, Sam didn't have much to show for all the hits he'd enjoyed and songs he'd written.

To give Cooke a quick cash infusion, Allen restructured Sam's BMI deal, getting $29,000 in guarantees against his songwriting royalties for the next two years and an additional $50,000 for him as the publisher. It was the Klein specialty, just as advertised: found money. Delighted, Cooke solidified the relationship, giving Allen Klein and Company a five-year contract to administer Kags Music and SAR Records. Having quickly demonstrated that he could deliver, Klein set about taking the measure of RCA and crafting the most advantageous deal he could for his most promising client.

Cooke's introductory letter got Allen in the door at RCA but didn't produce much cooperation from Yorke. That was all right with Klein; Sam's RCA contract wouldn't run much longer. And if RCA wasn't willing to give them the money they wanted, they'd get it somewhere else. Indeed, they already had a circuitous in at Columbia Records, where Sam, through his William Morris booking agent, Jerry Brandt, had been talking about helping his friend boxer Cassius Clay make a record.

Dave Kapralik was the Columbia A&R man for the Clay project. Klein approached him and said he'd be willing to bring Cooke to Columbia for the right deal—in his estimation, a 10 percent royalty. Kapralik nearly choked on Klein's grand expectations but quickly handed him off to Walter Dean, an attorney who oversaw Columbia's business affairs. Dean told Klein that no one at Columbia had a royalty rate of more than 5 percent and no one ever would, owing to what was known as the most-favored-nation clause. That contractual stipulation was given to stars and guaranteed them the company's highest royalty rate. Paying Sam Cooke 10 percent meant a host of other performers' percentages would have to be raised, and that wasn't going to happen.

If the clause was a negotiating ploy, it was a good one — but not good enough to prevent Klein from shrugging and saying they might be willing to take 5 percent on albums but that Sam definitely deserved 10 percent on singles since his hits sold themselves and Columbia didn't have to do anything. Not surprisingly, that didn't get any traction either.

Allen was disappointed; he'd thought Columbia a better and classier record company than RCA and a more suitable place for Sam. However, it occurred to him that if Sam left RCA, he would be leaving his catalog behind. Spurned labels could be spiteful and weren't averse to dumping previously unreleased or even substandard tracks on the market just as a former artist was promoting a record on his or her new label. Conversely, a smart record company could use a new hit to promote an artist's back catalog — if they had it — and keep it viable, and that meant more money for everyone. Maybe it made sense for Cooke to stay at RCA, though Klein ensured that executives there knew he was talking to Columbia. The news that Bob Yorke, who'd been so slow to deal with Sam, was no longer calling the shots was another positive. Still, Allen walked away from his Columbia conversations thinking about the most-favored-nation clause. As far as he was concerned, it was a label scam for limiting artist royalties. There had to be a way to beat it.

Yorke's new boss was Joe D'Imperio, an attorney who'd risen through the ranks at RCA to become vice president in charge of business affairs. One of D'Imperio's first moves was to reach out to Cooke and try to mend fences. The singer sent D'Imperio back to Klein.

It was the moment Allen had been waiting for. D'Imperio might be a new face but RCA had been giving Sam the runaround for far too long and Klein had a message to deliver: Things were going to be different. He drove the point home with an elaborate piece of theater.

A lunch meeting was set up at RCA with D'Imperio, executive Norm Racusin, Klein, and Cooke's partner and adviser J. W. Alexander. Looking to turn the page, D'Imperio was outgoing and gracious, emphasizing how much he thought of Sam as a performer and how happy the label was to have him; he suggested they forget about the past and talk about a new, extended contract.

Allen wasn't going to let the company off the hook so easily. He noted that while Sam's hits hadn't sold as well as they should have — for which he blamed RCA — he nonetheless believed that Kags Music, as the publisher of most of those hits, was owed a lot of money by the label, perhaps as much as two hundred thousand dollars. He expected the label to provide them with a complete accounting. Though D'Imperio didn't refuse, he clearly didn't like the idea and he reiterated how much faith they had in Cooke and that they'd like to craft a new agreement. Klein, who knew the label would resist giving them detailed financial information, played his next card. A few minutes after Klein and Alexander left the office, process servers came in and hit RCA with a demand for an audit.

Eager to gauge the reaction, Allen and J. W. hung around the building lobby. They were getting their shoes shined when an apoplectic Racusin burst out of the elevator waving the legal service, his face flushed. "I invite you here for lunch," he said. "And you serve me with *papers?*" It was clear what he thought Klein could do with the documents — and any further negotiations.

Allen feigned shock. "What? You've been served? Let me call my lawyer."

With Alexander and Racusin watching, Klein went to a pay phone and called Machat. "Marty? I'm at RCA. I came over to have lunch with Norm Racusin and he's just been served with papers. How could this happen?"

"Allen, you *told* me to do it!"

"Oh, this is terrible. I can't believe you did this!"

Klein made a show of apologizing profusely to Racusin and D'Imperio, but no one missed the message. Cooke got full access to his RCA accounting, and Allen had a stronger hand when, indeed, they sat down to negotiate the new deal.

• • •

*Without Each Other,* Klein's first foray into producing films, never found a distributor and never made a dime. It nonetheless may have been Allen's greatest investment, as it gave him the first experience with a business model he would use and expand on again and again over the years. Noting how Hecht-Hill-Lancaster had revolutionized the film industry, moving the locus of control away from the studios and to the filmmakers, Allen got to thinking. Why couldn't the same be done in the music business? You didn't need a studio to produce a motion picture; did you need a record company to produce your own records?

Though seemingly obvious now, at the time, it was actually a radical question. Fans might be interested in the performers, but in practice, pop records were a producer's medium. At the major labels like RCA, Columbia, and Capitol, casting was as important in making records as it was in making movies. The executives who oversaw the process were known as A&R men, for artists and repertoire, and it was their job to match performers with producers and material. With few exceptions, it was the record company, not the performer, dictating what was to be recorded and how it was to sound. Success and a growing artistic ambition might allow a Frank Sinatra to exert control over his material, but many others were perfectly content to follow the record company's lead. As Warner Brothers Records executive Joe Smith recalled, Dean Martin could hear one of his own records and wonder when it had been recorded.

At the small, independent record companies like Sun, Red Bird, Philles, and Scepter that were proving so important in the growth of rock 'n' roll and R&B, the situation was only a bit different. In virtually every case, those independents were run by or relied heavily on masterly producers like Phil Spector and Luther Dixon, men who had a deep appreciation for the music and were at least as likely as the performers to be its true architects. The independents weren't necessarily any more generous or artist-friendly than the majors, and their immediacy and savvy owed as much to a scratch-and-claw desire to succeed financially as it did to their understanding of the music and the young people they were making it for. They had broken out on their own for a variety of reasons, including a feel for the music, a belief in its commercial and artistic viability, and — certainly not least — a conviction that they could succeed on their own without the major labels. The producers and label owners reaped the rewards of independence, not the artists.

Klein represented the artist. He believed the deck was stacked unfairly against the artists in recording deals, and he now took the same doggedly indignant tone he'd used so effectively in audits into contract negotiations. His gleefully pugnacious style would resonate with artists and annoy the hell out of record executives, as would his voluble pride in his own audacity. He loved it when labels complained. It was the best endorsement he could earn. "Talk about *my* reputation, what about the record companies'?" he asked. "It's not like I was in church kicking over statues." Allen ingeniously recognized that a complete artist like Cooke — who could write, perform, and produce his own records — had a wealth of leverage at his fingertips. Sam Cooke didn't need RCA. RCA needed Sam Cooke. Klein let them both know it. Record-company contracts presupposed a pop performer's complete creative and commercial dependence; it was assumed that the singer should not make artistic decisions. That wasn't a true assessment of Cooke's artistic abilities and the value he brought to any recording agreement. Financing aside, he needed a record company only to manufacture, market, and distribute his work. Why should the company be involved in creative decisions that Sam was better suited to make? More to the point, Klein knew that an independent film producer like Hecht-Hill-Lancaster maintained ownership of the films it created. Why should RCA own Sam Cooke's recordings?

Allen explained the idea, first to Sam and later to RCA's D'Imperio, and had Cooke start his own company. Tracey Ltd., named for the singer's daughter, would produce and own Sam's recordings. RCA would pay for the sessions, and in return for that and a royalty, it would get exclusive distribution rights to Tracey and to Sam's recordings. Tracey — not RCA — would manufacture and package the records, which would then be sold to RCA, which in turn would raise the price and sell them to retailers. Klein told D'Imperio that Tracey was willing to give RCA exclusive rights for five years, after which all rights would revert to Tracey. The executive said that was out of the question — RCA wouldn't agree to fewer than thirty years.

That RCA would allow the rights to ever revert to Cooke was a surprise. Columbia had agreed to fifty-year reversions to the artists, but that was nearly the legal length that a sound recording could be copyrighted,* so the corporation wasn't giving much up. Other labels — notably Capitol in its dealings with Frank Sinatra — had staunchly refused such arrangements.

Whether out of a sense of fairness or simply because he was unconvinced that Cooke's work would still have significant commercial value after thirty years, D'Imperio allowed Klein and Cooke to open negotiations in an area previously closed: ownership of the recordings. In future years, reversion of masters to performers would be an important and lucrative bargaining point for recording artists, with term lengths shrinking. Not coincidentally, one of the most masterly negotiators in this area would prove to be another Klein graduate, Mick Jagger.

Klein was proposing that RCA sign a contract not with Cooke but with an outside company that controlled Cooke's rights. That would have two important and immediate results.

The first was that Tracey would press the records, which meant the company had the chance to make even more money. RCA, instead of manufacturing the records and paying Cooke approximately twenty-five cents an album as a royalty, would pay Tracey a bit over a dollar an album on average, out of which Tracey had to pay all royalties, licenses, and manufacturing costs, including pressing the records and making the covers. The margins were slim but there was certainly an opportunity to grab a few more cents out of every dollar. Klein insisted that RCA provide an accounting to Cooke every month rather than twice a year; if money was due, he didn't want someone else sitting on it.

Second, Klein argued that since Cooke wasn't signed to RCA, the most-favored-nation clause didn't apply and the executives were free

---

* The U.S. has subsequently extended the term to seventy years.

to set a higher royalty rate. In actuality, it didn't matter to RCA what the royalty rate was since Tracey was responsible for paying it out of the set price for the delivered album, and D'Imperio agreed to a royalty rate of 6 percent. The additional point proved more than a psychological victory for Klein; he would later say he convinced Cooke to let him, as Tracey's administrator, keep the approximately five cents RCA paid per album. Call the deal for Tracey a sleight of hand or call it brilliant, it was state-of-the-art; in his first negotiation of a major recording contract, Klein had taken the standard deal apart and put it back together the way he wanted it.

The RCA contract put ready money in Cooke's hands. A three-year deal with two option years, it guaranteed Sam a cash advance of $100,000 per year with an additional $75,000 for each option year. If the deal went to term, it was worth no less than $450,000.

According to Klein, he was trying to minimize Cooke's tax liability when he had Tracey pay the first $100,000 to Cooke in the form of preferred stock, an investment that mimicked a bond by paying set dividends and that Klein had become keen on. The certificates were deposited in Cooke's California bank account.

As Klein explained it to Cooke, Cooke would have to pay taxes only when he converted a portion of the stocks to cash. The reason they could do this, Allen said, was that he'd set Tracey up as a holding company that he, Allen, owned, and he'd registered the company in Nevada, where corporate regulations and taxes were light. If it had been Sam's private holding company, the IRS was certain to treat money paid to Tracey as personal income. This gave Cooke and Klein more latitude. "If he'd owned the company," Klein explained years later, "he would have had to pick up the income and not let it lay in the company."* Whatever the setup, it was hard to see Tracey as anything but Cooke's business; it was named for his daughter, and its president was his long-term partner J. W. Alexander. Sam was delighted.

---

* Though the government takes a dim view of schemes assigning income to outside individuals or entities, Tracey was never challenged, and Klein's plan was legally sound.

Yom Kippur is the holiest day of the Jewish year, a day for fasting and reflection. On Yom Kippur 1963, Allen found himself in a New Orleans hotel rather than a New York synagogue. Cooke was on tour and Klein was there to go over how they would handle the first $100,000 advance from RCA—and to collect his commission. It was a check that Sam was more than happy to write. Indeed, Cooke had a surprise for Allen.

"Would you manage me?" he asked.

Klein was at a rare loss for words. "I never managed anyone before," he sputtered.

Sam shrugged. "I was never a songwriter until I wrote my first song."

For Klein, who regarded Cooke with an admiration that bordered on awe, it was all the encouragement and validation he needed. Allen knew he'd gotten the job done with RCA—"It was the first time Sam ever saw money like that," he later said—but he hadn't expected or even angled for this. He quickly warmed to the idea.

Indeed, it wasn't long before Klein was actively looking for other artists to manage. He had a very specific type in mind: performers who, like Cooke, had the track records and musicianship to make their own records and fit into the independent-production model that Allen had extrapolated from the film business. The pop singer Bobby Vinton caught his eye. Vinton was on a roll—between the summer of 1962 and the fall of 1964 he'd scored four number-one singles—and Klein and Machat approached him and offered to handle him.

Vinton said he already had a manager. But he didn't have what Sam Cooke's manager said he could get him: a million dollars. It was a huge sum of money, even for a performer enjoying a hot run on the charts. Allen told Vinton he had a plan, and once again, he had borrowed it from somewhere else and reimagined it for his own purposes.

The month after Allen Klein became Sam Cooke's manager, another enterprising music manager, Brian Epstein, got an enormous break. The Beatles, his young English band, were a bona fide phenomenon at home, setting off fan riots wherever they appeared. But the United States was proving frustrating; executives at Capitol Records, the

American affiliate of the band's British record company, EMI, didn't like the Beatles and had steadfastly refused to release an American single. All that changed when the American television host Ed Sullivan, traveling in London, got a firsthand look at Beatlemania. Booking the band for three appearances on his Sunday-evening variety show, Sullivan forced Capitol's hand. By mid-January of '64, the Beatles' first Capitol single, "I Want to Hold Your Hand," was number one, a position it held for seven weeks; it was replaced by another one of their singles, "She Loves You," which Capitol had refused and EMI had licensed to another label. The first wave of what was soon called the British Invasion had crashed on America's shores.

Klein's initial contact with the newcomers was fleeting but significant. The Dave Clark Five, one of the Beatles' earliest and most successful rivals for America's affections — they were the first British Invasion band to tour the U.S. and made more than a dozen appearances on the *Ed Sullivan Show* — had signed a successful but short-term contract in the States with CBS's Epic Records. Both sides were eager to extend it. The band's London agent, Harold Davison, engaged Klein to negotiate on their behalf.

Unlike the situation with Cooke, little was expected of Klein in the way of strategy. On the contrary, Clark was the rarest of birds on the burgeoning British music scene: a hard-nosed businessman who recognized the financial value of his work, particularly his publishing, and who was firmly in control of his career. Promised 5 percent of the value of the deal rather than a continuing interest in Clark's career, Klein would later characterize his work for Clark and Davison as "a money deal," suggesting it wasn't anything of significance. Though the relationship was brief, that wasn't quite true.

Epic and Clark had little trouble coming to financial terms; they readily agreed on a five-year contract with a guaranteed advance of $250,000. The figure was excellent. The rub was taxes.

British income taxes at the time could be onerous, particularly on income earned abroad. If the Dave Clark Five took their $250,000 as a lump-sum advance, they would be taxed at a rate of approximately 90 percent, and possibly more. The idea of pocketing $25,000 — at best! — was hardly appealing. However, British tax laws could be more reasonable when it came to money acquired abroad in other ways, including as capital gains or as interest on investments. The idea, it was explained to Klein, would be to maximize tax advantages by investing the band's money in the U.S. and getting the payments over twenty years. Under that scheme, the band would eventually realize the full value of the contract.

It was Klein's first real exposure to Britain's Byzantine foreign-tax laws, and it gave him what would prove to be extremely valuable insights just as a horde of British recording artists and their handlers started searching for ways to hold on to money earned in America. Just as significant, Allen immediately realized that the scheme left money on the table — or at least underutilized it. He estimated that Clark would need to invest only around $80,000 in preferred stock to get a payout of $250,000 over twenty years.

Pondering his own commission in this arrangement, Klein projected that 5 percent of $250,000 invested over twenty years could net him $87,500. He just didn't want to wait that long. Armed with those figures, Klein convinced Davison that he should be paid his fee immediately rather than over twenty years — although why Davison agreed to let that much principal out of the investment is baffling; perhaps he viewed Klein as his only chance to circumvent an immediate and draconian tax bill. For his part, Klein could argue that the band still stood to make significantly more than $250,000 over the life of the annuity. "The artist doesn't get hurt at all," he claimed. "And that's how I made the deal and learned how to make money from the money."

With Vinton, Klein took the idea to "make money from the money" in a different direction; by investing recording and publishing advances, Allen guaranteed the singer greater income over the long run. "His idea was something that nobody was doing at that time," said Vinton. "Instead of giving me one lump sum to sign with him, if you spread it over twenty years, he could get a larger sum. It sounded good to me that he could get me a million over twenty years — it sounded awful good." When Bobby again expressed concern about already having a manager, Klein told him not to worry; he and Machat would take care of everything. "You sign with me and I'll get you out of your contract with your other manager," Vinton recalled being told. He agreed.

If not a towering talent to rival Cooke, Vinton was certainly a polished professional with an impressive track record, and he was just the kind of well-rounded artist Allen wanted. It didn't matter if the records were hokey or schmaltzy; Klein respected Vinton's success and musical abilities. "When I was involved with Bobby Vinton, everyone used to laugh: 'Sam Cooke and Bobby Vinton? How do you do that?' Bobby Vinton was a college graduate with a music degree who played every instrument. He started as a bandleader. I gravitated to artists who were creators, who did it, because I couldn't do it. I could be an appreciative fan, I might be able to help after I have my sense of things. But physically do it? I couldn't."

Born Stanley Robert Vinton Jr. in Canonsburg, Pennsylvania, Bobby had been working professionally since grade school, playing clarinet in a band led by his father. With a degree in music composition from Duquesne University and an army stint as a trumpeter on his résumé, Vinton was signed to Epic Records as an instrumentalist — and initially flopped. It was only the fear of being dropped that led him to try singing. His first effort, 1962's "Roses Are Red," went to number one and stayed there for a month.

The Jewish accountant and the singer dubbed the Polish Prince were an unlikely pair, one an unapologetic hustler, the other a guileless and unfailingly upbeat musician. Vinton was a devout Catholic and a family man who featured first his mother and later his daughter in his stage shows, and he relied on more than the best efforts of his record company and the machinations of Allen Klein for his success: before the release of a new single, he would visit St. Patrick's Cathedral in New York to pray that the record would do well. "I pray to the Blessed Mother," he said. "That's been my secret when I wanted hit records, help, whatever." Yet as different as they were, the two men grew close. Hard-working and serious about his career, Vinton had great admiration for Klein's keen intelligence and even keener chutzpah, and he loved to simply sit in the office and take it all in, watching and listening as Allen conducted business and worked the telephone. "I was from a small town," said Vinton. "I was a musician, a singer — the talent — I didn't know about wheeling and dealing and the way show business minds worked. He was like a professor of life and deals. He was just so bright compared to anybody else. And if he wasn't, he made you think he was. Yeah. He had the power of swaying everybody."

Vinton never doubted Klein. "I loved Allen Klein," he said. "Five or six years he represented me. He worked hard and liked to make waves. He figured the more waves he'd make, the bigger he would become. We were very good friends, but he didn't have too many friends in those days. All I did was defend him with so many people. They said, 'Why would you want to be with that guy?' I'd say, 'I don't care what you think of him. He has my best interests at heart.'"

Indeed, Vinton's best interests and making waves were synonymous to Klein, who appeared to relish nothing more than raising Vinton's profile by picking a fight. An otherwise flattering article about Vinton in *Life* magazine got Allen's dander up when it characterized the singer as "the most successful unknown in show business." Klein's pugnacious answer to the left-handed compliment was to post a billboard of Vinton on Broadway that trumpeted BOBBY VINTON — BIGGER THAN LIFE!

When Vinton's engagement at the Fontainebleau Hotel in Miami drew disappointing crowds despite having children's-television star Shari Lewis and her beloved hand puppet Lamb Chop as Vinton's supporting act, Allen was furious to discover the hotel hadn't bought any newspaper ads. Klein telephoned the *Miami News* and was told Fontainebleau owner Ben Novack was feuding with the tabloid. Allen's subsequent full-page ad did more to castigate Novack than publicize the singer's appearance: BOBBY VINTON THINKS THE *MIAMI NEWS* IS IMPORTANT EVEN THOUGH BEN NOVACK DOESN'T. The reviewer the paper subsequently sent weighed in with an unqualified rave. Said Vinton: "You know I was never going back *there*. So that's another one off the list. But I love the guy in spite of it all."

Klein's stunts could also backfire. When Vinton hosted the music variety show *Hullabaloo* in the spring of '65, Klein, with the aid of an assistant, Iris Keitel, took the liberty of making wholesale changes to the singer's cue cards just as the show was about to be recorded. The producer and director had a fit.

Knowing taping was starting, Klein seized the initiative. "Let's go," he told Vinton. "We're walking—put on your coat!"

In a swift turnaround, the executives begged Klein and Vinton to stay, asking why they were upset.

"You didn't honor Bobby's contract," Klein fumed. Vinton was performing a half a dozen songs on the show, including two with another Klein client, Chad and Jeremy, but everyone else was supposed to be limited to two numbers. Pointing to the show's summary, Klein accused the producers of reneging on the agreement by letting another act, the Youngfolk, perform three songs: "Come Judgment Day," "Skip to My Lou," and "Segue." It was explained to Klein that the last wasn't a song but a camera direction, and order, if not sanity, was restored.

Though Vinton would eventually host his own half-hour TV variety show in the late seventies—long after Klein had ceased to manage him—he believed *Hullabaloo*'s producers Gary Smith and Dwight Hemion were so mad that they effectively had him blackballed from television for five years. "I don't know who they hated more," he said, "Allen or me."

Whatever friendship Klein had with Vinton and Henderson, he eschewed handholding. "These performers aren't children," he said. "They're not delinquents who don't know what they're doing. They're grownups; they don't need personal managers like a parent or a warden. But they're not businessmen." Frankly admitting he knew nothing about making records, Allen nonetheless believed that part of his job as business manager—a term he claimed to have coined—was weighing in on artistic decisions and offering opinions about the work. He was particularly keen on the subject of whether a song would or wouldn't make a good single, and with an ear for melody and a remarkable memory for lyrics, he wasn't shy about lobbying for one or denigrating another. But the broader strokes—what might be best for the artist's career—were foremost in his mind.

Allen was mesmerized by Sam Cooke's talent and believed his future was unlimited. Cooke's aspiration to be a complete artist, to work and succeed beyond category, had Allen's wholehearted support. Klein's faith in Cooke's wide-ranging abilities and ultimate appeal was especially evident in the way he pushed the singer to pursue disparate goals. When Sam had something serious to say, Allen trusted that he had the vision and authority to succeed. Simultaneously, he pushed Cooke to refocus on his career as a mainstream nightclub singer, a lucrative area that had proven problematic and frustrating for Sam.

One of Cooke's few high-profile failures had been an appearance at the Copacabana in New York, the premier nightclub in the city and perhaps the country. The show had been poorly conceived — Sam, dressed in a tuxedo with a top hat and cane, was the opening act for Borscht Belt comedian Myron Cohen — and was poorly received; the club ended what was supposed to be a two-week engagement after just three nights. Though stung, Sam owned that the quick hook had been an accurate judgment: he hadn't been ready.

Returning to the Copa as a headliner and erasing the early humiliation became both a wish and a weight, as Cooke wanted to go back but feared another failure. Allen, certain that Sam could play for any audience in any venue, pressed him. "I thought it was essential that Sam return to the Copa and wipe out his memory," he said. To counter the singer's doubts, Allen, J. W. Alexander, and Joe D'Imperio took Sam to the club for a show by Nat "King" Cole. "I said, 'It's no big deal,'" Klein recalled. "'You're afraid of something you haven't seen.'"

Watching Cole seemed to do the trick. "He's just shucking," Cooke told Klein. "This is easy."

To make it happen, Klein first switched Cooke's agent, moving him from Jerry Brandt at William Morris to Buddy Howe at GAC. Brandt — young, brash, and much hipper than Howe — was a true Cooke fan. But Howe, an old show-business warhorse and the founder and chairman of GAC, had the ear of Jules Podell, the Copa's imperious impresario. It was the worst-kept secret in New York that Podell, a gruff-talking former bouncer, was a frontman for mobster Frank Costello. The loss of Cooke stung Brandt, who believed Klein had other motives for moving the singer.

"Allen wanted a new relationship where he was the focus," said Brandt. "Do you really think the William Morris Agency couldn't get a Copa deal? GAC was a minor agency. Allen had to be the man." Whatever the reason, Podell was uninterested in Sam at first; the singer wasn't the only one who remembered his last Copa appearance. But Podell came around when Klein hired two press agents and convinced RCA to back the gig by buying many of the club's tables in advance.

Cooke continued to waffle in the weeks leading up to the show, and Klein pushed harder. "I decided to take a billboard in Times Square and embarrass him into it," he said. The enormous picture of the singer was slugged SAM'S THE BIGGEST COOKE IN TOWN! Though Sam was tickled and the billboard proved a good promotional stunt for the Copa run, he remained nervous. It wasn't his usual audience, and he fretted that he couldn't perform his typical show.

At Howe's suggestion, a pair of warm-up gigs in the Catskills were booked for the preceding weekend. The first, at the Laurels Hotel and Country Club, was a disaster. The hotel happened to be hosting a firemen's convention, and since the conventioneers were to be fed that evening at an outdoor barbecue, no food or drink was available during the performance. Worse, Sam ditched his own material for an ill-advised grab bag of pop tunes and standards ranging from "The Sheik of Araby" to "The Girl from Ipanema." Though Cooke soldiered on tenaciously, most of the crowd wandered outside in search of dinner before the show's end.

Klein, who'd had a wisdom tooth pulled that morning, suddenly had a headache to match his sore jaw. He felt like a corner man whose champion fighter had suddenly forgotten everything that had earned him his title. When he got to Cooke's dressing room, Klein did not mince words.

"What the fuck did you just do?" he asked.

"I don't want to do it," he said.

"Stop trying to be someone else. All you have to do is your material."

The following night, at the Raleigh Hotel, Cooke revamped the show with the help of arranger and guitarist René Hall. Sam kept a fair number of standards, including "Frankie and Johnny" and "(I Love

You) For Sentimental Reasons," but refocused his performance on several of his hits. The high point was his handling of a pair of recent folk songs, "If I Had a Hammer" and "Blowin' in the Wind." The singer had found the elusive middle ground — the real Sam Cooke, but tailored for the dinner crowd. The Copa run proved a resounding hit both for Cooke, who cemented his reputation as an all-around performer and could now command big money dates in Las Vegas, and the club, which attracted a significant black audience for the first time. The Copa would soon host key nightclub appearances by several soul artists, among them Motown's the Supremes, the Temptations, Marvin Gaye, and Martha and the Vandellas. If Sam Cooke didn't transform the nightclub scene single-handedly, he certainly helped bring uptown downtown.

Klein, perhaps nervous about having been so confrontational, picked opening night at the Copa to surprise Cooke with a Rolls-Royce, paid for by Tracey Ltd. Yet he clearly had a sense of Sam and was pushing him in appropriate directions. "He was trying to be what he wasn't," Klein recalled. "RCA wanted Sam Cooke to be Nat King Cole. Sam Cooke wanted to be Harry Belafonte. I wanted Sam Cooke to be Sam Cooke."

Cooke was never more himself than on his unsurpassed American psalm, "A Change Is Gonna Come." As the Copa songs demonstrated, Cooke had been paying more than passing attention to the ongoing folk revival, and he was both moved and inspired by what he heard. Recalled Klein: "He said a black guy should have written 'Blowin' in the Wind.' *I* should have written 'Blowin' in the Wind.'"

Though Cooke keyed off the same timeliness and urgency that invested Bob Dylan's song, his musical roots weren't in folk but gospel. The resulting record was more than timely; it was timeless. Like the civil rights movement for which it served as an anthem, "A Change Is Gonna Come" does not crumble in angry, bitter despair but rises like an angel on wings of grace and spiritual transcendence. It is another profound dream: the triumph of faith over brutality and ignorance. Shortly after the song's release, the original recording was donated to an album benefiting the Southern Christian Leadership Conference, the organization closely associated with the Reverend Dr. Martin Luther King.

Klein loved the song, not just for the message, but for what it said about the messenger. Sam was clearly the rarest of popular artists, one capable of both entertaining and inspiring, and Allen took satisfaction and more than a little pride in the belief that he was helping to make it possible. When Allen heard "A Change Is Gonna Come," he knew it would also change the way the world viewed Cooke. Cooke had an appearance slated for the following week on *The Tonight Show,* and Klein lobbied hard for Cooke to perform the song.

Sam wasn't so sure—and RCA was dead set against it. "RCA was nervous as shit about 'A Change Is Gonna Come,'" Allen said. "It was not being released as a single—the single was 'Ain't That Good News.'" When Sam had a television appearance, the plan was for him to perform one middle-of-the-road number—in this case, "Basin Street Blues"—and his latest single. Nonetheless, Klein argued vociferously that this was the moment to make a career statement, that *that* trumped the marketing of any single. Sam first dismissed the idea, saying he didn't have the charts with him and that the *Tonight Show* orchestra lacked the proper instrumentation. But when Klein upped the ante by offering to pay for the additional musicians out of his own pocket, Cooke agreed.

For Klein, who sat in the audience during the New York taping, it had to be a moment of intense satisfaction. Sam's faith in him—his recognition that Allen could help his career—had been borne out. Even more satisfying, his insistence on "A Change Is Gonna Come" confirmed something about his own business style that Allen now believed even more fervently: he would make it by playing on the outer edges of the industry. Given the choice between taking the safe, well-worn path and following his gut—well, there was no choice.

As important as they'd quickly become to each other's careers, Klein and Cooke had surprisingly little in the way of a personal relationship. "I had very little to do with Sam socially," Allen admitted. There was one tragic exception: not long after Klein and Cooke began working together, Sam's infant son, Vincent, drowned in the pool at Sam's Los Angeles home. When Allen arrived in Los Angeles the following week to pay his respects, he discovered that the devastated singer had buried his grief by going right back to work. Allen told Sam he'd spent his lifetime wishing he'd had a mother and that his father hadn't shunted him aside, and he insisted they take their daughters for a day at Disneyland. "You can't forget you've got two other kids," Allen told him. "You got to be there for them."

Indeed, it wasn't until Cooke's own death the following year that Allen finally visited Sam's home — albeit to help his widow, Barbara, get a handle on Sam's finances. Killed in a bizarre and seemingly senseless incident — the singer, half-naked, was shot by the desk clerk at a Hollywood fleabag motel after a woman he'd met at a party ran off with his pants and money — it was an abrupt and demeaning end to what should have been a glorious life.

Sensational, seamy, and improbable as the facts appeared, Cooke's death started a hotbed of rumors, and Klein himself was skeptical enough to hire a private detective to check the official police version. He was quickly convinced there wasn't more to know. Still, a conspiracy theory needs little to flourish, and fans and disbelievers had a whole host of likely culprits to choose from, ranging from the Mob to Barbara Cooke to Allen Klein.

The stray fact fueling this last speculation was Tracey Ltd. Just a year earlier, Klein had created the company supposedly as a tax dodge to benefit Sam Cooke. Now Cooke was dead — and the person who owned the company that controlled his recordings and to which all the rights related to the master recordings would eventually revert was Allen Klein.

Was it luck? Prescience? Connivance? Whatever Klein had told Cooke, it soon became clear that Klein hadn't simply stumbled into an arrangement that gave him the lion's share of Sam's estate.

Theatrical producer Laurence Myers, a British business manager and an accountant by training, met Klein several months before Cooke's death and credited Allen with altering the course of his own career. "Allen taught me something without which I wouldn't have the lifestyle I do today," said Myers. "'Don't take twenty percent of an art-ist's income—give them eighty percent of yours.' The difference be-tween Allen and I is that I actually told them that was what was going to happen. And Allen certainly didn't. They found out sometime later." Myers paused. "So he was no accountant."

It's tempting to speculate what might have happened with Tracey Ltd. had Cooke not died. Sam was a thoughtful businessman and far more sophisticated than most artists. As happy as he was with the initial outcome of Klein's RCA negotiations, it's hard to believe he wouldn't have ultimately recognized the true value of the rights and revenues remaining with Tracey and short-circuited the company, perhaps forcing a renegotiation or splitting with Klein and limiting his future participation in his recordings. Instead, the opposite hap-pened. After Cooke's death, Klein grew Tracey, ultimately putting out more recordings with RCA and acquiring ownership of earlier Cooke hits made for the Keen label. And more immediately, he found himself with an unexpected opportunity: Soon after Sam died, Barbara Cooke told Klein she wanted to sell the rights she'd inherited to his music publishing. Klein advised her against it, he later said, but nonetheless bought them.

The perception that Klein stood to gain from his client's death fu-eled rumors that something nefarious was afoot. Silly as the stories were, they added something new and sinister to Klein's public and pro-fessional persona. Joe McEwen, one of the most knowledgeable A&R executives in the music business, came to work with and admire Klein in his later years. But as a young executive at Columbia Records in the seventies, he was leery of returning the routine business calls that occasionally came from Klein's office. "There were so many wild ru-mors about the guy," he said. "I thought he was some kind of mobster." The notion that Klein was violent or threatening was laughable. What wasn't funny was his clients' seeming ignorance of the ways in which Allen might benefit from their relationship. Allen knew the value of a proven talent better than anyone—he literally banked on it. It was no accident that he worked exclusively with established artists looking to improve their financial situations; he was not interested in developing or helping talented unknowns and never worked with them. Indeed, when Neil Diamond was a staff songwriter for Aldon, he asked Klein to take him on, but Klein declined. Rolling Stones manager Andrew Loog Oldham, who hired Klein as his own financial manager and asked him to renegotiate the band's recording and publishing contracts, later observed: "Allen comes in when your harvest is not as plentiful as your expectations on the sow. And part of the price is that he gets the farm." Regardless of the increasingly apparent cost of hiring him, Allen was attractive for two reasons. First, the artists knew the record companies were out to get them as cheaply as possible, and they were desperate for an aggressive advocate. Second, and more emphatically, Klein delivered. "He just got it quicker than everybody else and was able to do things for people and ask for numbers that had never been asked for before," said Michael Kramer, Allen's nephew and in-house attorney. Indeed, the deals Allen negotiated with the labels were much better than anything the artists had had before; his constructs were truly farsighted and state-of-the-art, and they were lucrative enough that he could pocket something and keep the customer satisfied. But satisfaction could be fleeting. When you hired Klein, you hired a pistolero; he'd run the rustlers and varmints out of Dodge, but then you'd have to figure out how to live with a mercenary in the sheriff's office. Said Myers: "His whole thing going in was 'I'm Robin Hood — I rob from the rich and give to the poor.' That's how he liked to see himself. He actually robbed from the rich and kept it. *Maybe* he gave it to the poor." Wild rumors aside, Klein's wheeling and dealing could indeed cost a client more than money. Although nowhere near homicide, his schemes could have painfully comic results.

Bobby Vinton returned to his Long Island home one afternoon to discover a moving van and a crew of workers emptying his house of its furnishings. Stunned, he and his wife, Dolly, were told that the singer had been successfully sued by his prior manager and that the furniture was being seized as part of the settlement. He immediately called Klein — who was just as surprised as Vinton, of course.

"Aah . . . yeah," Allen said. "Marty Machat was supposed to handle it. He said he had it under control."

Vinton was livid.

"My friend! I said, 'Allen, they took the bank accounts! They took all the furniture!' They took *everything!*"

Not quite everything. The moving men couldn't bring themselves to repossess the crib in which the Vintons' son, Robbie, was sleeping.

## 4

## THE YIDDISH INVASION

LIKE MILLIONS OF OTHERS, Allen Klein had become fixated on the Beatles, though his reason was unique. Allen knew they needed him as their business manager.

He certainly liked and admired their music, but it was more than that. The Beatles were *it*—the most important act in the world. Seemingly overnight, all popular recording artists could be divided into two categories, the Beatles and everyone else—and the latter group included Elvis Presley and Frank Sinatra. It was more than their revolutionizing the pop world and the record business, though; their influence was total in a way rarely seen before and certainly not since. Young people wanted to walk like them, talk like them, dress like them, *be* them. The world had suddenly changed, and the axis was now firmly planted somewhere between Liverpool and London. All of this Allen understood as quickly and surely and intuitively as anyone. That meant they needed him—and he needed them. It was that simple. And the benefits? Incalculable. But then, those would flow simply as a matter of course.

Klein didn't even have to make the first move. Murray Kaufman, a popular New York disk jockey known as Murray the K, had cultivated a relationship with the band on their first trip to New York (Murray often referred to himself on air as "the fifth Beatle"), and he told Allen that Brian Epstein, the Beatles' manager, wanted Sam Cooke as an opening act for an American tour. After booking a flight to London, Allen paid a visit to Joe D'Imperio, the RCA executive with whom he'd negotiated Cooke's recording contract, to tell him of his upcoming trip. What kind of advance, Allen asked, would RCA be willing to pay the Beatles if he could convince them to switch record companies? D'Imperio instructed Klein to offer one million dollars and a royalty of 10 percent.

In London, Klein relayed the offer to Epstein — but not before deciding it wouldn't be rich enough to sway him. "I can get you two million if you take the Beatles to RCA," Klein said, immediately fearful Epstein would agree and then discover Klein couldn't deliver. He needn't have worried.

"I'm sure that's very generous," Epstein replied coolly, "but I have loyalty. All of my acts are at EMI and I'm loyal to EMI." That was true enough — though that loyalty didn't particularly benefit the Beatles.

Epstein had discovered and was promoting the most influential act in the world, but even he couldn't imagine how singular the Beatles' influence and success would prove. Yes, the Beatles were a phenomenon, but few things are as transient as pop stardom. Epstein's insurance was a growing roster of lesser and developing acts with which he hoped to build his management company, NEMS Enterprises, into a talent empire. Indeed, Epstein was juggling his own career as a TV host for a regular British segment of the American music program *Hullabaloo* along with those of several other Liverpool acts, including Gerry and the Pacemakers, Billy J. Kramer and the Dakotas, and secretary turned singer Cilla Black. And while they had successfully ridden the coattails of Beatlemania — in some cases, with Beatles-penned songs — to hits on EMI, Epstein's attention and leverage was often squandered on a host of other bands that went nowhere.

Like Klein, Epstein had carved out his own place in the music business. But that, and the fact that Epstein was Jewish, was all they had in common. The son of successful merchants who owned a string of furniture and music shops — North End Music Stores, or NEMS — Epstein had grown up comfortable in depressed and provincial Liverpool. After weighing and then rejecting an acting career, he opted to throw his lot in with the family business. Though his primary responsibility was selling furniture, Brian was drawn to the music operation and its burgeoning record department. He kept close tabs on what was selling and wrote a regular review column for a local music tabloid that NEMS carried, *Mersey Beat.*

One record that caught his attention was "My Bonnie," by singer and guitarist Tony Sheridan, backed by a group billed as the Beat Brothers. Though recorded in Germany, the single was a strong seller for NEMS, perhaps because the Beat Brothers were actually a local Liverpool group with a growing following, the Beatles. Curious, Epstein and an employee, Alistair Taylor, ventured to the Cavern Club — literally a basement pub — for what turned out to be a packed and raucous show. Though neither particularly cared for rock 'n' roll, Epstein and Taylor were surprised by the size and passion of the scene and floored by the frenzied reaction to the rather tough-looking, leather-jacketed band. As Taylor liked to tell it, a somewhat flummoxed Epstein asked him what, if anything, he made of it all. "I thought they were awful, quite honestly," he replied, "but absolutely incredible." Epstein agreed. In short order, Brian introduced himself to the band as the owner of the local record chain and offered to manage them.

However little he knew about rock 'n' roll, Epstein recognized the Beatles were special. The crowd at the Cavern Club was wild for them. The music had drive and was wholly alive, and, equally important, the Beatles were true showmen: funny and clever with a sharp presence and personality. Epstein took just a little edge off them — he swapped their leather jackets for matching suits and encouraged the band to bow in unison — and then used NEMS's clout as an important record account to force labels to audition the band. Turned down at Columbia, Decca, Pye, and EMI, they finally won a contract with Parlophone, a small EMI affiliate. That was more than good enough — indeed, producer George Martin ultimately proved an ideal collaborator for the young band.

Unlike Klein, Epstein was an impresario, not a business manager. Although Epstein could launch and guide the careers of talented unknowns to fame, he had scant skill at engineering fortune. Epstein's own management contract was unusually generous (after going into his pocket to support the group in the early days, Epstein later commanded a whopping 25 percent of their gross income), but none of the Beatles' deals were particularly good. Some were awful. The EMI/Parlophone contract paid minimal royalties: each of the Beatles received just a farthing — one-fourth of a penny — per single sold. Music publisher Dick James kept the lion's share of income on songs written by John Lennon and Paul McCartney, and the Beatles' merchandising rights were virtually given away, a blunder Brian tried to hide from the band because it may have cost them as much as a hundred million dollars, an incredible amount at the time. Paul McCartney remained grateful that Epstein recognized and promoted the Beatles, but eventually he concluded that his manager was less than qualified to create or command a worldwide music empire. "He looked to his dad for business advice," McCartney said, "and his dad knew how to run a furniture store in Liverpool."

Aside from a botched attempt to correct the merchandising deal, Epstein showed little interest in seizing the Beatles' ever-growing leverage to renegotiate their record and publishing contracts. As in his discussion with Klein, he portrayed himself as a gentleman taking the high road. Just why he thought it more important to honor an egregiously below-market contract than to speak up for his clients is a mystery, although it's worth noting that Epstein's management deal paid him commissions for the full life of any contract he obtained, regardless of whether he was still the manager, and he was amenable to granting extensions. But the answer likely had much to do with the British record business of the time — a classic old-boy network in which the class system was firmly entrenched and outsiders were kept keenly aware that they had little standing. Any rock 'n' roll band signed to the prestigious EMI or Decca was advised to simply thank God, keep its collective head down, and use the service entrance. And that was likely to go double for its Jewish manager.

"If you got a record deal with EMI or Decca you were so grateful," recalled Myers. "They were an institution! With pressing plants and vans, you know? It was like signing a contract with Prudential Insurance: Who reads it? You're told the terms; how dare you question them? Signing a contract with EMI was an honor."

Epstein's disdain of RCA's greener pastures didn't put a crimp in Klein's patter, and he didn't miss a beat. "Do you want me to look after your American publishing?" he asked. Epstein again demurred. Klein, although disappointed, was not surprised. He certainly hadn't come to London without a backup plan.

Though Allen had taken Sam Cooke from the William Morris Agency, he'd nonetheless managed to cultivate Sam's former agent, Jerry Brandt. An earnest young hustler with an early appreciation for the financial potential of the emerging rock scene, Brandt smelled real money, and he was pushing William Morris hard to expand its involvement. He was in awe of the audacious Klein, particularly the way he was becoming a key player in the business while creating opportunities for himself as often as he did for his clients. Jerry regarded Allen with an unusual, and unusually visceral, mix of admiration and envy, reverence, and repulsion. "He was the smartest man in the world," said Brandt, "and possessed greed beyond belief. He took everything to the next level. He was the pied piper and I thought he was great."

Dissatisfied as an agent, Brandt hungered for a real score. Before Klein came on the scene, he'd been angling for a bigger role in Cooke's career. Bested, he now tried to go to school on Klein — or, better still, hook up with him. Eager to curry favor, Jerry fed Allen ideas and tips, passing along whatever he heard at the agency or on the street. Klein was more than happy to encourage him. "He captured me, called me fifty times a day," Jerry said. "His pitch was 'We'll be partners.'"

One of the British bands that Jerry was booking was the Animals, whose spine-tingling single, "The House of the Rising Sun," was an enormous hit in the summer of 1964. An electrified version of a folk tune already recorded by numerous artists, including Dave Van Ronk, Nina Simone, and Bob Dylan, the song was ubiquitous. It was impossible to go anywhere in America that August and not hear Eric Burdon's wailing, mournful vocal and the unearthly quiver of Alan Price's organ; the melody floated out of every open window, car radio, and transistor at the beach. At the height of Beatlemania, the Animals owned the airwaves for a long, hot month. In early September, when Brandt kicked off the Animals' first American tour with a two-week run at the Paramount Theater in Times Square, Klein came to the show. There, Jerry introduced him to the band's road manager, Peter Grant.

A former wrestler, Grant was a formidable-looking man who in later years would prove even more imposing as the larger-than-life manager of the band Led Zeppelin. At this juncture, however, Grant was still serving his apprenticeship with the Animals' handlers, agent Don Arden and manager Mike Jeffery, two characters of which many things were rumored and little really known.

Arden, a one-time Yiddish musical theater performer, was a tough-talking and much-feared figure in the London music business as both an agent and, later, a manager and record-company owner. Arden would cement his reputation while managing the Small Faces, first by holding the successful band members to an agreement limiting their total compensation to a weekly salary of twenty pounds each, then by reputedly holding rival manager Robert Stigwood out of a window by his feet for trying to poach the band. Also the manager of the pioneering heavy metal band Black Sabbath, Arden grew wealthy as the owner of Jet Records, whose most successful act was the Electric Light Orchestra. Moving to California and purchasing a mansion formerly owned by Howard Hughes, Arden was ultimately eclipsed by his equally enterprising protégée and daughter, Sharon Osbourne, from whom he was largely estranged. Nonetheless, some who knew him discounted much of the menace. "He was a pretend gangster," said Laurence Myers. Arden was, however, a genuine deadbeat.

"My first grown-up meeting in the music business was with Don Arden," said Myers, then the accountant and business partner of the Animals' producer Mickie Most. "Mike Jeffery, who was the manager, called Mickie and said, 'I'm in America. Don owes the Animals money and they're mad. Can you persuade him to pay us?'" Myers checked the accounts and found Jeffery was correct; the agent definitely owed the band money for a recent tour. He gathered the appropriate documents, and he, Grant, and Most arranged to meet Arden at his office.

Sitting in the waiting room, Myers had his first inkling that it would not be a typical business meeting. He could hear shouting coming from Arden's office. "*Listen, you Christian schmuck! I've had it with you!*" Ushered in a few moments later, the men found Arden sitting unperturbed at his desk. "Sorry to keep you waiting," he said. "I was on the phone with my bank manager."

To Myers's surprise, the meeting got off to a rip-roaring start, with Most and Grant—who'd known Arden for a while—immediately pounding the table and screaming. "I'm going to turn this desk over if you don't pay us, you asshole!" Grant yelled.

Stunned, Myers wondered what all the commotion was about.

"Hold it," Laurence said.

Arden looked at him curiously. "Yes?"

"I'm Laurence Myers. I am authorized to represent the Animals in this matter and I have my files with me. Here is a schedule. You owe the Animals six thousand twenty-seven pounds and forty-seven pence."

"Yeah."

"You agree?" Myers asked.

"Yeah."

"Well," Myers said, satisfied he'd settled the matter, "you're going to have to pay."

Grant pounded his fist on the desk as hard as he could. "Give him the fucking money!" he screamed.

Arden seemed not to notice Grant.

"Do you know what I'm going to do if you don't pay?" Myers asked.

"No," said Arden, finally looking interested. "What are you going to do if I don't pay?"

"I'm going to issue a writ."

"Oh," Arden said.

With that, Arden pulled out a paper-filled desk drawer that appeared to Myers to contain nothing but unanswered writs. Arden pulled the drawer all the way out, rose, turned, opened the window, and tossed the contents of the drawer into the street. Then he turned back to Myers.

"If you don't get out of my fucking office, you're going out the window too!"

The Animals didn't collect.

The stories about Animals manager Mike Jeffery were, if possible, wilder and woollier. A club owner from the Animals' hometown of Newcastle, Jeffery had a dubious reputation from the start; Eric Burdon intimated he had torched one of his own clubs for the insurance. Later, when the band was at the height of their popularity, Jeffery cited Britain's onerous foreign-tax laws and urged the band to let him park their money in an offshore tax haven. The money somehow disappeared. "I was frontman for a band that was screwing me from behind," Burdon later said. "We toured non-stop for almost two years, hardly a day off . . . for zero. We lost our monies in the Bermuda triangle." Yet when Animals bassist Chas Chandler heard the still largely unknown Jimi Hendrix in New York and wanted to move the guitarist to London and launch his career, he enlisted Jeffery as his partner. As with Sam Cooke's passing, Hendrix's death in 1970 would spawn a host of conspiracy theories — including, again, that his manager had murdered him. But Jeffery didn't need what investigators classified as a drug-and-alcohol-related accident to fuel outrageous stories about him (one of which was that he led a secret double life as a government spy). Nor did the theories end with Jeffery's own death, in 1973 in a Spanish air disaster; rumors abounded that Jeffery, who was terrified of flying, hadn't been onboard at all but had somehow engineered the crash in order to vanish with money pilfered from Hendrix. It was the sort of elaborately paranoid and romantic legend that flourishes in the entertainment business, but dishonesty and incompetence could have explained the events just as well.

Through Brandt, Klein learned that Jeffery managed the Animals and that producer Mickie Most made the records. Introduced to Grant at the Paramount, Allen said he could help everybody involved with the Animals make more money — a lot more money. For example, he said, the Dave Clark Five were going to be appearing in a film, *Get Yourself a College Girl,* with Nancy Sinatra, and he could get the Animals in the film as well. How did ten thousand dollars for one day of shooting sound?

*How did it sound?* It sounded like the right end of the rainbow. Jeffery jumped at the offer.

Rebuffed by Brian Epstein and the Beatles, Klein couldn't afford to go home empty-handed. He might just as easily have dealt with the Beatles' tour offer to Cooke from New York, but it had been too good an opening to let go. As would become his habit throughout his career, Klein affected the look of a cash-rich American wheeler-dealer in London, staying in a lavish suite at Mayfair's tony Grosvenor House Hotel that was beyond his means; he'd have to find a way to scrape up the money to cover the trip. He wasn't leaving London without convincing *somebody* to let Klein make him rich. Allen called Mickie Most.

One of the most underrated rock and pop producers, Most had made a huge splash with the Animals, but at that point he was also working with Herman's Hermits and a band managed by Don Arden, the Nashville Teens. In the coming years Most would produce enormous hits for Lulu, Donovan, the Yardbirds, Jeff Beck, and Hot Chocolate, as well as albums by artists as varied as Terry Reid, Chris Spedding, Suzi Quatro, and Kim Wilde.

Klein quickly recognized Most's brilliance. He had more than an ear for a hit. Looking for a particular sound on a session with Terry Reid, he made the guitarist play so far down the hallway that he was practically out of the building; he knew what he wanted to hear and he knew how to get it. He was also a whiz at picking songs for artists; though the Animals brought "House of the Rising Sun" with them, it was Most who found their follow-up hits "It's My Life," "Don't Bring Me Down," and "We Gotta Get Out of This Place" during New York shopping trips to Don Kirshner's Broadway office. For Jeff Beck, he found "Hi Ho Silver Lining"; for Herman's Hermits, "I'm into Something Good," "Wonderful World," "Dandy," "There's a Kind of Hush," and "Silhouettes." A former singer — *Most* was a stage name, taken when he began his career as a teenager — he'd followed his girlfriend and future wife,

Christina, back to her native South Africa, where he discovered a pau-
city of rock 'n' roll performers and became a national star by covering
Chuck Berry and Buddy Holly hits. With a string of South African
number ones, Most spent four years there and toured the entire con-
tinent. "Mickie was a bit of a tough guy," said Myers. "Being a rock 'n'
roll singer in South Africa would toughen anybody up. You had to go
out and survive in front of the crowd. Rednecks." Frequently forced to
engineer and produce his own records, Most came to prefer that over
being an artist. "It was fun performing but in South Africa it was eight
fights a week," he said. "It was a bit more pleasurable to be in the studio
than on stage." Returning to England in 1962, Mickie briefly played on
rock package tours, sometimes with the newly minted Rolling Stones,
while trying to establish himself as a producer. Mickie heard the Animals in Newcastle and offered the band and Jeffery a production deal:
his company would produce and own the records and try to license
them to a label. "I don't know how many offers you've had," he told
them, "but I'll bring you down to London and I'll pay for the recording session, and if you don't like it, then that's it — you've got nothing
to lose that way." They eventually agreed. The first record, a cover of
an old blues song, "Baby Let Me Take You Home," which Most heard
on his first trip to America in '63 and Bob Dylan recorded as "Baby Let
Me Follow You Down," cracked the top twenty. Their second single
was "House of the Rising Sun." Most and Myers had heard about Klein
and the Animals' sweet deal for *Get Yourself a College Girl* and they
weren't going to miss the opportunity to meet with him. Even after
Mickie's first visit to America, the country remained a mystery — a
vast, untapped, wealthy mystery. In that regard he wasn't alone; most
English acts and their managers viewed America as huge, distant, and
too big to master, while American music executives rarely came to
London. Yet here was Klein, the manager for Sam Cooke and a man
who seemed to know the score. Most and Myers said they'd be happy
to meet Allen for dinner.

Allen suggested that they drop by his suite at the Grosvenor instead
because he'd sent his evening clothes out to the cleaners. In reality,
Allen didn't have the money for dinner. He also preferred to control

the setting for meetings and negotiations, and the massive suite was a stunner. Most and Myers were impressed when the door was opened by a stylish and petite young woman who looked a bit like Elizabeth Taylor and who introduced herself as Betty Klein, Allen's wife. Myers, whose father-in-law, Jack Bloom, was a successful dealer in English antiques, frequently entertained Jewish buyers from America, and he had formed a different image of the Kleins based on the couples he'd met. "They were all nice middle-aged Jewish businessmen who came over with their six-two gentile broads," he said. "That's what I assumed I was going to meet."

Allen was also younger than he'd expected, and a good deal more intense than the furniture dealers. He had a simple pitch for Most that was as outrageous as it was irresistible.

"I can get you a million dollars," Klein said.

The proposition was straightforward: Give him a month to look over all the deals they had, recommend improvements and changes and point out other opportunities, and then let him negotiate on Mickie's behalf. There would be no fee for his work. If they were satisfied, he would earn his piece as Mickie's business manager in America.

Most and Myers didn't know it, but the pitch was a deluxe variant of the one Klein had been delivering for more than five years in America: "I can find you money at no risk." Though Klein's style was to come on like an outlaw and quote seemingly gigantic numbers, his read of the true business situation was conservative, basic, and — to him at least — obvious. Jerry Brandt, an excellent salesman himself and no stranger to business seductions as the head of the music department for William Morris, was blown away by Klein's ability to woo clients. "Allen," he asked, "what do you *tell* these people?" Klein shrugged. "They're all broke. I tell them I'll get them money."

The only difference this time was the amount — which sounded absurd to Most and Myers. They readily agreed to give Allen a shot, but both broke into laughter as soon as they got out of the suite and into the corridor. "We creased up," recalled Myers. "A million dollars? Back then, a hundred thousand dollars was a fortune. The queen didn't have a million dollars! We were very skeptical, but we figured there was nothing to be lost: if he gets us a million dollars, we'll sign something; if he doesn't get us a million dollars, we won't sign anything."

Myers, as Most's accountant and financial partner, became Klein's frequent contact as he sifted through the contracts. It was clear to Laurence that Allen was both measuring and wooing him, but that was fine. "Allen came to our home in St. John's Wood and we lied to each other," he said. "Neither of us had any money at all, but I said, 'One keeps one's money in Switzerland.' Then Allen said he kept his money in Canada. But my lies were smaller than his lies. I had a little money in Switzerland; he had *lots* of money in Canada!"*

In return for the invitation to Laurence's home, Allen called him and said he and Betty wanted to go out to dinner with Myers and his wife, Marsha. "I said to Marsha, 'Look — he's a big-shot American. We can't go where we normally go for dinner — it's too modest.'" Myers asked Klein if he and his wife would like to eat at Les Ambassadeurs, a tony and extremely expensive gambling and dinner club in Mayfair. Allen had heard of it and was eager to go. A reservation was secured through Myers's father-in-law.

"I know what you're like," Marsha Myers said to her husband on the way to the club, "don't you pick up the bill. They came to our house for dinner and we can't afford Les Ambassadeurs. They invited us. Don't pay the bill!" Myers told her not to worry. "I got us in, right?"

At that moment, in a taxi leaving the Grosvenor, an exasperated Betty Klein was thinking about the hotel suite they never should have taken and delivering a speech similar to Marsha's. "Don't you dare pay the bill tonight, Allen!" she said. "They've chosen the most expensive restaurant in London. We can't afford it."

Les Ambassadeurs lived up to Allen's expectations. The dinner proved excellent, the evening very pleasant. At last, however, the check arrived. Casting a wary eye at the bill, Myers felt a sudden burst of pain

---

* Whatever yeast he was adding to the story, Klein had, in fact, invested money in Canada at least twice, with United Telefilms and, disastrously, with Crescent Petroleum.

as his wife kicked him under the table and shot him a threatening look. Across the table, Allen visibly winced from a shot to his own shin. He looked at Betty, who gazed at him unwaveringly.

"Let's dance," Allen said as he took Betty by the hand.

Laurence knew he was in trouble. "I'll bet Allen never asked Betty to dance again," he remembered with a laugh. "Ever!"

Myers's own best hope was a long, leisurely trip to the men's room. Alas, when he finally returned, the Kleins were still dancing, the untouched check gathering dust on the table.

Hours later, Marsha Myers was still fuming at her husband. "Why in God's name did you pay the bill?" she asked.

Laurence gave a resigned shrug. "Look," he said, "they could dance all night. How long could you pee?"

Whatever the state of his own finances, Klein looked at Most's books and concluded that while Mickie was one of rock's best producers, he did not know as much about business as he thought he did. "Did you ever meet artists who want to be businessmen?" Klein asked. "Mickie Most is that. He was in such a mess." The biggest problem was the record deals he'd signed; Most and his acts were having huge hits, but as with the Beatles, the royalties were substandard. Allen gave Myers and Most a crash course in record-business economics.

For starters, Klein explained, there was an enormous gap between what a record sold for and what it cost to manufacture. In America, an LP retailed for four dollars, and the manufacturing cost, including the sleeve and packaging, was approximately sixty-five cents. For singles, which sold for just under one dollar, the manufacturing cost was less than five cents. A similar cost structure drove the British record industry. The record companies paid songwriters two cents per song. Even with other costs, like shipping and advertising, the record companies made dollars while the artists made cents. The artists were, of course, also charged for any advances or money used for recording. On top of that, the record companies had created a bevy of special accounting practices that effectively cut an artist's payday. For instance, the companies paid the artists for only 90 percent of records (an allowance for breakage that, while perhaps reasonable when records were sold on shellac disks, should have become obsolete with the introduction of vinyl records), and artists received half royalties for any foreign territories. That latter was particularly onerous for Most and his artists, as America was their biggest market.

But Klein wasn't going to challenge just the economics of the deal; he wanted to upend the entire relationship. Why should the artist be subordinate to the record company? Because that's the way it had always been? As far as Allen was concerned, the business had it backward. It wasn't the companies that were irreplaceable; it was the people who made the records. He was going to put the fear of God — and of Allen Klein — into them.

Myers accompanied Klein to his meetings with EMI Records managing director Ron Townsend and business affairs head Clive Kelly, and his education in the music industry was about to begin in earnest. He recalled how uneasy he felt; they'd think he was behaving like an impertinent ingrate and would surely toss him out on his ear.

"The old-school English — there was and, to a degree, still is a sort of strain of anti-Semitism, of disdain," he said. "And these guys were very old school. You could see it when we walked in, these two Jews. And the American Jew is even worse than the English Jew."

But Klein seemed not to share Myers's nervousness. Quite the opposite. He immediately took charge of the meeting and put the record executives on the defensive.

"Would you like a cup of tea?" Kelly asked. He leaned toward Myers. "Have some tea."

"I don't want any tea," Klein snapped.

Myers was surprised by Klein's obvious snub; it was like refusing to shake Kelly's hand. "Well," Laurence said sheepishly, "I might have but I don't want tea, then."

"You don't want tea?" Kelly asked.

"That's what we do," Klein said. "We don't have tea." He waited just a beat, then added: "Mickie's not going to make any more records for you."

Kelly and Townsend couldn't have been more stunned if Klein had urinated on the carpet.

"But he has a contract," Townsend said.

Klein shrugged. "Well, you may or may not have a contract. That's something we have to look at. But in the meantime, you are not to make any more records."

The color drained from the executives' faces. "We have a contract," Kelly repeated.

"You're not listening to what I'm saying. You're not going to get any more records."

Dumbfounded, Kelly and Townsend looked at each other and said nothing.

Klein smiled. "Now I'll have a cup of tea."

Klein's tactics were as much a revelation to Myers as they were to the record executives. "That was the first time I heard those immortal words," he said. "'You may or may not have a contract.' I have uttered them myself many, many times since." Though Laurence ultimately followed Klein's lead, it took him a while to really appreciate the leap Allen had made. "Allen told us, 'Your two artists are keeping MGM Records alive.' I mean, it sounded ludicrous. This is MGM we're talking about — MGM! But the Animals and Herman's Hermits were the only records they had that were hits; MGM had nothing. You don't realize how powerful you are. And that was a huge revelation. There was nothing for us to be sort of humble about. We'd thought we were very lucky to get our product out with huge EMI and MGM. And it suddenly dawned on us that actually, they were quite lucky to get the product from us. That was a sea change in thinking, and it spread."

One of the quickest ways to improve an English producer's income was to sever the American rights from the British contract, ensuring that American royalties would not be paid at a reduced foreign rate. Back in New York, Klein renegotiated the American recording agreements for Most's bands. Though they were all with MGM Records, he set up a series of other opportunities in the States, particularly at CBS, where Allen and Clive Davis negotiated deals for several acts soon to be recorded by Most, and at RCA, where Mickie was offered his pick of artists to produce, including Sam Cooke and Elvis Presley. Mickie thought producing Presley was a no-win proposition—"He'd done the best stuff he was ever going to do and there was no way I was going to be able to make records as good as those"—but he was eager to work with Cooke and later told an interviewer that he'd been traveling to New York to meet him when he'd heard the singer had been killed in Los Angeles.

Sure enough, when Klein sat down again with Most and Myers, he was able to present a package of firm offers that could earn them a million dollars. As per their initial discussions, Most readily agreed to make Allen his American business manager and allow Allen's company to make and administer deals for his records in America. Allen formed a pair of companies, Inverse and Reverse, to funnel Most's recordings to MGM and CBS, respectively. That meant Allen got his fee off the top directly from the American record companies and not from Most.

One of the ways Allen had been able to get to the magic figure of a million dollars was by building extensions and options into the renegotiated deals; they now ran far longer, and monies would be advanced at several points over the years rather than all at once. Paradoxically, the deals ran for so long that by the time they ended, they weren't particularly good. But when Klein struck them, they were so far out in front of other arrangements that Most was delighted and Myers became convinced Klein was a genius. In fact, Allen had again stood standard practice on its head. On Denmark Street, the hub of London's music business, Mickie Most's big score and the loud, ingenious Yank from New York who'd gotten it for him were the hot topic.

## 5

# "PEOPLE KEEP ASKING ME
# IF THEY'RE MORONS"

ANDREW LOOG OLDHAM was looking for a deal.

It was the spring of 1965, and London, following two deadly gray decades in which it had fought and won a brutal war for its life only to nearly succumb to its depressed aftermath, awoke to find its fresh, eye-popping popular art and culture scene was transforming the city into the tastemaking hub of the world. And Oldham, as co-manager of the Rolling Stones, was at the kaleidoscope's paisley center. He had just turned twenty-one.

The deal Andrew was hunting this morning was with an American publisher, Kags Music, that owned a song the Stones had recorded, "It's All Over Now." Written by Bobby Womack and originally recorded by his group the Valentinos for Sam Cooke's SAR label, the R&B record had been introduced to the Stones by the ubiquitous Murray the K. The New York disk jockey had suggested it could be a hit for them, and he'd been right. Though it got only to number twenty-six in the U.S., the record was the band's first number one in England. Oldham was hoping to use the Stones' success and growing popularity to pay reduced royalties to the songwriter and publisher, a frequently employed gambit. Indeed, Elvis Presley's infamous manager, Colonel Parker, wouldn't greenlight the recording of a song unless the singer shared in the publishing income. Andrew didn't have that kind of leverage; the Stones weren't Elvis, and since their version of "It's All Over Now" was already a year old, there was no question of refusing to record the song without preferential terms. Still, if you didn't ask, you didn't get. Like any good manager, Andrew was never shy when it came to asking.

A fashion plate, Andrew was a young man with tremendous taste and no self-control. "I still can't go by a watch shop without going into a dither," he admitted. He was looking forward to the meeting, which was at the outrageously expensive breakfast room of the Hilton where a plate of eggs cost seven pounds, about what a secretary made in a week. Yet he dawdled at the windows of the little gift shops off the hotel's marble lobby, daydreaming as he ogled overpriced jewelry. The Stones were really taking off; they toured Great Britain like fiends and their debut album had gone to number one there, staying on the charts for over a year. Yet they remained more rumor than fact in America, where other British Invasion bands, like Herman's Hermits, Freddie and the Dreamers, the Animals, and the Dave Clark Five, formed the bulk of the Beatles' rear guard. The Rolling Stones were still small potatoes in massive, all-important America. "We didn't mean shit," said Oldham. Yes, the money they all wanted was starting to come in, but only in little waves. Their tsunami was still somewhere out on the ocean, far from landfall. With a sigh he left the jewelry store and went into the breakfast room. It wasn't difficult to spot the right table: J. W. Alexander, Sam Cooke's partner in Kags Music and SAR Records, was the only black man in the restaurant. He wasn't alone, though, and he and his companion rose as Oldham approached and introduced himself.

J. W. smiled and nodded toward the other man. "This is our business manager, Allen Klein."

Klein didn't show it, but he was surprised. Allen had assumed that he was going to be meeting Eric Easton, the agent who was the Rolling Stones' other manager and who was said to handle most of their business arrangements. Klein didn't know anything about Oldham. He sure as hell was young, he thought.

Chatting over breakfast, Andrew soon came to the point: the Stones had done well with "It's All Over Now," producing an unexpected payday for Kags, and deserved a rebate.

"Why?" asked Klein. "Your record blocked us from having a hit with the Valentinos. I should charge you double."

It was soon apparent to Oldham that the only thing he was likely to get that morning was breakfast. Still, it was a thrill to meet Cooke's partners, and he began to pepper them with questions, first about the late singer and then about the American music business.

To Andrew's way of thinking, the British record industry was hidebound and moribund. The culture gap between the music and the street scene that fed it on one side and the old farts at the record companies that he relied on to market the Stones on the other was maddening and almost unbridgeable. Indeed, Oldham's guile, cheek, and extraordinary self-assurance had frequently been his chief weapons in forcing the business to take notice of the Rolling Stones, and it had impressed the band. "He was smarter and sharper than the assholes that were running the media, or the people running the record companies, who were totally out of touch with what was happening," Keith Richards said.

It wasn't like that in America, Andrew knew. He'd been to the States with the Stones, and he'd worked briefly with Bob Dylan and his hip and unorthodox manager Albert Grossman when they were in London. But his most lasting impression had come from befriending the brilliant American record producer Phil Spector, who had given Oldham a crash course in the business. Aside from having prodigious studio talents, Spector was a hard-nosed entrepreneur who knew the ins and outs of the music-publishing and record industry, and he exerted dictatorial control over the careers of his performers. Oldham idolized him.

Andrew told Allen and J. W. that, like Spector, he was starting his own independent record company, something of a rarity in Britain. He and his partner, Tony Calder, were calling it Immediate Records. But as he talked, it became clear to the others that Oldham had a lot on his plate at the moment; the Stones' recording contract with Decca was about to expire, and he wasn't quite sure what he was going to do. Oldham didn't mention that Easton had negotiated the band's initial Decca contract, nor that he and his partner were on the outs. The Stones were only just beginning to hit their stride commercially, and now they had to stay on the charts and continue to make hit records. In that regard, the record company was key.

"To keep the thing going is basically what everyone is about," Andrew recalled. "*Keep it going.* We have places to go, we have things to do. We definitely are in trouble in America from the point of view that we have absolutely no vinyl licks at all. And all the people that we kind of sneer at in England are all doing very well."

Andrew was particularly worried that if Easton negotiated the next recording contract, he would be cut out and finished as co-manager of the Stones. The longer he talked to Allen Klein about what Klein had done for Mickie Most, Sam Cooke, Bobby Vinton, the Dave Clark Five, and Bobby Darin, the more he believed he'd chanced upon his lifeline.

"I can't handle this thing with Eric Easton — and I've got to find somebody who can," Oldham recalled thinking. "Those kinds of people did not exist then. It wasn't 'There are five people I can go to.' What Allen did was not done; he was in the business of repelling all boarders. I just happened to walk into the Hilton and meet him. That's it."

Oldham had Klein's full attention. Allen suspected he wasn't hearing the whole story and that Easton was likely holding some big cards, but he was nonetheless impressed by Oldham, whom he'd been ready to dismiss as a kid. "He was a sharkster," Klein recalled with admiration. "He wanted to make money. I thought at the time, and I say it now, if he and I were the same age at the time we met, he would have kicked my ass."

But they weren't. Klein, who already knew how to reel in a fish and which bait worked best, didn't say anything about the Rolling Stones. Instead, he offered to work with Andrew on Immediate, suggesting he could negotiate an arrangement for him with a British company and help line up a distribution deal for the label in America, probably with CBS Records. In fact, the company's annual convention was coming up in Florida the next month. If the two men went together, Allen would introduce Andrew to Clive Davis, with whom he'd already negotiated several deals, as well as anyone else he wanted to meet.

Oldham was delighted and ready to bite. But Klein gave the reel one more crank before setting the hook.

"So, Andrew," he said. "Are you a millionaire yet?"

Oldham wasn't born within a mile of a million dollars. London in 1944 was a grim, war-weary city; Andrew's most striking childhood memory was coming home one evening to discover the woman he and his mother, Celia, shared an apartment with dead in the kitchen, her head in the oven.

Celia Oldham, an Australian of mixed English and Jewish heritage, was a bookkeeper by trade but a nurse during World War II. That was how she met an Army Air Corps lieutenant from Texas, Andrew Loog; he was killed in action over the Channel six months before Celia gave birth to a boy. Twenty years later, the son she named Andrew Loog Oldham would get his first look at the home state of his presumed father when the Rolling Stones played four poorly conceived, poorly paid "teen shows" with trained monkeys as their opening act at the Texas State Fair in San Antonio. But in postwar London, any wide-open spaces were likely to be marked by rubble, and whatever roaming Andrew undertook was in his head. He wondered, for example, if his mother's longtime lover — a successful and married Jewish businessman who helped to support them — was actually his father. The two of them did have the same ginger hair.

A mama's boy, Andrew had a hyperactive mind given to soaring flights of fancy. At eight, he sneaked into the local cinema to see *Moulin Rouge* and got his first proof that there was indeed a life of color and romance somewhere. He emerged movie mad and somewhat barmy.

By the time he was ten, Andrew was decidedly odd and precocious. A good deal more sophisticated about clothes and fashion than most grown men, he already had pronounced and unusual tastes. He was a rabid fan of stars and glamour, and at an age when most boys were clipping photos of footballers, Andrew idolized the actor Laurence

Harvey and the American singer Johnnie Ray. In later years Oldham
would suggest that Ray, both a heartthrob and gay, was the forerunner
of rock singers like Mick Jagger, David Bowie, and Freddie Mercury,
performers whose androgyny made them sexually attractive to women
yet nonthreatening to men. True or not, the same could be said of Oldham, whose infatuation with Ray bordered on the bizarre; reading that
the singer used a hearing aid, Andrew took to wearing one. When he
discovered Elvis Presley, he was thrilled not just by his music but by
his look and his clothes, particularly that pink-striped jacket with the
black velvet collar. As far as Andrew was concerned, Elvis was great,
and "as attractive as Natalie Wood."

In 1956, the basement of London's tiny 2i's coffee bar in Soho was
earning a reputation as a hub for skiffle and the nascent rock scene.
There, on a makeshift eighteen-inch-high stage in a room that could
barely accommodate fifty, the members of the first generation of British rockers, including Jet Harris, Cliff Richard, and Vince Taylor, made
their mark. Show-business impresarios and idol makers Jack Good and
Larry Parnes trolled for marketable hunks there, launching a bevy of
faux rockers with suggestive names, Tommy Steele, Marty Wilde, and
Vince Eager, among others. It wasn't just a place to check out rock and
measure the emerging scene—it *was* the scene, and the only school in
town. Mickie Most worked at the 2i's as a singing waiter; Peter Grant
was the bouncer. Oldham, just twelve, hung around so much that they
started handing him odd jobs. Like Most and Grant, Oldham was as
fascinated by the process and milieu—you certainly couldn't call it a
business—as he was by the music. The scene was exciting and alive,
like *Moulin Rouge* only here and now, and he needed to understand it
and participate. Unabashed and forward, Oldham was the kind of kid
who didn't know he was a kid. He had no trouble talking his way backstage at a Shadows show. He knocked on the door of Shirley Bassey's
home, not to meet the singer but to get pointers from her husband
and manager, Kenneth Hume, who wound up inviting him in for tea.
Andrew was fourteen going on forty.

One place Oldham didn't fit in was a classroom, and although his
mother repeatedly attempted to see him properly educated, sending

him to a succession of English boarding schools that she couldn't afford, Andrew was tossed out of all of them, the last one when he was
sixteen. He landed on his feet as a gofer at Mary Quant's Bazaar, the
King's Road boutique that, along with John Stephen's Carnaby Street
shops, was the epicenter of a London fashion revolution.

Though Oldham's career had yet to come into focus, he couldn't
have picked a better teacher than Mary Quant. Just twenty-one years
old when she launched Bazaar, Quant was as young as the consumers
she served. She was in tune with them, designing and selling mini-
skirts, white plastic boots, tight ribbed sweaters, knit leggings, and
shiny plastic raincoats, and a great advocate of affordable fashion.
Along with her husband and business partner, Alexander Plunket
Greene, Quant took youth marketing in new and surprisingly lucrative directions, creating not just shops but designer fashion lines that
catered to young buyers; by the mid-1960s, Mary Quant would be a
worldwide brand. When the teenage Oldham showed up at Bazaar's
back door looking for a job, he was already so much of a fop that he
carried a silver-topped cane, and he was so cocky he simply assumed
they would hire him — and he was right. Yet he kept his mouth shut
and eyes open enough to learn.

To Andrew, fashion, film, and music were all of a piece, all expres-
sions of the same attitude and chance: a London coming back to life,
a hope that the possibilities and excitement seen in America's movies
and heard on its rock 'n' roll records might also be had in Britain. He
came to view Quant's empire, built on what he later poetically dubbed
a "cockney-Chanel non-uniform uniform," as one of pop culture's first
achievements; her style, sensibility, and enterprise built a bridge between the American birth of rock 'n' roll and the coming of Britain's
Beatles. Helping, hustling, and making contacts, Andrew augmented
his income and education with evening jobs, waiting tables at Soho
jazz mecca Ronnie Scott's as well as at the late-night Flamingo Club, a
jazz turned R&B venue on Wardour Street regarded as a melting pot
for music and fashion. He imagined he might make a career for himself as an emcee and impresario of rock shows and picked the stage
name Sandy Beach.

Regardless of what he was up to at any particular moment, Oldham, like Klein, was actually becoming both the pitchman for a coming world and an indefatigable promoter of himself as its prophet. Allen sold himself with numbers, knowing the client's greed would do the rest; as a would-be style guru, Andrew had a harder sale to make. Few saw the cutting edge of a just-emerging pop culture, let alone recognized its power, but Andrew had a finely honed eye and the temerity to believe that someday soon, everyone would see the world his way.

In 1961, Oldham took an assistant's job at an old-line London public relations firm, Leslie Frewin and Associates, promoting a chain of staid men's shops he wouldn't have been caught dead in. Nonetheless he learned enough about PR to start offering himself as a freelance publicist to people and projects that did appeal to him, and he convinced a dancer on the weekly pop-music TV show *Cool for Cats* to become his first five-pound-a-week client.

The mainstream record companies had their own in-house publicists, and with the exception of the respected music publicist Les Perrin, there were no models for an independent PR man in London, particularly when it came to cadging work from peripheral figures on a pop scene just starting to coalesce. Making the rounds of the few independent record producers in hopes of landing a project, Andrew found a mentor in artist manager Ray Mackender.

Mackender, an insurance underwriter for Lloyd's who'd worked with Cliff Richard, had abiding interests in both pop music and young men; he managed the beefy singer Mark Wynter and had helped guide him to a big UK hit with a cover of Jimmy Clanton's million-selling American record "Venus in Blue Jeans." Ray gave Oldham a job as Wynter's publicist and showed him the ropes. "He taught me how to work," Oldham said. "He gave me his press lists and contacts, his fire and agenda." By keeping an ear open at record companies for news of visiting American artists in need of London press, Oldham snagged short-term jobs with a broad range of performers running the gamut from Little Eva to Bob Dylan. He may have worked only a week with Dylan, who was in London to perform in a BBC television drama, *Madhouse on Castle Street,* but it was a wonderful entrée, his version of Klein's Bobby Darin story. It also gave Oldham a brief but intimate look at the then-close relationship between the iconoclastic yet savvy Dylan and his innovative and idiosyncratic manager Albert Grossman.

Yet the American music man who had the most profound impact on Oldham was producer Phil Spector. One of pop music's true geniuses, Spector was known for an over-the-top production style dubbed the "wall of sound." His records were broadly drawn dramas of teenage romance that should have been bombastic kitsch but instead were earnest, heartfelt, and thrilling, glorifying rather than exploiting the subject; Spector's singles were *Romeo and Juliet* at 45 rpm with all the sword fights, soaring hearts, family battles, and tragic defeats. In their scope, daring, and unapologetic sentimentality, the records were precisely the kind of grandiose creations that pierced Oldham's overwrought heart. When he heard Spector was coming to London to promote one of his acts, he telephoned the producer's New York office to say he could get him ink in the London newspapers. In fact, Oldham knew that the *Evening Standard*'s Maureen Cleave already planned an article on Spector; Andrew simply made it his business to stand next to her at the airport when she met the producer's flight. It worked — he was in.

Mary Quant and Ray Mackender had schooled Andrew, but Phil Spector was his Harvard. Not only did Spector know how to make records, he also had a deep understanding of the recording and publishing businesses. And certainly just as important to Andrew, Spector had both style and a perverse sense of entitlement that fell somewhere between boorish and outright criminal. Behind it lurked a pervasive and nasty bitterness. Now firmly in control of his own career, Spector had learned his lessons the old-fashioned way, making early publishing and recording deals he'd come to regret — including his partnership with publisher Lester Sill in their company, Philles Records. Seemingly born with a chip on his shoulder and a bruise in his heart, Spector grew increasingly cynical and hard, the deals he offered artists as one-sided and exploitative as any in the business. He adhered to the tough, ugly business mantra Screw or Be Screwed.

Spector delighted in acting bratty, and Andrew was soon doing the same. "Phil looked more like an act than most acts," he recalled, "and behaved like one too. I had the opportunity to model myself after a perfect little hooligan." But Oldham wanted to do more than adopt Spector's habits and sunglasses—he had his ears open as well as his eyes. Spector counseled him to make sure he was firmly in the driver's seat if he ever managed an artist. And, most important, Andrew should absolutely not use the record company's studio or sign the act directly to a label. Instead, he should set up his own production company to maintain ownership of the recordings, pay for an independent studio, and lease the recordings to the record company. That approach, Spector assured him, would keep control in his hands and earn him a great deal more money than he'd make if the record company was in charge. Hanging out with Spector was exciting and eye-opening, but it was while Oldham was ferrying Wynter on an otherwise pedestrian trip to Birmingham in January of '63 that he caught his real break—or, more accurately, had the prescience to see, hear, and seize an opportunity.

The event was a taping of an episode of the pop TV show *Thank Your Lucky Stars* that featured, in addition to Wynter, the Beatles playing their just-released second single, "Please Please Me." It was Oldham's first exposure to the band. Though he would later wryly suggest he could tell in rehearsals that they'd be huge because "like Napoleon and Hitler they combed their hair forward," he knew exactly what he was hearing. "There was nothing calculated about artists like Dylan and the Beatles," he said more earnestly. "They were simultaneously omniscient and naïve." After asking John Lennon who their manager was, Andrew was pleased to find Brian Epstein on hand, and he immediately pitched himself as a London publicist for the band. Dissatisfied with Parlophone's efforts, Epstein agreed to give Oldham a try. "Brian gave me the job because at that point Liverpool was a long way from London and you didn't make long-distance calls unless there was a death," Oldham said.

Dropping Wynter and Mackender for the Beatles and Epstein, Oldham set out on his own. He rented a desk for four pounds a week in the Regent Street offices of Eric Easton, an old-line showbiz agent.

Oldham couldn't have timed his relationship with the Beatles much better. The band's first single, "Love Me Do," had made a strong showing, getting into the top twenty; "Please Please Me" became their first unqualified hit, reaching number one in *Melody Maker* and *New Musical Express*. And although the Beatlemania juggernaut had yet to get up a full head of steam, Oldham got a glimpse of the madness to come. During a package show at a theater in Bedford (at which the Beatles were still second on the bill, below sixteen-year-old singer Helen Shapiro), Oldham stood alongside Epstein behind the orchestra seats and watched as the audience went into an absolute frenzy, shattering windows and making it impossible to hear the band. To Oldham's mind, the future he'd longed for had arrived, and it was even more powerful than he'd imagined. "I heard the whole world screaming," he said. "The power of the Beatles touched and changed minds and bodies all over the world. I didn't see it—I heard and felt it." Andrew did all he could to stoke the machine. The band had to be in London often and he ferried them around in cabs to print and radio interviews, yet he never really connected with them on a personal level. Unlike Oldham, they were tough, clear-eyed working-class kids from one of the hardest neighborhoods in one of England's hardest cities, and they'd come to do business. Lennon, clearly the group leader, was particularly difficult to read, by turns sullen, abrasive, and charming, depending on his mood. Andrew, whose own natural mode was a camaraderie of thieves, kept himself in check—they were the clients, right? He focused on the job at hand, which was getting them as much press as possible. And if not the most important band in the world quite yet, the Beatles were still a hell of an entrée for Oldham. After dropping their names, he found it considerably easier to push his other acts as he made his ceaseless rounds of publications, clubs, and watering holes favored by journalists in a daily quest for ink.

In the De Hems pub in Soho, Andrew cornered *Record Mirror* editor Peter Jones, seemingly to no avail. The next issue was full—no room for any of Oldham's darlings—but Jones liked Andrew and was impressed by his unflagging energy and so gave him a tip: one of the *Mirror*'s writers had just filed a rave review of a show by an unsigned

R&B band, the Rollin' Stones, that the *Record Mirror* would publish in the coming week.

The group had a steady Sunday-night gig at what was called the Crawdaddy Club when the band played there but was on all other nights simply the tiny potted-palm-studded ballroom of the Station Hotel in suburban Richmond. And though the band didn't have a record deal yet, the review was unstinting in its praise, suggesting it was the vanguard of a new London scene. Jones thought Oldham might be the person to do something with them. "He was the young, hip youth about town—you couldn't even really call him a young man," Jones said of Andrew. "He had a lot of energy and hustle and I thought he might want to go hear them." Richmond was the last stop on the London tube line, and Oldham wasn't wild to drag himself out to the sticks on a Sunday evening; he later admitted he was more interested in buttering up Jones than in hearing the band. Nor was the stripped-down performance he witnessed—hard-charging, unadorned covers of Bo Diddley, Jimmy Reed, and Muddy Waters tunes—to his taste. Andrew preferred the more nuanced, pop-inflected R&B offered by Leiber and Stoller, Phil Spector, and the Brill Building crowd. "It didn't mean dick to me," he admitted. But in the end it was the singer, not the song, and he found the band, and particularly vocalist Mick Jagger, mesmerizing—"authentic and sexually driven." The jazz singer and pop chronicler George Melly would later suggest there was something more than a frisson of sexual excitement working its way up and down Oldham's spine. It was the hot flash of the main chance, and Andrew was not going to blow it. "He looked at Jagger as Sylvester looks at Tweetie Pie," Melly cracked. Andrew had no doubt he could do something with the band. What he couldn't do was get them work—that required an agent's license, and you had to be of legal age to get one. Indeed, any contract was thorny, since Oldham, Jagger, and guitarist Keith Richards were all minors.

The answer, of course, was right down the hall. On Monday morning, Andrew popped into Easton's office and begged the agent to come hear the band with him the following Sunday night with an eye toward booking and co-managing them. In Oldham's recollection it wasn't an easy sell — Easton had been loath to miss his favorite TV show, *Sunday Night at the London Palladium*. But "he was in awe of what he saw," said Easton's son Paul, adding that both the band's performance and the huge lines outside the Station Hotel convinced Eric that the act was well worth a shot. Easton and Oldham introduced themselves to guitarist Brian Jones, whom drummer Charlie Watts had identified as the leader of the band. Jones, along with pianist Ian Stewart, had organized the original rehearsals that drew in Jagger and Richards. Childhood friends from suburban London, Mick and Keith were a matched pair no matter how the deck was shuffled, but they shared a passion with Jones for electric Chicago blues and the music of pioneering rockers Chuck Berry and Buddy Holly. Sharing a flat in Edith Grove, the three had an almost messianic zeal about their band; they might be struggling now, but they were going to bring the true gospel to London — although Jagger, who had a small and much-needed stipend as a student at the London School of Economics, hedged his bets.

"God, the Rolling Stones had so little work," Jagger recalled. "I wasn't totally committed — it was a good, fun thing to do — but Keith and Brian didn't have anything else to do so they wanted to rehearse all the time." Indeed, Jagger was the last to commit fully to the band, dropping out of school only well after they were launched — a move that still enraged his father, Joe, a teacher and college athletics coach.

The consensus in the band was that Oldham and Easton could be a good team. Andrew was obviously someone who understood them; his Beatles association was extremely impressive. "He was our age and we thought he was good news for the group," said bassist Bill Wyman. Easton, although ignorant about rock music, was an established and respectable agent, and it was essentially a done deal after the introductions. It was Brian Jones — as the band's titular head and someone old enough to sign a binding contract — who came to Easton's offices a few days later while the underage Jagger and Richards waited for him around the corner in a coffee shop. On May 9, Jones signed a management contract on behalf of the band with Jagger acting as witness. A short and straightforward document, it stated simply that Easton and Oldham would procure work for the band and represent them

exclusively, a job for which they would receive 25 percent of whatever
the band earned. Within the month, the group had also signed a production deal with Impact Sound, a company owned by Easton and
Oldham, to record the Rolling Stones. Andrew hadn't forgotten Spector's admonishment; Easton and Oldham were going to own the band's
recordings and lease them to a record company. That kind of deal was
increasingly common in the American record business, but it was still
rare in Britain.

With the Rolling Stones firmly in hand, Easton and Oldham had surprisingly little trouble getting Decca, one of England's recording gi-
ants, interested. That had less to do with the managers' faith in the
band than with the fact that the label, and in particular its A&R man
Dick Rowe, had come to rue passing on the Beatles. Decca was hardly
alone in that regard; no one except George Martin's little Parlophone
had been willing to give the Beatles a shot. But because Parlophone
was part of Decca's archrival EMI, Rowe, who otherwise had an admi-
rable track record as a producer and talent scout, had been hung with
the unflattering sobriquet of the Man Who Turned Down the Beatles.
Rowe had already heard George Harrison touting the Stones, so he was
all ears when Easton came calling, and Rowe and Decca proved willing
to take a flier on the band largely on its managers' terms.

Those terms looked terrific — for Easton and Oldham. Decca agreed
to pay Impact Sound a royalty of 14 percent on a single by the Rolling
Stones. But Impact Sound had guaranteed the Stones only a 6 percent
royalty — meaning the managers pocketed more than half of any recording income after costs. On top of that, the management agreement
gave Oldham and Easton a 25 percent commission on that 6 percent.
The band, however, couldn't have been happier: They were going to
put out a record! And on Decca!

Oldham bought a few hours at Olympic, one of London's top studios, and produced two tracks with the band in early May. It was a case
of the deaf leading the blind; Andrew was savvy enough to know what
to ask for in a production deal but at a loss as to how to actually make
records. Instead, he bluffed his way through, relying on the engineer

to supply the technical know-how and the Rolling Stones to bring the noise. He huddled with them before the session, agreeing to record songs originally done by artists on Chicago's Chess Records — Chuck Berry's "Come On" and Muddy Waters's "I Wanna Be Loved (but Only by You)," and then egged them on during the recording.

"Andrew's music input was minimal," Richards said. "He wasn't a natural in the studio, he was not very musical. He knew what he liked and other people liked, but if you said E7th to him, you might as well be saying 'What's the meaning of life?' … That was the genius, I think, of Andrew's method of producing, to let us make the records. And to provide a lot of energy and enthusiasm." Rowe had enough reservations about the end product to summon the band to Decca's studio and rerecord the songs himself — a move Andrew feared was a ruse to sidestep the production deal — but his results weren't as exciting, and the original Olympic recordings became the Rolling Stones' first single in June 1963.

That first 45 revealed a good deal less about the Rolling Stones' musical tastes than about Oldham and the band's aspirations. "Come On" wasn't an effort to capture the driving R&B sound of a Stones performance; it was an attempt to make something flat-out commercial, its Beatles-inflected bounce a bid for airplay. The strategy worked moderately well and it certainly didn't hurt that Oldham was buying up as many copies around London as he could, a naked ploy to drive the record up the charts. The debut reached twenty-one, which was good enough to get a further recording commitment from Decca and help Easton book gigs. Though still largely confined to London clubs, the band was now performing almost every night. That didn't mean they were proud of the record, though; Jagger ultimately deemed it "shit" and the band refused to play the song live. "It was nothing to do with what we were doing," Keith Richards admitted. "I quite cold-bloodedly saw this song as just a way to get in. To get into the studio and to come up with something very commercial." Having gotten this far, the band now had one overriding goal: to keep it going. Oldham felt the pressure as sharply as the musicians.

Although faking it in the studio, Andrew had a keen understanding of image and promotion and strong feelings regarding how the band should sell itself. More than that, he had a romantic but well-formed faith that fame was something valuable in and of itself and that pop culture was only just beginning to appreciate its own power. He was confident the Stones could succeed and that he could create a look and buzz around them and make them stars. He'd watched Mary Quant do it, had taken note of the way Brian Epstein had cleaned up the Beatles.

Following Epstein's lead, he outfitted the band in matching houndstooth jackets and set up photo sessions with fashion photographers. The Stones were having none of it; to Oldham's horror, they "forgot" to wear the uniforms to the shoots. But then, Oldham was also having his own self-serving memory lapses: he'd neglected to tell pianist Ian Stewart about the photo shoots.

To Andrew, the mature, square-jawed Stewart wasn't teen-heartthrob material. Andrew told the others that Ian didn't look right, and besides, six bodies were too many for fans to care about. Though Stewart was an integral part of the band and had been a driving force in its inception, the others readily agreed to jettison him, assuring Stewart that he would still play on their sessions, have a job as road manager, and "always be a Stone." Like Oldham, the musicians had their eyes fixed firmly on success and seemed to feel no more than a soupçon of guilt over dumping Stewart; certainly no one spoke up for him. For his part, Stewart was stung and blamed Oldham. But he rightly saw Andrew as very much on the same page as the others and instrumental in their eventual success.

"I honestly don't like Andrew Oldham as a person," Stewart said. "I just don't like his attitude. He's a brilliant guy, actually. And if it were not for him, I don't think the Stones would've gotten to where they are now. They would have made it no matter what, but Andrew was very careful about the exposure and image of the group."

When Andrew looked over the band's stark first photos, shot against the brick and mortar of the Thames Embankment and on London street corners and back alleys, his heart sank. Even with Stewart gone, the band lacked glamour. In fact, the black-and-white prints made them look downright scruffy, although nowhere near as menacing as they seemed to hope. Didn't the Stones get it? Hadn't they seen how handsomely a few minor concessions to mainstream tastes were paying off for the Beatles? God, even parents were starting to take to them! It struck Andrew as ironic; the Beatles were working-class toughs before Epstein applied a bit of polish and made them ditch the leather jackets and smile for the camera. And what did Andrew have? A group of nice middle-class boys who'd make a bland pop record in a second if it got them on the radio but who dressed and carried on like they'd just been paroled from Borstal. The situation frustrated and depressed Oldham. Then it inspired him.

He should have seen it from the start: The world already had its Beatles — why should the Rolling Stones join their growing army of imitators? Though a chance meeting between Andrew and his former clients led to the Stones recording a tune by Lennon and McCartney, "I Wanna Be Your Man," as their second single, Andrew soon became enamored of the notion that the Rolling Stones should do more than just avoid imitating the Beatles; they should become the anti-Beatles. "The Beatles looked like they were in show business, and that was the important thing," Oldham said. "And the important thing for the Rolling Stones was to look as if they were not." The Stones were perfectly capable of being smug and obnoxious — Keith nearly started a fistfight on the set of the television show *Thank Your Lucky Stars* when he baited an Irish band in matching blue uniforms, calling them cunts and "the Irish fucking navy"—but they were still about as dangerous as Coca-Cola and just as eager to be sold. Rolling up his sleeves, Oldham began looking for any excuse to portray the Stones as hooligans.

Newspapers were eager to follow Oldham's lead, readily reporting that the band members were unkempt, dirty, and out to upend the empire. Moaned the *Daily Express,* "They look like boys whom any self-respecting mum would lock in the bathroom." Even the music press, which should have known better, was more than obliging. In an issue of *Melody Maker* that also featured an article speculating on just how much longer the Beatles would continue to interest fans now that they had been around a whole year — which spoke volumes about the life expectancy of pop acts and the world in which Oldham and his clients were trying to make their way — Ray Coleman filed an early report of life on tour with the mangy Stones headlined "Would You Let Your Sister Go with a Rolling Stone?" Coleman led with the shocking news that, aside from not wearing matching outfits onstage, the band didn't even bother checking themselves in mirrors because "hair-combing is rare."* When refused the use of the restroom at an East London gas station on a late-night drive home from a performance, they relieved themselves outside, leading to court dates, fines of five pounds apiece for Jagger, Wyman, and Watts, and a bumper crop of headlines for Oldham. The *Evening Standard*'s savvy pop reporter Maureen Cleave clearly saw the method in Oldham's madness, noting both Jagger's tenure at the London School of Economics and Watts's prior career as a graphic artist and then playing along tongue-in-cheek by accusing the band of doing "terrible things to the musical scene — setting it back, I would say, by about eight years." For good measure, she let Andrew run wild. "They don't wash that much and aren't all that keen on clothes," he told her. "And they don't play nice-mannered music. People keep asking me if they're morons." The strategy proved artful, slyly subversive, and massively appealing; it turned the fame equation on its head. Supposedly, you succeeded in entertainment by sitting up straight, being nice, and behaving yourself. The Rolling Stones zealously aspired to play music that was serious, authentic, and in revolt against almost anything heard or seen on radio and television, yet they were as earnestly interested in commercial success as any other entertainers were. An air of standoffishness and a feigned indifference to all the contradictions and compromises their position entailed soon came to define their persona. Oldham, in seizing and promoting the notion that the Stones were a very, very bad bunch of boys indeed, wasn't conjuring an image out of thin air; they *were* disdainful and hostile toward the status quo. But through exaggeration and repetition, it became more than that — a crusade and a thumb in the eye. Oldham played a huge role in making the world notice the Rolling Stones, and the strategy

---

* In fact, Brian Jones paid obsessive attention to his hair, often washing it several times a day.

succeeded so well that, at least in its early days, the band was more famous for being infamous than for their music.

"There's a theory that Andrew Oldham saw us from the start as wild rebels," said Wyman. "That is not so. Andrew never did engineer it. He simply exploited it exhaustively . . . And we listened to Andrew because he had made things happen: he said he'd get us on radio and TV and concert tours, and he had." Easton, who was booking the band furiously — they had a gig, and sometimes two, virtually every night — was also a hit, particularly with Wyman. Five or six years older than the other Stones (a fact then kept from fans), he didn't find the agent nearly as off-putting as the others did. They were inclined to gravitate toward Oldham, their contemporary and coconspirator, and before long Andrew had replaced Brian Jones as Jagger and Richards's flat mate.

The band remained far behind the British Invasion pack in the U.S., but they were bona fide stars at home. A four-song EP featuring "I Wanna Be Your Man" released in January 1964 went to number one in the UK, as did the Stones' self-titled debut album four months later. It topped the charts for twelve weeks.

Success bred new challenges for the Stones. Material was quickly emerging as one of the band's biggest problems; they couldn't possibly sustain a career just rerecording hits by Chuck Berry, Bo Diddley, and Buddy Holly. Oldham remained unsteady in the studio (Easton was forced to step in and produce several tracks when Andrew simply didn't show up), but he dutifully scoured the American music scene for appropriate songs and unearthed not just "It's All Over Now" but producer and songwriter Jerry Ragovoy's "Time Is on My Side," which had been an American hit for the New Orleans R&B singer Irma Thomas, and Jerry Leiber and Mike Stoller's "Down Home Girl," which had been an American flop for another New Orleans R&B singer, Alvin Robinson. He found some nuggets, but the search was exhausting, and the band's need for hits endless. The Rolling Stones had to have a new single for the market every twelve weeks, and Oldham lived in constant fear that the Stones were just one or two commercial missteps from losing their career; three months off the charts and no one would remember them. With the competition for outside material fierce, he saw just one answer: the Rolling Stones had to start writing their own songs.

Jones was proving a versatile player on the band's early recordings, adding slide guitar, dulcimer, keyboards, recorder, and marimbas and other percussion instruments, but he didn't have it in him to become a songwriter. "Brian was loath to pay attention to anything but himself," Oldham said. "He didn't respect the pop-song structure and thought it involved little more than rhyming 'Moon' with 'June.' Mick and Keith knew there was more to it than that and appreciated how hard it was to keep things simple." Andrew presented the pair with two pressing reasons for them to become songwriters: first, they were running out of good sources for material, and second, there was real money to be made in publishing. Royalties were paid to performers on recordings, but there was an additional stream of income for songwriters, who received payment not just for records sold but also for airplay and public performance. Every time the Rolling Stones had a hit, the songwriters got paid — why shouldn't they be those songwriters? Mick and Keith got it right away.

Still, it would require a leap; Richards had never thought of himself as anything but a guitarist. Songwriting entailed a different set of skills, and as far as he was concerned, it was like asking a carpenter to be a stonemason. Oldham encouraged him to think of himself more broadly. He wasn't just a guitarist, he was a musician whose band needed songs — and no one knew more about what they should sound like. With Jagger and Richards willing but unsure how to proceed, Oldham took control of the situation: he literally locked them in the apartment and told them that he was going to his mother's for dinner and if they hadn't come up with something by the time he got back, he wouldn't let them out.

"It was Andrew who really forced Mick and me to sit down and try it and got us through that initial period where you write absolute rubbish, things you've heard, until you start coming up with songs of your own. Andrew made us persevere," Richards said. The first good results, a tune Keith and Mick titled "As Time Goes By" and that Andrew suggested revising and renaming "As Tears Go By," was deemed strong enough to be recorded by Marianne Faithfull, a stunning blond girl Andrew had met at a party and gotten Decca to sign. A few months later, in early 1965, the Rolling Stones would record and release their first original single, "The Last Time." It went to number one at home and, just as encouraging, cracked the top ten in America.

Those American victories were still hard-fought and too far between. To the Stones, who'd found their musical roots in America, the country had always been the promised land, but the reality they encountered on their first tours proved even more exciting than they'd dreamed. Everything they saw in America, from Harlem's famed Apollo Theater to the Sunset Strip and the deserts of the West, was spectacular. And the radio — twenty-four-hour rock, country, and soul stations at the push of a button! They found it all nothing short of amazing, particularly the chance to record at Chess Studios in Chicago. But conquering the nation was another story. After the UK, the scope and size of the United States felt awesome, the trail they should follow for success decidedly less well-worn. Struggling to break the band in America, Easton booked a series of short tours in 1964 with GAC in New York acting as the band's agents. At the time, there was no established concert circuit for rock 'n' roll, and agents often turned to wrestling promoters to organize their clients' performances. The results were strictly catch-as-catch-can; the band sold out two shows in New York at Carnegie Hall but also found themselves playing fairgrounds and farm arenas and poorly attended shows in cities like Omaha. In Detroit, the Stones played for a thousand ecstatic fans, but it was hard to look out at the mostly empty fifteen-thousand-seat Detroit Olympia and be happy. They blamed Easton, whom they now felt wasn't up to the job. "Once it got to America, this cat Easton dissolved," said Richards. "He went into a puddle. He couldn't handle that scene." Perhaps most discouraging was their television appearance on *The Hollywood Palace,* a variety show. Most of the Stones' three-song performance was left in the editing room, replaced by nasty jibes from host Dean Martin, who cracked that the band members didn't have long hair, just small foreheads, and then introduced a trampoline act as the musicians' father. "He's been trying to kill himself ever since." An angry and humiliated Jagger phoned Easton in London and blasted him for putting them on the show.

Oldham was unlikely to be the target of the band's ire; he was as much a peer and a coconspirator as he was their manager. Despite Andrew's limits in the studio, the Stones trusted his taste, fed off his energy and enthusiasm, and recognized that he'd played more than a passing role in their growing fame. Andrew had strong opinions and a definite sense of style, and much of it rubbed off on the band, particularly Jagger. Onstage, the singer's campy androgyny — a flick of the hips delivered with a roll of the eyes — was a page torn out of Oldham. Andrew "slung his fur coat around his shoulders and waved his hands a lot," said Simon Napier-Bell, who managed T. Rex. "Jagger never used those mannerisms before Andrew took them on. It was Mick falling in love with Andrew's campness."

Conversely, Andrew respected the Stones and was savvy enough to follow their lead and adopt their opinions. When the band decided to release a cover of a straight blues song, Howlin' Wolf's "Little Red Rooster," as a single, Oldham argued furiously that it was a commercial mistake and that they should pick a pop tune instead. But when it became obvious the Stones weren't going to change their minds, he did a complete about-face. Decca and Easton continued to object, but Andrew insisted they had to follow the Stones and that having a hit with a blues record would prove they were more than a pop band. With the help of the Stones' fan clubs, Oldham mounted a big first-day buy, goosing sales of "Little Red Rooster" until the unlikely single entered the British charts at number one.

Increasingly at odds with Easton, Andrew wasted no opportunity to bad-mouth his partner to Jagger and Richards. Yet it was becoming apparent that the biggest threat to Oldham's position wasn't Easton, but Oldham.

Precocious, charismatic, and brilliant, Andrew was also insecure and manic, and he switched from confident euphoria to deep depression and self-doubt as quickly as if he were twisting a radio dial. And the more successful the band became, the more he worried and acted out. He was incapable of holding on to money, and it wasn't unusual for Andrew to get on a plane and disappear to France, to Spain, to America — it really didn't matter where. Vanishing was a dangerous habit for any manager, and the Stones — particularly Jagger and Richards — were proving to be quick studies as each success hiked their self-confidence. In the beginning, Andrew's grasp of PR, his religious zeal for pop, and his worship of fame were a needed tonic, and he seemed like a magician who pulled press coverage and recording contracts out of a hat. But the longer they watched Oldham's act, the better they recognized his bluster and misdirection.

Like everyone else in the young rock business, Andrew was self-invented, and he had to search hard for maps and role models. Constantly trying on the different personas of his idols, he didn't differentiate between their brilliance and their affectations. His youth, emotional insecurity, susceptibility to drugs, and faith in outrageous behavior as a tool for escaping a life of drudgery repeatedly resulted in ridiculous actions, and he evidently believed that the hipper you were, the more you should be able to get away with. Phil Spector might not get called out for his abominable behavior because he was a brilliant producer, but it seemed lost on Andrew that the abominable behavior wasn't *why* Spector was a great producer. Indeed, as far as Ian Stewart could tell, Andrew was very confused and knew "nothing about music whatsoever. I mean, you can still be a record producer and not know anything about music," he said, "but when Andrew started this producing bit, he was more interested in the image of Phil Spector, running around in big cars, with bodyguards, collecting money, and buying clothes. That's how he thought producers should act." Feeling the pressure to remain the enfant terrible, Oldham became more irrational and outrageous, his actions sometimes even thuggish. After all, it had worked for Don Arden. Oldham soon had custom cars, a hulking driver with a reputation as a bone breaker, and the well-earned CV of an obnoxious and out-of-control brat who nonetheless likened himself to Sergei Diaghilev. If that wasn't enough, he found yet another badge of authenticity to grab in the outsize number of London pop and rock managers known to be gay. Though Andrew had married his teenage girlfriend, he strove to suggest, without actually saying it, that his sexual tastes were wide-ranging and that he fit the cliché of the gay manager. Indeed, years after his relationship with Jagger and the Stones ended, Oldham would continue to play a coy game of did-I-or-didn't-I regarding his personal relationship with the singer.

Easton, as unflinchingly middle class as any man who ever worked in the music business, could only scratch his head — but then, that was much of the point of Andrew's behavior. "I think Andrew frustrated my dad," said Paul Easton, who recalled the band's road manager Mike Dorsey showing up at their house in Ealing after the first American tour and urging Eric to keep a tighter rein on Andrew. "He would disappear; he wouldn't do the little things that needed to be done." That Oldham was chugging his own snake oil and actively cultivating a legend as both a Svengali and a dangerous character didn't bother the Stones — at least not yet. And if Andrew's high jinks weren't Easton's speed, the band could certainly appreciate the joke, as long as it didn't veer too close to home. But during the Stones' first U.S. tour, while Andrew and the group were in Chicago to record at Chess Studios, Oldham had an emotional meltdown. He startled the band members by pulling a gun they didn't even know he had.

"Andrew was a lover of speed, but this time he was drunk too," recalled Richards, who attributed the incident to Oldham's marital problems. "He started waving a shooter around in my hotel room . . . Mick and I got the gun away from him, slapped him around a bit, put him to bed and forgot about it." Perhaps they really did forget about it. After all, there were many moments when it seemed to them that Andrew Loog Oldham had been born for the music business. But as the Stones' fame and ambitions grew, the question was whether Andrew could grow as well. By the following spring, when Andrew marked two years as the band's co-manager, he was feeling far from secure. He was desperate to bolster his position by showing he was on top of the business, and eager to jettison Easton.

Allen Klein was just the ticket. Oldham would continue to do what he always did, taking the pulse of the emerging scene in order to pitch and advise the Stones, while Allen handled the money and the business. If Andrew could keep it together, they promised to be a formidable team.

# 6

## THE KING OF AMERICA

ALLEN KLEIN SPENT his first week as Andrew Oldham's new business manager hunkered down in his New York office listening to records by the Rolling Stones and poring over every contract, document, and letter pertaining to them that his new client could supply. The good news was there was a lot of room to improve their deals. But Allen wasn't sure if what he had in his hands was the whole story. The quality of his information and the depth of his preparation were issues over which he endlessly fretted before any negotiation. Indeed, Klein had an axiom he liked to repeat to employees and associates: It's okay not to know; what's dangerous is not knowing what you don't know.

Eric Easton, not Oldham, had negotiated the band's publishing and recording contracts, and Klein couldn't be sure there weren't extensions in the works or even contracts and discussions that Andrew didn't know of; Oldham had already moved out of Easton's offices and stopped speaking to him. Andrew — and not the Stones — was Allen's client, and Klein wasn't sure that gave him enough authority to negotiate on the band's behalf. He knew he wouldn't get anywhere without the Stones' imprimatur.

He told Oldham he was sure he could get the Stones rich new record deals in both Britain and the U.S. but that he wouldn't negotiate without their permission. Andrew said they should speak with Mick Jagger.

There were a lot of reasons to pick Jagger. Brian Jones, the founding force behind the band, had been the original leader and the one who'd made the production and management agreements with Andrew and Eric, but the others quickly stopped trusting him when they discovered Jones had negotiated an additional five-pound-a-week bonus for himself. Worse, success didn't agree with Brian. He had a yen for the spotlight, scant self-discipline, and a taste for drugs that he couldn't handle. Whatever real enthusiasm he had for the music, Brian was a nightmare of a band mate and increasingly undependable. When he discovered LSD during an early American tour, he simply disappeared for days on end and failed to show up for concerts. Before long, the others, particularly Jagger and Richards, were imagining how much nicer life would be without him.

"I never saw a guy so much affected by fame," Richards said. "He became a pain in the neck, a kind of rotting attachment." Oldham, who shared their frustrations, was busily monitoring and manipulating the band's factionalism, particularly as it related to Easton. He viewed both Jones and Wyman as Easton supporters. "Bill and Brian did not feel threatened by Eric Easton, but they did feel threatened for different reasons by me, Mick, and Keith," Oldham said. "Brian had been 'the leader' of the group at a time when he was carrying on the negotiations with Eric and I, and he enjoyed the power of going back and telling them what had been said. He just didn't like letting that go. He was definitely siding with Easton." For his part, Andrew counted on Richards and Jagger continuing to emerge as the driving force behind the band's records and, consequently, the ones whose opinions mattered most. Keeping their confidence was very much on his mind, particularly in regard to the Decca contracts. "Mick and Keith were looking at me to see what I could do about it or would I turn into somebody that was disposable," he said. "Meeting Allen changed that. I was back on probation for a couple of years."

Jagger was vacationing in the U.S., enjoying the fact that the Stones' latest single, "(I Can't Get No) Satisfaction," had just topped the American charts and given them their long-sought U.S. number-one hit. He agreed to fly to Miami, where Klein and Oldham were attending the CBS Records convention at the Doral Hotel. Perhaps because of what Oldham had said to Jagger about Klein's negotiating prowess beforehand, the meeting was brief. "[Jagger] came into this bungalow and I said, 'Listen, do you want me to help Andrew do this thing?'" recalled Klein. "He said yes. That was it."

Using Klein was the obvious call. For starters, the band didn't have the financial knowledge and business experience to stand up to Decca; they desperately needed a gunslinger, and Klein's reputation preceded him. Closer to home, while "Satisfaction" spent a month atop the American charts, Jagger couldn't have missed the fact that the dreadful record chasing it, "I'm Henry the Eighth, I Am," was by Herman's Hermits — an act Klein handled. And it certainly didn't hurt that neither Jagger nor the other Stones would have to pay Klein's fee. Allen was Andrew's business manager and his 20 percent payment was to come from management. "I did not get one penny from the Stones," Klein said. "My money came out of Easton and Oldham's end. And each one of the principals, the five Stones and Oldham, got paid their money directly from Decca. I never touched them. I had nothing to do with that."

As soon as the convention ended, Allen went back to New York, picked up attorney Marty Machat, and took the redeye to London. Arriving Monday morning, they checked into the Hilton and met that day with the Stones. They had already been briefed by Oldham, who'd insisted Klein was the man to get them what they deserved from Decca. Wyman, the Easton stalwart, was the only one to raise an objection, and he was quickly and loudly overruled by the others. "Don't be so fucking mercenary!" said Richards. "We've got to trust *someone*." Nonetheless, it proved hate at first sight for Wyman — or at least a toxic mix of mistrust and snobbish condescension. Though ostensibly one of the bad boys of rock 'n' roll, the bassist found Klein — who opened the door to his Hilton suite dressed in a red T-shirt and sneakers — indefensibly déclassé. But when Klein piled everyone into a pair of rented Rolls-Royces for a five o'clock meeting with Decca chairman Sir Edward Lewis at the company's headquarters, he marshaled the Stones like a field commander. Everyone, including Wyman, did as he was told.

"I don't want you to say anything," Allen said. "Let me do the talking. You just sit there and look angry." That was fine with the Stones; it was one of the things they did best. Anyone with sunglasses was encouraged to keep them on during the meeting, but there was to be absolutely no talking under any circumstances.

Klein, who still wasn't sure if he really knew everything that was in the existing contracts, seemed to be having his own last-second gut check. Just as all of them were about to enter the conference room at Decca, he grabbed Oldham and dragged him into the men's washroom.

"Who makes the records?" Allen asked him.

Andrew, who had been known to exaggerate his role, gave them all the credit. "They do," he said.

Klein nodded. "Let's go."

Sir Edward, flanked by his attorney and label executives, was waiting in the office. The Stones played their roles to the hilt, silently filing in and leaning sullenly against the back wall. Klein knew Andrew had left all of the prior dealings with Decca up to Easton, and he assumed the negotiations had been cozy and gentlemanly, so he did what he always did: he put the executives on the back foot by speaking brusquely and seizing control of the meeting.

"I'm Allen Klein," he said, sitting down. "I speak for everyone."

"Where's Eric Easton?" Sir Edward said.

"I asked him to come. He didn't come."

"Well," said a manufacturing executive, "we don't want to have a talk without Eric Easton."

"Why? Does he play an instrument?"

The room was silent for a moment.

"What do you want?" Sir Edward asked.

"I want to see royalty statements. You signed the band in 1963. It's 1965 and they've never received a royalty statement. I'd also like to see the license agreements for every territory. It's Monday. I'll be back tomorrow at the end of the day."

"We're still curious why Eric didn't come," one of the executives said.

Klein shrugged and stood up. "You'll have to ask him. We're leaving. Just get me the royalty statements and get me the contracts. I'll be here tomorrow night."

On Tuesday Klein received everything he'd asked for as well as a new contract the company had proffered to Easton. It gave the Rolling Stones an opportunity to make $300,000 if they continued to sell in the future, but it was very much in Decca's favor, with none of the money guaranteed or paid as an advance against future royalties. Klein considered it a ridiculous and insulting offer, one that Oldham agreed was likely financed with money the group had already earned. By the end of the week, Klein had a vastly different arrangement in hand: $600,000 guaranteed as an advance against royalties for a one-year contract, to be paid over several years to ease the tax burden. The day the Rolling Stones signed the contract, Klein gave the jubilant musicians checks for the first year's advance.

But that wasn't the half of it. In a repeat of the strategy Klein had employed for Mickie Most, he severed the Stones' American contract. That meant if Decca's American subsidiary, London Records, wanted to continue to release Stones records in the U.S. and Canada, its executives would have to make their own deal. They soon did — for the same price Decca was paying to get the rest of the world.

The idea to limit the contracts to one year was also Klein's; he was assuming that a formal split with Easton would be finalized in a year, and he wanted to exclude him from claiming a portion of any subsequent contracts. Indeed, Klein would soon renew the two contracts for the following year under essentially the same conditions, this time for $700,000 each. Suddenly the Rolling Stones, who had never received a meaningful advance, were guaranteed $2.6 million.

It was a fortune — far more than the Beatles were guaranteed, as Klein made sure to point out to the press. And though he couldn't know it, the dart hit its mark; upon learning of the deal, Paul McCartney threw it up to Brian Epstein, wondering why the Rolling Stones had a better deal than the Beatles — and whether Epstein should have hired Klein himself.

McCartney may have been frustrated, but Oldham and the Stones were ecstatic. Keith Richards judged the hiring of Klein "the best move Oldham made . . . he was brilliant at generating cash." Jagger was less effusive but clearly happy. Oldham was off probation. Cut out, Easton promptly sued Klein and Marty Machat for inducing the Stones to breach the recording and management agreements signed by Brian Jones.

With the record company settled and cash in hand, Klein turned his attention to Andrew's management and production contracts. In Allen's opinion, Easton and Oldham had overreached, paying themselves too big a share. It was bad enough that the managers got a larger cut of the royalties than the band, but taking a 25 percent commission on top of that was double-dipping and unconscionable. It was also unlikely to stand legal scrutiny if any of the Stones wanted to challenge it. At Klein's insistence, the band received a pair of letters from Oldham. The first said their royalty was being changed from 6 percent to 7 percent "because of your phenomenal success in the recording business, which we appreciate." The second, explaining that a commission on royalties would no longer be charged, was more forthright. "As we are receiving producing royalty on these same gramophone records it would not be ethical or fair for us to receive the 25% commission on your share of the royalties. We therefore consider that portion of the Agreement eliminated." Even Bill Wyman was impressed.

Marianne Faithfull, who was also managed by Oldham and signed to Decca, was given a similar adjustment. "[Klein] raised my royalty rate from two percent to twelve percent," she said. "That's still not really great — I get a lot more on my current recording contract and he wouldn't be Allen Klein if he gave you everything, would he? — but it's much better and it's good because that's when I had my hits. I liked Allen — it was a very good relationship." It didn't hurt that Allen had a tremendous crush on her.

Klein set up a new U.S.-based publishing company for the Stones' songs, Gideon Music. The company owned the copyrights previously held by several earlier Stones' publishers as well as the rights to any new songs Jagger and Richards wrote. Klein, who had come onboard just as "Satisfaction" became an enormous worldwide hit, believed in Jagger and Richards as songwriters. Already the owner of several publishing companies, he offered to be their publisher and administer and finance the work himself.

"I hadn't seen them perform," Klein said of the Stones. "And I didn't really like 'Satisfaction,' because I'm not a dancer. But I was impressed with 'As Tears Go By' and loved 'Play with Fire.' I said, 'Whoa — they're good writers!' That's what did it for me."

The deal Klein offered the Stones was better than anything they were likely to get from another publisher. Whereas the typical publishing agreements of the time were split fifty-fifty between a publisher and a successful songwriter, Gideon Music paid seventy-two cents on every dollar earned to Jagger, Richards, and Oldham, with Andrew receiving 15 percent of that and the rest split evenly between the two songwriters. Klein also guaranteed them a minimum of a million dollars — a huge advance for 1965 and a figure that, with the Stones' increasing success, soon went up to three million. As with virtually all the band's deals engineered by Allen, the guarantee was paid out annually in twenty installments to minimize the tax bite. Any additional money earned would be paid out at the end.

"I thought he was crazy to make that deal and I told him so," said Klein's nephew Michael Kramer. Then a young assistant in the office, Kramer was a fan of the Stones but warned his uncle they weren't a pop act built for top-forty radio. "The Stones didn't sell huge. Herman's Hermits *killed* the Stones on singles." Kramer asked Klein, "What are you banking your twenty-eight percent on? The guys who wrote one big hit, 'Satisfaction'?" In fact, Klein wasn't risking much at all; he quickly arranged for Essex Music, a British company owned by American music publisher Howard Richmond, to act as Gideon's worldwide subpublisher outside North America. The advance from Essex covered the first payment promised to Jagger, Richards, and Oldham.

· · ·

As pleased as the Rolling Stones were, the piece of the puzzle they really hoped Klein could deliver was America. In every key aspect — touring, record sales, and airplay — the Stones still lagged badly behind many of the other British Invasion bands. "Satisfaction" looked like the watershed hit they'd been waiting for, and they were eager to seize the moment.

The record *December's Children (and Everybody's)*, released exclusively in the U.S., was less an album than a grab bag of tracks both old and new, and it coincided with an American tour. Unhappy with the way the group's first U.S. tours had been handled by Easton and their American agents at GAC, Klein suggested the Stones switch to Jerry Brandt at the William Morris Agency. Eager to have them, Brandt, along with Klein, convinced WMA president Abe Lastfogel that the band was a key signing and would generate so much money that the agency should move off its standard 10 percent commission and charge the Stones only 7.5 percent — a unique discount not even given to Frank Sinatra. The savvy Brandt, who later owned and operated two of New York's watershed rock clubs, the Electric Circus and the Ritz, proved an ideal agent for the Stones, even going on the road with them. Also traveling with the band were Allen's nephew Ronnie Schneider, whose job was to settle accounts with promoters after every show, and promotion man Pete Bennett, hired by Klein to ensure the Stones' records were played on the radio. The band quickly took to calling Bennett "our Mafia promo man," but it was an indication of how many services Klein provided. Essentially a financial manager, Klein knew he had nothing to contribute to the Stones' music and was grateful that Oldham was there to deal with creative and recording issues, but Klein's company oversaw all of the Stones' American manufacturing, promotion, and publicity, which it arranged with established PR firms like Solters, Roskin, and Friedman. Catch-as-catch-can American tours were now a thing of the past; the Stones found themselves kicking off a six-week North American tour at the cavernous Montreal Forum, playing shows — sometimes twice a day — in large arenas with a minimum guarantee of $10,000 a performance, and traveling by private chartered jet. For good measure, Klein bought the same Times Square billboard he'd used for Sam Cooke and Bobby Vinton and plastered on it a giant reproduction of the cover of *December's Children*. The Stones were so mobbed by fans in front of New York's City Squire Hotel, it took them fifteen minutes just to get from their cars to the lobby. For Keith Richards, it was the difference between night and day. The Rolling Stones were finally — *finally!* — stars in America, and their hooking up with Allen Klein was a good bit of the reason.

"Klein was magnificent, at first, in the States," he said. "The next tour, under his management, was cranked up several gears. A private plane to get us about, huge billboards on Sunset Boulevard. Now we're talking."

Marianne Faithfull, then Jagger's girlfriend, agreed. "Letting Allen Klein have that much financial control probably wasn't a good thing for the Rolling Stones," she said. "But it wasn't a bad thing either, because it meant that the work got out in America. It's worth whatever it costs to be properly sold in America. Because otherwise they might never have been more than another little British band."

The thirty-eight-date tour netted each of the Stones $50,000. The next U.S. tour, in the summer of 1966, took them from Massachusetts to Hawaii and proved even bigger. By then the band had racked up two more American number-one hits, "Get Off of My Cloud" and "Paint It, Black." For the New York show at Forest Hills Tennis Stadium, Klein, the master of the exaggerated gesture, hired a helicopter to ferry the band from their midtown hotel to the concert; he dragged a queasy Oldham, who suffered from vertigo, up to the stadium's corrugated roof to watch the performance.

At tour's end, Klein chartered the *Princess,* a seventy-foot yacht docked at the Seventy-Ninth Street Pier, for the Stones to unwind on. For two weeks, the band used it to cruise New York Harbor and as the site of their first New York press party.* When the Beatles performed at Shea Stadium in late August, Klein, the Stones, and Bobby Vinton

---

* The party on the *Princess* marked the first assignment in the exceptional career of photographer Linda Eastman, who covered the event for *Town and Country* magazine. Linda later married Paul McCartney, and Linda's brother, John Eastman, became a key Klein adversary.

took the *Princess* to Queens. Allen, who still longed to step into the Beatles' business, was angling to host a shipboard party for both bands after the concert. But the scene at Shea proved far too hectic, and not just because of Beatlemania. Vinton recalled that several Beatles fans — "Brooklyn guys" — recognized Jagger and tried to take a swing at him.

"The Rolling Stones weren't as big as the Beatles then but they were coming up," Vinton said. "People were buying their records, but they were kind of the bad guys. We're walking along with Jagger and it seemed like everyone wanted to take a punch at him! So Allen started running, I started running, and Mick Jagger started running. They were just punching Mick Jagger but you figured maybe they'd start on us next."

Unable to connect with the Beatles, the Stones didn't stay long. Cruising back to Manhattan, they made the unhappy discovery that the ship's radio wasn't working. The only record onboard, a Vinton single, "Long Lonely Nights," was played over and over again until an exasperated Jagger couldn't take it anymore. "I'm tired of this goddamn record," he said, getting up and turning off the player. "I don't give a shit if he is on the boat with us!"

For Klein, the most lasting memory of the evening was the self-confident, almost blasé reaction the band had to seeing the Beatles play a fifty-thousand-seat stadium. "The Stones were not impressed with the Beatles at Shea," he said with a mix of surprise and admiration. "They were never in awe."

The Beatles remained Klein's white whale, his longed-for prize and validation. Yet it was increasingly clear to the industry that with or without the Beatles, Allen Klein and Company was already the vanguard management firm. Allen had moved his offices to the Time-Life Building in midtown and begun to manage the British singer and songwriter Donovan. And when Ray Davies of the Kinks needed someone to renegotiate and improve that band's recording and publishing deals, Peter Grant steered Davies to Klein. Though gimlet-eyed and proud of it, the twenty-two-year-old rocker had never met anyone like Klein. He had no idea what to make of him.

"You got talent?" Klein barked upon being introduced.

When Ray didn't respond, Allen turned it up a notch. "Oh, come on, let's cut this phony humble act. Of course you got friggin' talent — so much so that you're making Reprise Records and Louis Benjamin at Pye a goddamn fortune," he said, naming the American and British labels for which the Kinks then recorded.

Marty Machat acted as the foil, and Klein and the attorney put on a show for Davies, enumerating precedents, plotting strategy for taking on the labels and all but guaranteeing their capitulation. The plan, in a nutshell, was a variant of a Klein favorite: threaten to break the contracts and force a renegotiation. In this case, Allen and Marty would tell Pye that the contract was void because Davies had been a minor and had not received proper legal representation, and they would threaten to sue; they would tell Warner that its contract was no good because the Pye contract that supplied them with Kinks records for America wasn't going to hold up. The scheme would have the added bonus of getting the two labels sniping at each other.

When Davies asked Klein what he should do, Allen told him to just go home, continue to work, and leave the rest to them.

It was obvious to Davies that Allen counted on the dishonesty of the record companies — and perhaps, for that matter, on the dishonesty of everyone. "I will succeed," he recalled Klein telling him, "because I believe all men are born evil. That's how I stay in business and that is why we will win. So don't worry." A few months later, Davies sat with Allen in the penthouse suite of the Hilton in London while he negotiated simultaneously with Pye and Reprise, and what Ray saw chilled him to the core. "To say that he bullied them into a new deal with the Kinks would be an understatement," Davies said. "Doing deals was Klein's passion as well as his living." Allen's tactics were so abrasive and alien to the British business establishment that Davies's own solicitor fled the suite in tears — and Klein was on *their* side.

Klein relished his pugnacious and foul-mouthed reputation, playing it for all it was worth. His clients loved that Allen scared the hell out of music executives, so he advertised himself as trouble. *Yea, though I walk through the valley of the shadow of death I will fear no evil,* a Christmas card to friends and associates declared, *for I am the biggest bastard in the valley.*

It wasn't all an act; he could be a terrific and terrifying bully, and not just with opponents he sought to intimidate but with the people who worked for him. Machat, who received a monthly retainer of six thousand dollars as well as a piece of the deals he worked on, took the brunt of the abuse.

Attorney Eric Kronfeld, who began his career as Machat's junior associate, initially viewed Klein as "the devil personified," largely because of the way he casually and continually humiliated Machat in meetings. "Marty would say something and Allen would just look at him and go, 'Shut the fuck up. You don't know what you're talking about. You're an idiot.' Literally."

No one was immune or exempt from abuse until Allen's son, Jody, joined the company in 1985, and even though Allen didn't savage him, he looked to be choking back the insults. Michael Kramer, who first joined his uncle Allen's company as a gofer and later became ABKCO's in-house attorney after Allen put him through law school, eventually had to quit and go out on his own.

"I love my uncle but he had demons," Kramer said. "You couldn't tell him anything, you didn't know anything." After Allen sent Michael to MCA to get information about a new contract for Bobby Womack but forbade him to say anything or even acknowledge questions from label executives—"Just keep your fucking mouth shut"—Kramer finally decided he'd had enough. Uncle Weasel might have put him through law school and given him a career, but the price demanded in return could never be paid. Michael resigned and opened his own law practice.

Predictably, Kramer's departing raised his stock in his uncle's eyes and precipitated an all-out love offensive. Allen dreaded being alone, couldn't personally fire an employee, and had a particular terror of familial abandonment. His first response was vindictive; he doubled the salary of Michael's secretary so she couldn't follow him. But he was soon insisting that employees consult Kramer on any and all legal questions. "All of a sudden I'm a genius," Michael said. "Anybody in the office says something, it's 'You don't know — call Michael.'" Over the next eight years Michael refused Allen's multiple entreaties to return to the company, telling Klein he preferred to have him as his uncle rather than his boss. But in the early nineties, when Klein was in a difficult legal wrangle with Bertelsmann Music Group over Sam Cooke's masters, Michael agreed to come back and help solve the problem.

The honeymoon ended in the very first meeting with BMG. "We're talking and I say something and Allen cuts me off. 'Shut the fuck up. You don't know what the fuck you're talking about.' About five minutes later, the same thing: 'You're an idiot. Shut your fucking mouth.'" During a break in the meeting, Kramer took Klein out into the hall and finally laid the issue to rest. "Allen, you're my uncle and I love you," he said. "But if you ever talk to me like that again I'm going to beat you so badly you won't be able to get up."

Paradoxically, many who bore the brunt of Klein's abuse felt they understood him, even while cowering through the boss's outbursts. He was clearly obsessed: obsessed with being one step ahead, obsessed with knowing more than anyone else, obsessed with winning. Allen didn't go into a meeting thinking he'd simply bully an adversary and bluff his way through the negotiation — although he certainly could and did. He prepared tirelessly. "No one could read a contract like my uncle," Kramer said. Allen pored over documents, learning and looking for angles, then entered meetings with the knowledge that after he finished the bullying, he would inflict the real damage by being far better prepared than the opposition.

It wasn't just contracts and documents that concerned Allen; he thought about business strategies incessantly and could be doggedly single-minded. Andrew Oldham's wife, Sheila, found him obsessive, bright, persuasive, and nearly impossible. "The whole time Allen Klein was with the Stones he was trying to get the Beatles interested in him," she said. "We used to spend days and days and days when Allen would just talk and talk and talk . . . It was all the psychological things: 'Well, if you did this, they would do that and if you did something else . . .' How to get it right."

He seemed to have no off switch. Klein frequently strategized in the shower, where it was his habit to argue both sides of an issue out loud.

The notion of managing the Beatles had become an obsession for Klein. They were the best, he was the best — nothing else made sense. It was difficult not to wonder if Klein had pursued Donovan as a client in some measure because he knew the singer was friendly with them. Anyone Allen did business with — whether an artist like Ray Davies or a producer like Mickie Most — had to hear how he was going to get the Beatles. Klein was so sure of himself that he bet Mickie's wife, Christina Hayes, ten thousand dollars that he would become the Beatles' manager within the year.

That was an awful lot of money for Allen to bet on what sounded like a long shot. Christina couldn't resist. "We shook on it," she recalled. "And Mickie went white."

The Kleins and the Mosts were friends. They vacationed together; the Mosts stayed with the Kleins when they came to New York. Still, as far as Christina was concerned, this bet was at least as much business as friendship — and when it came to being a businessman, Allen wasn't as unfailingly gracious and generous as he was as a friend.

Mickie was pleased at the way Allen renegotiated and enriched his contracts, but Christina said Mickie was disappointed in later years when additional payments never materialized. "Mickie used to say, 'He's the brightest man in the music business.' But he also used to say, 'Why can't he be one hundred percent all right?'" She made it a point to remind Allen of the bet.

She needn't have worried. In London, the first time she saw Klein after she'd won, he handed her a shoebox stuffed with ten thousand dollars. "What do you say we go thirty thousand on a year's extension?" he asked. There was no way she would do that; the smaller bet had been harrowing enough, and if Allen was ready to triple it, he probably *was* going to get the Beatles. Still, Allen got a bit of his own back.

After handing over the money, Allen took Christina out to dinner, but she quickly noticed that the limousine wasn't headed in the direction of the restaurant. "He knew I have a middle name that I hate," she said. "And we drive by Piccadilly Circus, and going round and round on the news ticker is 'Christina *Winifred* Hayes.'"

It wasn't just the Beatles that made him obsessive. When wooing a new client, Klein would obtain and very nearly memorize every item on the artist he could find, from press clips to contracts. "He had an amazing memory," said former ABKCO employee Paul Mozian. "It was a gift. Just the way he thought and could put deals together on the fly. He always had in-house counsel when I was there but did the crafting and the thrust of the deals himself." But beyond that, there was something about Klein's thought processes that was so idiosyncratic as to be nearly bizarre. When he was formulating ideas, particularly in office-strategy sessions, they often came out jumbled and difficult to decipher. The only thing clear was that Allen's mind was racing, entertaining and trying to express several trains of thought simultaneously. It was sometimes impossible to keep up with him, particularly when he was working through a problem or a plan. Attorney Gideon Cashman compared it to chasing a grasshopper.

"Flashes would go off in his mind and send him in different directions," he said. "So there'd be no continuity. I had to pay the closest attention to him — and if my attention lagged I was a dead duck. Then he's fourteen blocks ahead on some other point, having skipped three other parts. I wouldn't know where the hell I was and have to fake it." As much as it frustrated listeners, the gap between what went on in Allen's mind and his ability to explain it frustrated him more than anyone. It was clearly a source of his rage.

"Allen would get very angry and shake his hands — not his fists, but his hands — and his eyes would roll practically in a temper; his voice would be more a shriek than a scream," said Beverly Winston, Klein's assistant in London. "I think that a lot of the time he lost his temper out of frustration, because his mind worked faster than anybody else's. Like, *Why can't you see?* The reason you couldn't see was because he was ahead of himself and hadn't explained it properly." Whether he and his colleagues were plotting a negotiation, hammering out a contract or a proposal, or discussing how to woo a client, the issue was examined over and over and over again until Klein was convinced that he was in control of as much as possible. In negotiations, the process frequently went on and on, which sometimes led the other side to grow impatient and play its hand but just as often frustrated Allen's own people. Harold Seider, Klein's in-house attorney for several years, said Allen frequently avoided decisions so the negotiations dragged on longer. Recalled Seider: "I used to send him memos saying, 'What do you want to do?' And they would sit there. Eventually I sent him a memo that said, 'Please check the appropriate box: yes, no, maybe.' Never even did that."

Putting Allen's contracts and proposals on paper could be just as daunting as negotiating them. When a contract or deal was being worked on, normal business hours went out the window. If Allen wanted you around, you didn't leave, even if it meant working twenty-four or even thirty-six hours straight.

"He would have you do things a thousand ways," said Emily Barrata Quinn, one of Klein's former assistants. "No computers — typewriters. We were forever cutting and pasting and retyping." She and Allen's other assistant, Reggie Golodik, often worked late into the night. "I gained about fifteen pounds because Allen placated us with dinner orders from any restaurant we wanted."

Still, in the rare instance he met a similarly far-thinking opponent, Klein proved just as happy to make a bed as rumple it. Clive Davis had been negotiating and socializing with Klein for several years as a CBS Records attorney before becoming president of the company. In that latter role he was primarily concerned with modernizing the roster and making Columbia the leader in the rock world. Klein had just the kind of clients Davis was looking for, and Donovan proved a key signing for both the executive and Columbia's sister label, Epic. "We never had an argument," said Davis, who met George Harrison at Klein's home in Riverdale. "We were always direct with each other and accepting of the fact that we had separate objectives. We clicked. Our dealings were very professional and not at all confrontational. He was very

effective and very successful in relating to independent-thinking artists." Indeed, after Klein replaced Ashley Kozak — an associate of Brian
Epstein — as Donovan's manager, Donovan called him a major factor
in both his commercial and artistic success. "What did I want?" asked
Donovan. "I wanted the music heard and marketed. I don't know how
Allen contacted Ashley but it was the best thing that could have happened to me." In fact, Klein owed his introduction to Donovan's music
to Peter Grant, who played him a copy of "Catch the Wind," just one in
a string of folk-inflected singles that included "Universal Soldier" and
"Colours" with which the singer/songwriter was beginning to make
his mark. Friendly with the Beatles (a fact unlikely to have escaped
Klein's notice), Donovan was becoming increasingly ambitious and
experimental in his work. He envied the band's relationship with their
producer George Martin and was searching for a similar association,
someone who could help him expand the parameters of his music.
Klein suggested Mickie Most.

While Klein set about renegotiating Donovan's existing recording
contract with Pye in the UK and moving him from the small Hick-
ory Records to CBS in the United States, Most took Donovan into the
studio to see if they could come up with a single. After listening to
the songs Donovan had been writing, he suggested hiring John Cameron, a young Cambridge graduate, as an arranger. Together, Most and
Cameron provided Donovan with just the kind of support and broader
context that Martin, an arranger as well as a producer, had given the
Beatles. The first track they completed was "Sunshine Superman."

Most knew it was a hit. More than that, he knew it would be a big
record for Donovan, one that would redefine him as far more than a
folksinger. A classic summer anthem, it was also something new and
unique: a psychedelic pop record propelled by bright percussion and
a funky-sounding harpsichord. Knowing that Klein was in the midst
of negotiating new deals and that they would have to sit on the record
for several months, Most fretted that other artists would hear the song
before it was released, mimic its unique sound, and beat them to the
punch. "Listen," Mickie implored Donovan, "please don't play this record for Paul McCartney."

Donovan couldn't wait to hear what the Beatles thought of his latest record and refused to follow Most's advice. Whether history proved the producer prescient is debatable but he certainly knew who the competition was. In America, where Epic released "Sunshine Superman" in July 1966, the record went to number one. But in the UK, where contract negotiations held up its release for another six months, it got only to number two. In the interim, the Beatles had a pair of UK number ones, "Paperback Writer" and "Eleanor Rigby."

Most also remained a Klein client, although he no longer required as much attention. At Allen's urging, Mickie had taken advantage of British tax laws favoring income on one-time capital gains and sold the masters and recording contracts of several acts, including the Animals and Herman's Hermit's. The buyer was Klein.

Klein's holdings were becoming as impressive and productive as his client roster. Along with the Most recordings, he owned or had an interest in Sam Cooke's records and publishing as well as a growing number of other copyrights purchased from clients like Jocko Henderson. With the addition of the Rolling Stones, Klein was clearly a player and a power in the business. He liked that—but not for the usual reasons. "He didn't sweat about money," said one friend, employee, and collaborator, producer Julian Schlossberg. "Money wasn't a god to him. He just didn't want anyone to screw around with him."

More to the point, he didn't want anyone to leave him again—ever. The legacy of his orphanage childhood was the abhorrence of solitude. Allen simply could not be alone, and now he had the power to make people stay.

For those around him, the results could be comical. Any new acquaintance or business associate could count on a trip to Newark, where the guided tour included the former site of the orphanage, the old playgrounds in Weequahic, and the cemetery where his family members were scattered in plots he at first couldn't find and so eventually had consolidated. Friends and employees might be invited to kill a little time playing hearts, only to have the card game turn into an epic, days-long battle. Michael Kramer, leaving the office one afternoon to attend an evening class for law school, was waylaid by his uncle, who begged Michael to keep him company on a limousine ride to the airport for an overnight flight to London, promising that the driver would then take him to school. Once at the terminal, Klein told his nephew to walk him to the gate—and then, finally, to keep him company on the flight. It wasn't until the next morning, when Allen was checked into his suite at the Dorchester and eager to take a nap, that Kramer was turned over to Alf Weaver, Klein's London chauffeur, to be dropped back at Heathrow.

Allen's need for female companionship was just as acute. Despite being married and wanting to stay that way, Klein seemed unconcerned with being faithful to either his wife or, later, Iris Keitel. A former Miss Brooklyn, Keitel was young, cute, and recently divorced when she joined the company in the sixties as a secretary and then became Klein's confidante and mistress. But having a girlfriend on the payroll didn't necessarily put a crimp in his nooners, which he announced with a wink and the news that he was "going out for a cheeseburger."

Nor could he countenance silence. "So what do you think?" he asked whenever there was a lull in conversation. "So what do you think?"

Perhaps his greatest financial lever was largely invisible: the day-to-day control of his clients' money. Klein's usual recommendation to his British clients looking to skirt the prohibitively high taxes charged on income earned abroad was to place the money in corporate accounts controlled by Klein and then take payment slowly over several years—often as many as twenty—rather than all at once in a lump sum. In fact, it worked; the money became income only as it was paid out, which allowed the clients to keep considerably more. With Bobby Vinton, who was an American, Klein followed a similar strategy, investing Vinton's advances and paying them out like an annuity over the years so that the amount he earned was actually much greater than the original advances. Everyone was happy; as far as the majority of his clients were concerned, Allen Klein was a financial genius.

They didn't know the half of it. Klein's clients, particularly the Rolling Stones, had already been paid millions of dollars that, for tax reasons, they were leaving largely untouched in New York's Chemical

Bank. Klein was bound and ready to pay them every penny to which they were contractually entitled. In the meantime, however, he put that money to work. It quickly earned a good deal more than Klein had guaranteed to pay his clients, and he wasn't bound and ready to pay them that. After all, leverage — including making money from money — was his specialty.

# 7

## ABKCO

*WHAT KIND OF SCHMUCK reads a newspaper in a steam room?*

Abbey Butler squinted in disbelief through the wet haze of the Luxor Baths at the squat, towel-draped man in the next chair hunched over the *Herald Tribune*. It had to be some kind of joke — the damn thing was sopping wet, collapsing in on itself, and altogether impossible to read. He couldn't resist saying something.

"What are you trying to read that's so important?" he asked.

"I want to know the price of MGM."

"Thirty-seven and a half," said Butler.

The man with the newspaper gave him a long, funny look. "What's General Motors?"

"Fifty-seven."

"How do you know that?"

"I'm in that business." Butler, then a young broker with Diamond, Turk, and Company, a small New York firm handling trades on the New York and American Stock Exchanges, explained that he'd developed the ability to commit key daily prices to memory to avoid having to constantly telephone for quotes.

Impressed, Butler's companion began chatting him up, mentioning that he was in the music and film business and that his father-in-law owned the health club. Later, as they were leaving the club, Klein gave Butler his card. "I'd like you to come up to my office one day," Allen said. "I have some money I have to invest and I really don't know how to do it. I'd like to talk to you about it."

Butler made it his business to visit the office in the Time-Life Building before the week was out. Klein explained that he was looking at long-term investments of approximately twenty years for his clients. He said he was particularly interested in preferred stocks, which had the dual benefit of being taxed at a lower rate and accruing dividends — enough, at 5 percent, to more than pay what was pledged annually to the artists. At Klein's request, Butler agreed to research General Motors.

A few days later, Butler told Klein that GM preferred did indeed appear to be the kind of investment he was looking for, and Klein asked for a day to consider what he was going to do. The young broker, who rarely took an order as big as a thousand shares in those days, was optimistic; it sounded like Klein might be ready to place that kind of big order. With a little luck, he might even buy two thousand shares. But when Klein called him back the next day, he didn't ask for a particular number of shares.

"I want you to start an account in the name of Nanker Phelge," he said, "and buy one million dollars' worth of GM preferred."

Butler was stunned. "One million?"

"Right."

"Allen, that's a lot of money. I'll need a bank reference before the senior partner will approve it."

Klein gave him the name and telephone number of a vice president at the Chemical Bank branch in the Time-Life Building. When Butler's boss did indeed insist on bank approval, Abbey called the man.

"I have an order from Mr. Allen Klein," Butler told the banker. "It's for an account called Nanker Phelge and it's for one million dollars. I'd like to know if it's okay to execute the order. Do they really have one million dollars?"

The banker did not answer directly. "Any order that Allen Klein gives you, the money is good."

The trade was cleared. By the standard of the time, it was huge; it took three days to find and purchase a million dollars' worth of General Motors preferred. When he finally had all the stock, Butler dropped by Klein's office. Allen again surprised Abbey by writing a check for the full amount on the spot.

Delirious, Butler skipped back to his office, imagining it would be a long time before he booked another deal like that. But when he got there, the telephone was already ringing. It was Klein with instructions to set up a new account in another name, and once again the order was for a million dollars.

Klein opened approximately a half a dozen accounts in quick succession. Although they were all in varying amounts, each was for a large sum of money. Eventually, Butler's curiosity got the better of him. "Allen," he said, "you got to explain to me what you do and what this is about." It was then he learned that the accounts contained money paid to the Rolling Stones, Herman's Hermits, Bobby Vinton, the Kinks, the Animals, and Donovan.

Butler liked Klein and loved his business, and the two were soon spending a lot of time together traveling to London and Italy, where Klein was pursuing film projects. Allen began thinking out loud about finding a public company to buy and use as a vehicle himself. The basic idea was that he would get control of a publicly traded company, fold his own Allen Klein and Company into it, raise the profile and price, and then use the stock to finance other acquisitions and deals. The question was, what company made the most sense to acquire?

Klein was going to be making several movies. Allen had remained friendly with Tony Anthony, the actor he'd partnered with on his first picture, and he'd agreed to coproduce a spaghetti Western that Anthony was starring in, *A Stranger in Town*. He'd also convinced MGM Records to advance money against Herman's Hermits' future royalties in order to produce a film with them, *Mrs. Brown, You've Got a Lovely Daughter*, while the Rolling Stones had purchased the film rights to a

British novel, *Only Lovers Left Alive,* that Oldham wanted to develop into a vehicle for them and for which Klein had cajoled a million dollars in seed money from London Records. With all those projects on the board, Allen believed an existing entertainment company would be the best fit. He asked Butler to take a look at MGM and see whether buying up its stock made sense.

Despite MGM's racking up some of the biggest hits of the sixties — including *Doctor Zhivago* and *2001: A Space Odyssey* — its financial performance was uneven and its record division comparatively weak next to RCA and Columbia; with Herman's Hermits, Klein controlled the act that was likely the corporation's biggest seller. The company also looked as if it was about to be in play. Philip Levin, a New Jersey real estate developer and one of MGM's largest shareholders, was mounting a proxy fight against management and clearly eyeing a takeover. After hashing over the situation with Butler and Marty Machat, Allen decided to go for it. "If anybody is going to make a bid for MGM, it's going to be me," Allen said. "Start buying the stock," he told Butler.

"How much do you want to spend and how much can I pay?"

"Just start buying it. Buy everything you can for the next couple of days."

Butler did just that. The money wasn't actually Klein's — it was from the various artists' accounts — but Butler shrugged, figuring Klein managed and controlled the money and that was good enough. Nonetheless, Klein's juggling of accounts was frequently felt in London, where Laurence Myers, who was now handling the Stones' day-to-day expenses for Klein, and Jo Bergman, the Rolling Stones' office manager, had trouble getting enough cash from Allen to pay the bills.

Before long Klein had bid the price of MGM up from the midthirties to the midfifties. Along the way, he amassed 160,000 shares, a significant holding that didn't go unnoticed in either *Variety* or the business pages. When the next MGM shareholders meeting was held, on February 23 in New York, Allen attended with the express aim of stopping Levin and hopefully tipping things his own way.

Though Klein didn't personally speak, he used Butler as his mouthpiece, feeding him questions to ask from the floor and prodding him to make a speech in favor of current management and against Levin. "When I sat down, Allen gave me a pat on the head and then we went home," Butler recalled.

Klein's bid for MGM never got off the ground. Levin briefly got control of the company before ceding it to Seagram heir Edgar M. Bronfman Sr., who lost it a few months later to hotelier Kirk Kerkorian. Nonetheless, the shareholder meeting wasn't without repercussions. Butler's remarks were included in newspaper reports of the meeting, and he found himself called on the carpet at Diamond, Turk, and Company, his actions deemed inappropriate for a broker. Upset, he called Klein and asked if he could stop by his office. Butler wasn't sure what he expected Klein to say; he was worried about his future and wanted Allen to know his ass was in a sling. But what Klein suggested caught him completely off-guard.

"Why don't you buy seats on the exchanges and start your own firm?" he asked.

"Allen, I don't have that kind of money." A seat on the American Stock Exchange cost approximately two hundred thousand dollars at the time; one on the New York Stock Exchange twice that.

"I'll lend it to you."

Speechless, Butler just stared at Klein, a man he'd met just a few short months earlier in a steam room. Then he burst into tears.

It was the kind of generous and seemingly impetuous offer that Klein would repeatedly toss off as he became ever more successful. Yet, although he might have acted out of kindness, Klein was always complicated. He could have had several competing motives, some of them large, some of them selfish, and all of them legitimate. It frequently seemed Allen's best and most thoughtful deals answered to more than one master. He was, after all, the strategist who as a matter of course contemplated several competing and complementary ideas at once, examining and refining them over and over and over again.

Butler was certainly useful to him. He was also typical of the advisers and professionals that Klein often elected to work with: young, hungry, and decidedly junior. When Klein needed outside counsel for litigation, he hired a top-notch firm but rarely relied on a senior part-ner. Instead, Allen would identify a young associate and direct all his requests and calls there, often monopolizing his time. Flattered and grateful, the younger attorneys invariably saw cultivating Klein as a unique opportunity and were at his beck and call. Abbey Butler him-self did not underestimate Klein's value.

"Abbey was a terrific hustler," said Harold Seider, Klein's in-house attorney at the time. "And Allen made him rich." In return, Klein got his own personal brokerage firm.

With MGM seemingly unattainable, Butler uncovered another, albeit significantly smaller, target trading on the American Stock Exchange: Cameo-Parkway Records. Begun in the basement of Philadelphia songwriter Bernie Lowe's home, the company had enjoyed a string of hits in the fifties and early sixties with Chubby Checker, the Dovells, Dee Dee Sharp, Bobby Rydell, the Orlons, and the Tymes, in no small part because of Lowe's close relationship with Dick Clark and his daily television show, *American Bandstand*. As was the widespread practice of the time, Clark regularly received an interest in the label's hits and just as regularly spotlighted them on the show. But the label's power waned with the congressional payola hearings and the British Inva-sion. By the time the show moved from Philadelphia to Los Angeles, in 1964, Cameo-Parkway wasn't even captivating its founder, and Lowe sold the company to a pair of investors in Texas who quickly demon-strated that they had no idea what to do with it. Klein, in comparison, didn't have just one idea of what to do with the company—he had about a dozen.

Klein wanted control of Cameo-Parkway for the same reason he'd wanted MGM: so he could engineer a reverse merger, in this case us-ing Cameo-Parkway stock to buy Allen Klein and Company, essen-tially making Cameo-Parkway pay to be taken over. Once his assets were in a public company, Klein would be able to do many things. Along with looking to enhance its value, run up the price of the stock, and make a personal killing, he hoped to use the company to finance other acquisitions. He hadn't completely given up on the idea of gaining control of MGM, and he also had his eye on a venerable privately held publisher, Chappell Music.

A public company could also be a useful tool for paying his artists. Klein still had a problem to work out, particularly with the Rolling Stones. He'd been able to optimize their — and his — income while minimizing their British tax bite by staggering their guarantees over many years. But the band was becoming more and more popular all the time and was certain to earn a good deal more than the guarantee. Under the recording and publishing agreements, they were to receive that additional money as a balloon payment sometime in the future. The problem was the same old one: how to collect a big lump payment without losing most of it to the Inland Revenue.

One traditional tool was the drop-out year. To encourage citizens to work overseas in Britain's colonies, the government granted a year's tax amnesty — provided the individual spent the entire year abroad and did not set foot in Great Britain. Klein, who was familiar with the strategy, had discussed with Jagger the idea of taking all the money that way, and he'd tried to employ it with Donovan, who moved to Japan. But Donovan soon decided that he didn't like being apart from Linda Lawrence, his girlfriend (and the mother of Brian Jones's son). He returned to England before the year was up, forfeited seven million dollars, and married her.

The Stones weren't that sentimental, but Klein saw another possibility that didn't require them to become exiles: instead of taking their money as income royalty, for which they'd get creamed, the Stones could get paid in stock. As he had with Tracey, Allen set himself up as the owner of Nanker Phelge U.S., the company that controlled the rights to manufacture Rolling Stones records in America. If Allen paid them in stock rather than cash, the Stones could then sell the shares and take the money as capital gains with nowhere near the tax penalty.

In early 1967, with Cameo-Parkway trading at just about $2 per share, Klein and Butler made their move and approached William Bowen, the company's principal stockholder, about a takeover. Bowen was eager to unload his investment, and by July, Klein had acquired 297,000 shares of the sparsely traded stock — a 48.5 percent stake — from Bowen for $1.75 a share. Butler bought Bowen's remaining 50,000 shares at the same price.

Rumors of Klein's interest, circulating before the deal was consummated, started to drive the stock up. In the first six months of 1967, fewer than 136,000 shares of Cameo-Parkway had traded on the AMEX; in July alone, the figure was nearly double that, and the stock topped the $10 mark. Things were looking good; Klein's stock-market killing seemed guaranteed. And then, as a trickle of rumors became a flood of speculation, the insanity began.

Klein's plans for a reverse acquisition were no secret. It quickly became known that Cameo-Parkway had filed to be renamed ABKCO, an acronym for the Allen and Betty Klein Company (although Allen later joked that the B stood for Bad), and investors interested in the entertainment business were intrigued by the notion of a company whose assets included the contracts for the Rolling Stones, Donovan, and others, not to mention the chance to tie their money to the industry's storied wheeler-dealer. On top of that, Klein wasn't willing to wait for the Securities and Exchange Commission to bless the reverse merger before he took advantage of his new financial tool. The Dreyfus family, with extensive music holdings in America and Europe, was entertaining bids for the publishing firm Chappell. Its extensive copyrights included the work of Jerome Kern, George and Ira Gershwin, Rodgers and Hammerstein, Cole Porter, Kurt Weill, Lerner and Loewe, and Jule Styne. Allen desperately wanted it.

As the SEC had yet to welcome ABKCO officially to the AMEX, Klein began raising money by peddling warrants — the right to purchase shares in the future — to Wall Street. Though their value and even their legitimacy was undetermined, he had no trouble finding takers.

"We went on a dog-and-pony show," said Harold Seider, "which is where I acquired my disrespect for Wall Street. The only thing that motivates them is greed and most of them are stupid beyond belief. We were raising money to buy Chappell and these guys were willing to give money in return for warrants in Cameo-Parkway at a penny apiece or something."

In fairness to Klein's backers, the chance to buy cheap warrants was nearly irresistible: Cameo-Parkway's stock was heading for the stars. Trading at ten dollars per share in August, it rose steeply over the next few months, climbing into the thirties, forties, and then fifties.

Seider, who as Klein's attorney had become a vice president and director of Cameo-Parkway, attributed the rise to a perfect storm of intense interest and keen skepticism. As the stock rose, speculators shorted the company, believing the price was grossly inflated and would have to drop. But its popularity with short-sellers had just the opposite effect; because the pool of available stock was so limited—there was a maximum of 240,000 shares available in the market—the price kept rising as desperate short-sellers hustled to find enough stock to cover their positions. Between August 1, 1967, and February 15, 1968, when Cameo-Parkway peaked at 76⅝, two million shares changed hands.

The dramatic price run-up led to a great deal of speculation regarding who was getting rich. "Abbey was pushing the stock and Allen was not oblivious to it," Seider said. Cameo-Parkway had become a hot story on Wall Street. Marty Machat's associate Eric Kronfeld handled much of Klein's legal work on the Cameo-Parkway deal, and his failure to tip anyone off made him very unpopular at home.

"My father-in-law was particularly furious with me," he recalled. "I said, 'Well, if I'd said or done anything, I'd probably go to jail. It's called insider trading.' He said, 'Oh, yeah? Who'd know?' He was mad at me for months."

Seider believed the biggest pool of winners was drawn from Butler's friends and neighbors. "Abbey was having all the people where he lived in Brooklyn buy the stock," he said. "They were the ones selling to the shorts. They were buying homes; people were getting rich in the neighborhood." Asked in a shareholders' meeting why the stock was rising so dramatically, Seider just shrugged and attributed it to the law of supply and demand. "It was true! It wasn't that anyone was playing games."

Indeed, when the government ultimately stepped in and halted trading in Cameo-Parkway in order to stop its runaway inflation, it didn't blame the company or Klein and Butler. According to Seider,

"The SEC guys were saying, 'What went on?' I said, 'Please — we're not crooks. We're just *stupid*.' At the time they weren't as aggressive."

By then, however, Klein had raised enough money to make a bid for Chappell, which was expected to fetch $45 million. Klein's strategy was to blow away the competition from the outset; he bid $60 million. Armed with a check for $6 million as a deposit, Seider and an ABKCO accountant, Joel Silver, figured they'd close the deal on a Friday night. But though they worked through the night on a contract, the Dreyfus family balked and changed their minds over the weekend, perhaps numbering themselves among those who didn't see a future in Cameo-Parkway stock. "They didn't believe Allen could come up with the total financing," said Kronfeld. "They chose not to deal with him." Though the bid failed, Klein's interest in the company and his willingness to pay a premium looks prescient today: Chappell subsequently became the cornerstone of Warner Music's publishing operation, a company valued at $1.5 billion.

In the end, the Cameo-Parkway acquisition produced decidedly mixed results. Though the company did ultimately change its name to ABKCO Industries, the American Stock Exchange opted not to reinstate it for trading. Whether Klein's apparent failure to complete an SEC audit of Allen Klein and Company's assets was the root cause or whether the exchange was still worried about what it had witnessed, it announced that the new company "will not meet the applicable listing standards of the Exchange relating to net worth and earnings." Instead, ABKCO continued to trade over the counter, and the stock rocket fell to earth. And in the coming years Klein would find he did not like all the oversights and restrictions that being the head of a public company placed on him.* Nineteen years later, in 1987, Klein took ABKCO private. Klein's failure to complete the audit was typical. Ironically, while Klein was hyperaggressive and belligerent in negotiations, he ducked every other confrontational situation.

---

* Klein was not alone in this regard. The British music mogul and entrepreneur Richard Branson would come to the same conclusion several decades later when he briefly took his company, Virgin, public and then just as quickly reversed course and went private again.

For starters, he couldn't fire anyone. When a termination became unavoidable, he would convince someone else to do it; it fell to Abbey Butler to fire Morton DaCosta, the director of *Mrs. Brown, You've Got a Lovely Daughter*. In business he'd discovered that ignoring an unwanted outcome frequently produced another and sometimes more advantageous one — although not always. In 1963, when the IRS sent an agent on a relatively mundane matter regarding late filing of employee-withholding documents — the taxes had actually been paid but the paperwork hadn't been properly filed — Klein made the agent wait several hours and then didn't meet with him, a decision that would come back years later to cause Klein far-reaching and irreparable problems. Similarly, on the day SEC officials came to the office to discuss the Cameo-Parkway stock imbroglio, Klein left the job of meeting with them to Seider, electing instead to go to the movies with his assistant and mistress, Iris Keitel.

ABKCO's inability to meet AMEX standards told a truth about Klein, as did his ostrich-like behavior toward the IRS: he didn't have the stomach or patience to play by any rules but his own. Yet he was hard-working and had prospered because artists desperately needed the kind of brash and creative representation he could provide. And now that ABKCO was public and Klein had had to reveal a great deal of information about his business practices, it was more obvious than ever just how clever and original Allen was. In the final analysis, he wasn't really a financial manager. He was in the business of creating new streams of revenue — for himself as well as his artists.

Two surprising facts stood out in ABKCO's statement to its shareholders. The first was that the company had no management contracts with any artists. The second was that it did have contracts to manufacture records and made more money doing that than it did from management.

At the core of ABKCO's financial engine was an arrangement Klein referred to as the "buy/sell agreement." Beginning with Sam Cooke's work and continuing with Mickie Most's recordings and the Rolling Stones', ABKCO — and not the respective record companies — controlled the right to manufacture records in the United States. The artists didn't switch American record companies; Cooke remained with RCA, the Animals and Herman's Hermits with MGM, the Rolling Stones with London Records. But each acquired a new middleman in ABKCO. When Allen picked up a client, he negotiated new recording contracts that increased the advances and royalties for that artist. At the same time, Klein frequently negotiated another deal, one in which his company would manufacture and deliver the records to the label at an agreed-upon price.

In the case of the Rolling Stones, for example, the musicians were due a royalty of 7 percent — half of the 14 percent initially negotiated by Easton and Oldham — of a record's list price. An album such as *Beggars Banquet* might retail for $4.98 at the time, meaning the Stones would get approximately thirty cents per record after standard contractual allowances against returns and breakage. By contrast, Klein's share of the Rolling Stones' royalties was 20 percent, all of which was paid out of Oldham and Easton's share, meaning he was already making roughly twice as much in record royalties as any member of the band. But he made a separate payday on the difference between what it cost ABKCO to manufacture Rolling Stones records and what London Records paid him to do it. If, for example, London paid ABKCO $1.25 per album, ABKCO used that money to pay royalties, the cost of making and packaging the record, and other associated and incidental fees. When all was said and done, there was plenty of wiggle room; the performers and songwriters got paid what they had been promised, and whatever was left over belonged to ABKCO.

The buy/sell agreement was unique to ABKCO and starkly demonstrated Klein's business savvy. Since the average artist was promised just pennies on a $4.98 album, Klein recognized that the record companies had tremendous financial leeway, and he used that knowledge not only to get the artists more money but to deal himself into the equation: he demanded a segment of the business — manufacturing — on which the labels themselves traditionally made a profit. Initially, as with Mickie Most, it was a way for Klein to say he was getting his fee out of the American record company and not deducting a commission out of the client's money.

On the surface, this didn't appear to harm the artists; they got whatever royalties they had been promised, and it was always a good deal more than they'd received before meeting Allen Klein. The rub was that he advertised himself as a business manager but didn't enlighten his clients or maximize their income as one might reasonably expect a business manager to do. He improved their incomes dramatically but didn't necessarily spell out where and how he'd participated or how much he was earning. He knew, as he'd told Jerry Brandt, that artists were financially abused by the record companies and desperate for money, and he sold himself to them as someone who could get that money for them.

When Klein met a prospective client, it was his habit to simply ask, "What do you want?" Invariably, the answer was money—and a young artist, a Mick Jagger or Keith Richards, could be counted on to name the highest figure he could think of, likely a million dollars. Klein knew he could get that, and he would tell all the young artists so. What he would not tell them was that they were asking for the wrong thing. But then, Klein wasn't a CPA and didn't have management contracts with his clients. As far as he was concerned, he provided the best and most aggressive financial representation in the music business; he could make it rain like no one else and was entitled to a commensurate fee.

# 8

## ROCK 'N' ROLL CIRCUS

IN THE EIGHTEEN MONTHS since Klein had taken charge of the business affairs of the Rolling Stones, Andrew Loog Oldham had continued as their manager and producer. And that was exactly as Klein wanted it. Indeed, when the band severed ties with Easton, Brian Jones — who didn't get along with Oldham — suggested to Allen that he, Allen, become the manager. Klein wanted none of it.

"Oldham managed the Stones," he said. "I managed Oldham. That was the deal. I did not want to manage the Stones. I didn't want the obligation. And I couldn't do it." Klein believed he had good ears for a pop tune and rarely hesitated to offer suggestions to Sam Cooke or Bobby Vinton, but he recognized that the Stones were not in his musical comfort zone and that he had nothing to contribute creatively.

On a personal level, he had great affection for Keith Richards and respected Charlie Watts. The others he could do without, particularly Bill Wyman, who kept a close eye on his money and liked to complain. Klein, gauging that Richards and Jagger were calling the shots in the band and that Wyman would never transcend his status as a late addition who'd been hired because he had a professional amplifier, treated him as an incidental member of the Rolling Stones. After Jagger and

Richards bought homes with funds obtained literally overnight from Klein, Wyman wanted to do the same, and he stewed while Klein made him wait months for the money. As for Mick Jagger, he and Klein were wary of each other from the start.

"Jagger — I spent some personal moments with him but I didn't want to get involved," Klein said. "I always wanted Andrew to be there. I didn't want to spend the time. I mean, that's a full-time job. Keith — he was easy. He didn't demand a lot of time. He was gentle, kind, really terrific."

In the studio, Oldham sought to remain a factor in the group's music. But his inability to bring real technical and artistic know-how to the recording process, as engineer Glyn Johns or arranger Jack Nitzsche might, made Oldham less valuable as the band became increasingly sophisticated and self-assured. More pointedly, he was distracted by his own drug use and his quest for success and celebrity, unable to take an accurate read of his shrinking role and changing status. In the early days, the Stones had needed the press-corps Svengali with a mile-a-minute rap as their hip cheerleader and coconspirator, but no more. And there was a growing sense within the band that they didn't need to generate publicity anymore; in fact, they needed to avoid it. Their outlaw status, so helpful in launching their career, was starting to feel like a burden. Watching the ever-increasing, ever-evolving mainstream acceptance of the Beatles — the perpetual yardstick of creative and cultural success for any band at the time, particularly the Stones — the group wondered if they'd made a mistake. "There'd been a big change around November 1966 where in some ways the Beatles were allowed to come back and retire [from touring] and flaunt their wealth and drive around in Rolls-Royces and go to the Prime Minister's house," said Oldham. "The Rolling Stones were not."

Jagger in particular seemed to be chafing under the relationship. Once close to Jagger, Oldham now seemed to spend every moment with the singer either arguing with him or placating him. The launch of Andrew's own recording career via the Andrew Loog Oldham Orchestra and of his own label, Immediate Records, gave him new creative platforms, not to mention a separate path to continue to pursue fame, fortune, and excess. Though Oldham still knew precious little about making records, he and partner Tony Calder did have an eye and ear for the right artists; the Immediate roster included singers Rod Stewart, Chris Farlowe, P. P. Arnold, and Nico as well as numerous seminal bands such as John Mayall and the Bluesbreakers, the Small Faces, the Nice, Fleetwood Mac, Humble Pie, and Savoy Brown. And if his relationship with the Stones and Mick Jagger remained precarious, perhaps Immediate could provide the rapprochement; aside from giving Oldham another outlet, it also supplied Jagger and Richards with additional income by way of covers of their songs, with Chris Farlowe's version of "Out of Time" reaching number one in the UK.

But the relationship between Oldham and the Stones would soon take a ruinous turn.

On February 12, 1967, a small army of eighteen policemen descended on Redlands, Keith Richards's recently purchased home in Sussex. The raid came just as Richards and several others were coming down from an LSD trip. The contraband recovered was modest: there were a couple of roaches around the house; Jagger had a few amphetamines purchased from a druggist in Italy; and a friend, Robert Fraser, had heroin. But it was enough to get them hauled off to jail, and the tabloid *News of the World* made a meal of the bust, reporting with particular gusto that Marianne Faithfull, fresh out of the shower, had greeted the police clad only in a fur rug.

Though the men were released on bail, it immediately became apparent that the government was serious about bringing a case for jail time against Jagger and Richards. It was an obvious call to arms for Oldham, who had to know that at moments of crisis, a manager proves his worth by taking charge. It was his job to devise a strategy, hire the proper legal and public relations firms, and defuse the situation. Instead, he abandoned his clients and fled to America.

"I was out of there," Oldham admitted. "I was already not dealing with a completely full deck, but if you have five policemen in your house, you've got a good reason to think you're going to end up in jail. So I left the country." It fell to Klein to pick up the slack. He flew to

London and huddled with publicist Les Perrin as well as Joynson and Hicks, the Stones' solicitors, to select a barrister for Jagger and Richards's court case.

Allen suggested the band leave the country to get away from the press, and they took off for an extended stay in Morocco. The situation had become even more complicated when *News of the World* incorrectly attributed a prior drug incident involving Brian Jones to Jagger, who demanded a retraction and threatened the paper with a defamation suit. Richards came to believe that Jagger's threat against the tabloid worked heavily against them, as the paper's best defense would be their conviction on the drug charges, and he later suggested the newspaper conspired with prosecutors in a "stitch up." Whether this was true or not, Jagger, Richards, and Fraser were all convicted at trial in June and sentenced to prison: Jagger for three months in Brixton, and Richards and Fraser for a year and six months, respectively, at Wormwood Scrubs.

As incredible as the episode was, its least likely feature may have been the identity of their eventual savior. The day after sentencing, William Rees-Mogg, an editor at the conservative London *Times,* published a scathing essay decrying the thinness of the case and the injustice and idiocy of the sentences. Inspired by Alexander Pope, the editorial, entitled "Who Breaks a Butterfly on a Wheel?," caused an outcry and forced the court to vacate Jagger's and Richards's sentences.* Jagger, said to be devastated by the sentence, wound up spending three nights in prison, all of them, reportedly, in the infirmary. Richards spent only one night in prison and said he was treated well by his fellow inmates, but he was nonetheless relieved to be out. He soon turned wryly philosophic. "The judge managed to turn me into some folk hero overnight," he said. "I've been playing up to it ever since."

The day Jagger and Richards were released from jail, policeman Norman Pilcher, who'd already busted Donovan for drugs and would later target George Harrison and John Lennon, arrested Brian Jones for marijuana possession. Klein sent Perrin to bail him out and that

---

* Robert Fraser's sentence was not vacated and he served his time.

evening invited Jagger, Richards, and Marianne Faithfull to his pent-house suite at the London Hilton to celebrate their release. Allen was at first stunned and then enraged when a package delivered to his suite for Marianne proved to contain a small box with a false bottom from which she produced a ball of hashish. Klein grabbed it from her, flushed the hash down the toilet, and tossed the box off the balcony. He couldn't believe it — Jagger and Richards had just gotten out of jail!

"You people are stupid!" he snapped.

Marianne just pouted. "You didn't have to throw it away."

The Beatles and their friend Donovan were spending the last week of August at Bangor University in North Wales studying transcendental meditation at a retreat with Maharishi Mahesh Yogi. On Wednesday, August 23, the Beatles' manager, Brian Epstein, called to say he would join them the following Monday, August 28. But on Sunday, Epstein's body was discovered in his Sussex home, his death later ruled an accidental drug overdose. He was thirty-two, and his passing left the Beatles shocked and rudderless. "I knew that we were in trouble then," Lennon would later say. "I didn't really have any misconceptions about our ability to do anything other than play music. I was scared." Allen Klein heard the news of Epstein's passing on the radio Sunday evening, driving alone across the Henry Hudson Bridge to his home in River-dale. "I got 'em!" he said aloud.

With Epstein gone, Allen knew the Beatles were facing a rat's nest of financial and contractual problems, the kind that only a few people had the ability to sort through. And while it would be more than a year before Klein actually became involved with the Beatles, there was something to his sense of inevitability. As he himself would ask, who else was there? The Beatles would comb the British financial world, in vain. And in the music business, the alternatives to Klein were either unavailable or unsatisfactory. Frank Sinatra's attorney, Mickey Rudin, was certainly savvy enough to handle the group, but he was unlikely to be comfortable in their milieu. The Beatles knew Bob Dylan's manager, Albert Grossman, but the insular and affected Grossman already had a stable of artists and liked the world arranged to his own tastes, so it was doubtful that he would take on such a monumental task. Robert Stigwood, a rising force in management with the Bee Gees and Cream, had already been in and out of a brief and ugly partnership with Epstein and the Beatles; he wouldn't cross that bridge again.

No one wanted or needed to manage the Beatles as much as Allen did. His deepest secret wasn't that he used creative and questionable ways to make money off his clients; indeed, given the right audience, he was likely to crow about that. His secret was that he would have managed the Beatles for nothing. Klein saw handling them as final and irrefutable proof that he was the best.

For all the ingenuity and work that Klein brought to the pursuit of money, money was not an end in itself, or even how he kept score. He didn't like losing it — he stopped playing the stock market after dropping a million dollars on National Video — but he always spent it lustily. And once he and his family were secure, money became a tool for vindication. Professionally, he needed to be acknowledged as the best and brightest in the game. In his private life, he had to be adored.

Bluff and rough in battle, even downright nasty, in other situations, Klein wore his hunger for approval on his sleeve and waved his generosity like a big red banner. Once Allen had made it, no one out with him ever paid for a meal, a cab, an evening's entertainment, an airline ticket (first class, of course), a hotel suite, or a vacation again. He had to pay.

"He was probably the largest spender I ever met," said his friend and attorney Leonard Leibman, recalling a time when Klein discovered a key in his jacket pocket for a suite at the Plaza Hotel that he'd used once three months earlier and forgotten to check out of. "He would have jets waiting on runways for three days. And you never saw a bill when you were with Mr. Klein."

Producer Julian Schlossberg attended the Cannes Film Festival with Klein in 1973, and on the way there they stopped in Rome to screen versions of *Andy Warhol's Frankenstein* and *Andy Warhol's Dracula,**

---

* Actually directed by Warhol protégé and collaborator Paul Morrissey.

Following the death of his mother, Klein was sent to live with his grandmother, Anita Brown, on Newark's South Nineteenth Street.

When Klein was four, he was placed in Newark's Hebrew Orphanage and Sheltering Home, where he and his sister Naomi remained for five years, until their father remarried in 1941. Allen, third from left, and Naomi, second from right, on a rare day out for their sister Esther's wedding.

*Unless otherwise noted, photographs reproduced courtesy of ABKCO Archives. Used by permission.*

Klein enlisted in 1951. His years in the army provided his first exposure to the world beyond Newark's cloistered Jewish community and spurred an intense period of self-examination and reinvention.

With help from the GI Bill, Klein worked part-time and put himself through New Jersey's Upsala College. If his years in the army were characterized by extensive reading and soul-searching, his approach to college was strictly practical: to become an accountant and launch a career.

Ill-suited to the button-down world of accounting—Klein was fired by a Manhattan firm when he proved incapable of coming to work in the morning—he instead formed Allen Klein and Company to provide bookkeeping and auditing services to the music industry. Following his first successful audit, for performers Jimmy Bowen and Buddy Knox, he treated himself to a new car.

Klein's aggressive record-company audits earned him the loyalty of performers and the enmity of label executives. In 1963 his career took a dramatic turn when singer Sam Cooke, impressed by the job Klein had done, made him his manager. To help Cooke secure a historic 1964 appearance at New York's Copacabana, Klein urged him to retain General Artists Corporation founder Buddy Howe (left) as his agent.

With the British Invasion, Klein became a leading figure in the burgeoning rock industry, managing business and negotiating deals for numerous British artists, including the Dave Clark Five, the Animals, the Kinks, Herman's Hermits, Lulu, and Donovan. Receiving gold record awards in 1964 with one of his key British clients, the producer Mickie Most.

Klein began a long and controversial association with the Rolling Stones in 1965 when he negotiated new multimillion-dollar recording contracts for the band. It was also the start of a tempestuous lifelong relationship with the band's original co-manager and brilliant style guru, Andrew Loog Oldham, with whom Klein is pictured at the London Hilton, celebrating the Stones' new contract.

*Mirrorpix*

Mick Jagger's ever-increasing role in the Rolling Stones—and growing sophistication regarding the music business—led to a wariness between the singer and Klein. For his part, Allen liked to refer to his opulent home in Riverdale, New York, as "the house that Jagger built."

Mick Jagger and Keith Richards after being released on bail following the infamous drug raid on Redlands, Richards's home in Sussex. Despite his role as the band's manager, Oldham had feared the police would target him next and fled the country, leaving Klein to work with the band and their lawyers. Chichester Magistrates' Court, May 10, 1967.

*Daily Mail / Solo Syndication*

Klein, who rarely hesitated to voice an opinion about their work to most of his clients, including Sam Cooke, John Lennon, and George Harrison, considered himself unqualified to comment on the music of the Rolling Stones and steered clear of creative discussions. "Oldham managed the Stones," he said. "I managed Oldham." A rare moment in the studio with Jagger and Richards, London, 1968.

A record label's worst nightmare. "He was a sharp, bullying sort of an individual," one record company owner said of Klein. But artists, ranging from Bobby Vinton to John Lennon, delighted in his ability to strike fear and get results. "Talk about my reputation, what about the record companies'?" Klein asked. "It's not like I was in church kicking over statues." Riverdale, New York, 1971.

*Michael Cooper / ABKCO Archives*

As the new business manager for the financially strapped Beatles, Klein attempted to regain control of their music publishing from Dick James, who instead sold Northern Songs to Lord Lew Grade's ATV in 1969. The tense dealings were hampered by the growing rift between John Lennon and Paul McCartney. With Lennon and Yoko Ono in London during negotiations.

*C. Maher / Hulton Archive / Getty Images*

Paul McCartney's refusal to accept Allen Klein as the Beatles' business manager led him to sue Lennon, Harrison, and Ringo Starr to dissolve the Beatles' partnership. "He's nothing more than a trained New York crook," McCartney said of Klein. "It had to be done." Arriving at the London High Court with his wife, Linda, to hear his suit argued, February 19, 1971.

*Popperfoto / Getty Images*

Following McCartney's suit, a court-appointed receiver oversaw the Beatles' business, but Harrison, Lennon, and Starr continued to have Klein manage their solo careers. With Harrison and Ravi Shankar during a press conference at New York's Madison Square Garden announcing the Concert for Bangladesh, July 27, 1971.

*New York Daily News / Getty Images*

Ringo's interest in pursuing an acting career led to his appearance in *Blindman*. The film was one of several spaghetti Westerns produced by Klein, who made a cameo appearance as a bandito dynamited in the film's opening sequence. On the set in Spain, 1971.

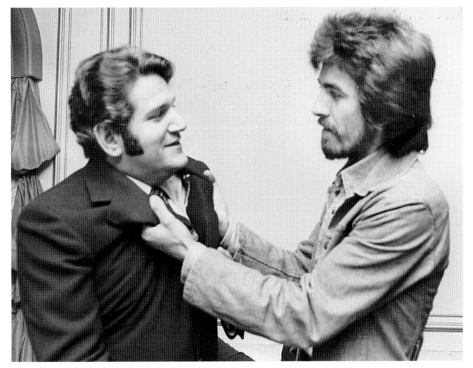

Though most devoted to Lennon, Klein took pride in—and gave himself credit for—promoting George Harrison's post-Beatles success. The two would later sour on each other, with Harrison frustrated over Klein's inability to settle with McCartney and Klein viewing Harrison as an ingrate. The broken relationship would lead to a decades-long legal battle when Klein later inserted himself into a plagiarism suit over "My Sweet Lord." In happier times: Riverdale, New York, 1970.

Klein's orphanage childhood and street-brawler reputation appealed to John Lennon, who saw Allen as the antithesis of Lee and John Eastman, the father-and-son attorneys who were Paul McCartney's in-laws and choice to manage the Beatles' affairs. "Allen's human," Lennon said. "Eastman and all them other people are automatons." Unlike others, Klein had also assiduously treated Ono as Lennon's equal. With Lennon and Ono at a dinner for songwriters in New York, 1972.

Unhappy with his American music-publishing deal, Pete Townshend, guitarist and primary composer for the Who, turned to Klein, who helped retrieve his rights. Townshend (far right) and Klein are pictured in New York with Terry Doran (far left), head of promotion for George Harrison's Dark Horse Records, and Rich Totoian, national promotion director of A&M Records.

Klein's biggest undertaking as a film producer was financing *The Greek Tycoon*, a thinly disguised reworking of Aristotle Onassis and Jacqueline Kennedy's marriage, starring Anthony Quinn and Jacqueline Bisset. Filmed in Europe and the U.S., the project kept Klein hopping around the globe and led to a friendship with Quinn (far left), with whom Klein is shown dining in Greece.

Klein's work with Sam Cooke led to a lifelong relationship with Cooke's friend and protégé, singer/songwriter Bobby Womack. In the 1980s, Klein advised Womack in his legal battle with Beverly Glen Records and negotiated a deal that brought him to MCA Records. Shown at the record company's offices in Universal City, left to right: Irving Azoff, chairman of MCA Records; Klein; Susan Markheim, vice president of MCA Records and executive assistant to Azoff; Womack; Jheryl Busby, president, black music, MCA Records.

*Jim Shea/From the collection of Susan Markheim*

Swinging from the heels. Playing softball with the ABKCO team in Central Park, 1979. As captain, starting third baseman, and owner of ABKCO, Klein was the lead-off hitter—every inning. At the company's employee basketball games, he took every free throw.

John Lennon's admiration for Chilean filmmaker Alejandro Jodorowsky's tripped-out psychedelic Western, *El Topo,* led Klein to distribute it and then finance its follow-up, *The Holy Mountain.* The two fell out when Jodorowsky backed out of directing an adaptation of the sadomasochistic bestseller *The Story of O,* and Klein punished Jodorowsky by keeping his films from being shown for over twenty years. The two reconciled shortly before Klein's death in 2009.

As business manager for both the Beatles and the Rolling Stones, Allen Klein may have been the most powerful player the record business ever produced. Complex and contradictory, he was an aggressive artists' advocate who sometimes left his clients believing he'd taken too big a piece. "He was charming," said an associate. "And he was ruthless."

which Klein was considering releasing in America. When they missed their subsequent flight to Nice, Allen chartered a private plane rather than wait several hours for the next commercial flight. "And he did it without fanfare," said Schlossberg. "It was fun to be with a guy like that."

In return, Klein expected to have everything his way. There was an ABKCO softball team; Allen played third and led off every inning. There was an ABKCO basketball team; Allen took every free throw, despite the presence of two employees who'd attended college on basketball scholarships.

Money was for making life pleasant, indulging whims, and skipping lines. A season-ticket holder for the Knicks and Rangers, Allen habitually tipped the lot attendant at a garage across from Madison Square Garden to park his Rolls-Royce by the entrance so he wouldn't have to wait to retrieve it. One night when Betty parked the car, Allen was miffed to discover it wasn't waiting for him at game's end. He walked to the head of the cashier's line and snatched the ticket from the man about to be served. "You paid for dinner," Klein said in a loud voice. "I got this one." He pushed the man's ticket, and his own, into the cashier's cage along with a hundred-dollar bill.

In London, Allen used Alf Weaver, who'd driven Frank Sinatra, as his chauffeur. It was Weaver's responsibility to settle Klein's bills. When dining out, Allen and his guests would simply rise and leave after eating; Weaver would then come in and pay.

Allen was fond of London's exclusive gaming clubs, although he was an embarrassment to anyone who ever placed a wager. Klein's modus operandi was to take a few guests and simply bet hunches, and a night of gambling usually ended as quickly as it began. After betting and losing several thousand dollars playing the same number at the roulette wheel four or five times, he would wander away in search of the free dinner the clubs served.

Klein's approach to fine dining was just as casual. "Allen didn't know wine but he did know price and he always went to the bottom of the list," said Michael Kramer, who recalled one dinner at Le Gavroche in London when he and Peter Howard, ABKCO's UK attorney, dined with Allen, Betty, and their two youngest children, Jody and Beth. "He ordered a '45 Lafite-Rothschild. This is when the Rothschild '45 and '61 are *the* wines and it must have been two thousand dollars. Peter is a wine person, and for him this is like Bo Derek is going to come to the table naked." The bottle was decanted and allowed to breathe. Allen signaled the sommelier to pour for everyone, including Jody and Beth, who quickly surmised it was excellent for gargling. In short order, the decanter was knocked over, and the wine spilled all over the table. "I think Peter was fighting the urge to suck the tablecloth," Kramer said.

Klein worked hard for the Stones. Aside from all the financial administration, ABKCO was responsible for a wide range of functions, including manufacturing and promoting the Stones' records, dealing with radio stations, hiring publicists, handling advertising, coordinating and supervising American tours, and overseeing the design and manufacture of their record sleeves. He was more than glad to have Oldham as a buffer. Unfortunately, it was increasingly clear that the relationship between Andrew and the band was barely extant. Jagger and Richards didn't forget that he'd cut and run at their most vulnerable moment. When the Stones returned to the studio after the drug trial to begin work on a new album, *Their Satanic Majesties Request,* something had clearly changed.

Previously focused and businesslike in sessions, the band now came to the studio without tunes or a set agenda. Instead, they ran tape endlessly, experimenting or just noodling around. Oldham, who was contractually obligated to pay all recording costs, suspected the band members were out to bankrupt him and force his resignation.

"Suddenly they weren't arriving in the studio with songs," he said. "There's actually nothing to do. Three weeks this is going on—and three weeks in the sixties was a very long time. I was bored and had no idea what I was doing there. They had spent eighteen thousand pounds. You couldn't spend eighteen thousand pounds on a Rolls-Royce regardless of what you put in it!"

His suspicions were correct; the band believed Oldham had little left to contribute and were out to dump him. "His box of tricks was exhausted," Richards said. By comparison, Jagger was continuing to grow; if anything, he was just beginning to hit his stride. Over the coming decades, the singer's focus and increasing sophistication, both artistic and financial, would become a primary driver of the Rolling Stones' ever-expanding popularity. He no longer needed or wanted Oldham—or anyone, for that matter—to tell him who the Rolling Stones should be or what they should do. "There was something between Mick and him that couldn't be resolved that I can only speculate on," Richards said. "They were falling out of sync with each other. Mick was starting to feel his oats and wanted to test it out by getting rid of Oldham." Jagger never denied it. While allowing that the band was taking too much LSD during those album sessions, he admitted that much of the dithering was simply "to piss Andrew off because he was such a pain in the neck." Said Jagger: "We wanted to unload him [and] we decided to go on this path to alienate him. Without actually doing it legally, we forced him out. I mean, he wanted out anyway. We were so out of our minds." Klein, however, saw a more straightforward reason why the singer wanted to be rid of Oldham. "What bothered Jagger was that Oldham was making five times as much as him," he said.

Mick and Keith were now making significant additional income as the Stones' songwriters, but the math was correct regarding record royalties: management still received 50 percent while the five musicians split the other half equally. Since Easton was out of the picture, Jagger wanted Eric's share—25 percent—to go to the band. Klein, however, placed the money in escrow pending settlement of Easton's suits against himself, Machat, Oldham, and the Rolling Stones.

Whatever role Oldham had played in the beginning, he wasn't fulfilling it now, and there was certainly an argument to be made that the underage Jagger and Richards had been taken advantage of with the original contracts—even if Oldham himself had been only nineteen. Nor could there be any doubt regarding who was making the Rolling Stones valuable, both artistically and commercially.

Dejected, drugged, disoriented, and undergoing shock-therapy treatment, Oldham resigned toward the end of 1967 and went deeper into his tailspin. "You don't want to lose the second-biggest group in the world when you're twenty-three if you can help it," he said with pithy understatement. "It has ramifications." Announcing the split, Jagger predicted the band would not be hiring another manager. "Allen Klein is just a financial scene," he said. "We'll really be managing ourselves."

Continuing to handle the Stones' business while steering clear of any other duties was exactly what Klein wanted. It was, after all, an extremely unusual situation: Allen was definitely administering the band's business and had his hands on all the financial and marketing levers but he wasn't contractually the business manager for the Rolling Stones—Oldham was his client. And active or not, Andrew was still due a share of the Stones' income, and Klein would get his 20 percent there. And of course, ABKCO made money manufacturing the Stones' records and would continue to be their music publisher for at least the next three years. Still, Klein wondered where he really stood. "Jagger came in and said, 'I'm going to run things, you take care of America and I'll take care of the rest,'" he recalled. "But I knew that wasn't going to happen."

Jagger's public statement that the Stones would be managing themselves essentially meant that *he* would be managing them. No one else in the band had the focus, desire, or power to do it. And once again Mick proved a quick study, able to scale a steep learning curve.

In public, Jagger presented himself as indifferent to commerce. "I do the minimal amount of business as possible because I'm not actually interested in it," he said in 2014. But those who negotiated with him had a different experience. Former CBS Records chairman Walter Yetnikoff recalled Jagger challenging him one afternoon in a Paris café to see who could more quickly compute the estimated value-added tax on Stones albums sold in Europe. Yetnikoff lost. "When it came to numbers, Mick was sober as Saint Augustine," he said. "He's a skilled negotiator who never lost sight of his advantages as a pop icon."

• • •

The advisers and aides Mick surrounded himself with were first rate.

One of Jagger's priorities was to find the Stones a new producer, someone who, unlike Oldham, had the studio skills to enhance their recordings. The self-produced *Their Satanic Majesties Request* had proved a shoddy, sloppy affair and surprisingly bloodless. It included one or two memorable moments, particularly "2000 Light Years from Home," but aping the Beatles had never played to the Stones' strengths, and hoeing the same psychedelic row as *Sgt. Pepper's Lonely Hearts Club Band* produced a thin harvest. The Stones needed to be the Stones — and they needed a producer who could underscore that and bring at least the intimation of discipline to the studio. They selected Jimmy Miller, an American producer who had worked with numerous British bands, including many on Island Records, most notably the group Traffic. Not coincidentally, Island's founder and the manager of Traffic, Chris Blackwell, was acting as an unofficial adviser to the Stones.

Blackwell was Jagger's kind of man. Enterprising and iconoclastic yet oddly patrician, he lived and played on the fringes while remaining glamorous and to the manor born. Raised in a wealthy and prominent Jamaican family — his mother, Blanche, was Ian Fleming's mistress, their relationship the inspiration for a play by friend and neighbor Noël Coward — he had struck out on his own in the record business, ultimately proving he had extraordinary taste. He scored his first hit record in 1963 with "My Boy Lollipop" by the teenage Jamaican singer Millie Small before moving into rock with the Spencer Davis Group. Straddling two worlds, he continued his association with both rock and ska and reggae; Blackwell and Island would later make worldwide stars of Ireland's U2 and Jamaica's Bob Marley and the Wailers.

"Jimmy Miller came to the hotel to negotiate a producer contract on one of the Stones albums," said Harold Seider. "And Chris Blackwell came. I was very impressed with Chris, understood that he was thinking and not just a hustler."

Miller's first project with the Stones, *Beggars Banquet,* marked a key transition for the group as an increasingly erratic and drugged-out Brian Jones faded from the picture. With the exception of some lovely slide work, Jones was all but absent from the album, and Richards stepped to the fore. "He'd show up occasionally when he was in the mood to play," Miller said of Jones, "and he could never really be relied on. The others, particularly Mick and Keith, would often say to me, 'Just tell him to piss off and get the hell out of here.'" Though not included on the album, the hit "Jumpin' Jack Flash" was produced at these sessions.

After firing Jones, Jagger brought in guitarist Mick Taylor on the recommendation of John Mayall. During their first session together, recording "Honky Tonk Women," the band received word that Jones had drowned in his pool. They didn't stop working, but a previously planned free concert a few days later in London's Hyde Park was recast as a memorial.

"Honky Tonk Women" proved an enormous hit that went to number one on both sides of the Atlantic and solidified the transition begun with *Beggars Banquet*. With Miller at the recording console and Taylor replacing Jones, the band found another gear; from 1968 through 1972 the Rolling Stones whipped off an unsurpassed run of extraordinary albums that also included *Let It Bleed, Sticky Fingers,* and *Exile on Main Street.*

Having put paid to the Stones' creative issues, Jagger turned to the financial side of the ledger, where his key move was to retain British merchant banker Prince Rupert Loewenstein as an adviser. Recommended to Jagger by his friend Chris Gibbs, a London antiques and rare-book dealer, Loewenstein was unknown to Klein until 1968, when Jagger sought Allen's opinion on having Loewenstein set up companies for the Stones in tax havens like Liechtenstein. Allen advised caution. The Beatles had at one point set up a similar offshore tax dodge but abandoned it, supposedly because government officials in England threatened to tar the band as ungrateful tax cheats. Klein also worried that the money would be beyond the band's daily control and in the hands of someone else.

"I never wanted to allow money to go offshore," he said. "He told me about Loewenstein and that he was planning an offshore company.

I said, 'Look, you want to trust somebody, that's okay just as long as it's limited. It's tough enough to trust someone you know. You can get fucked.' And that was the last thing. That's why he went with Rupert Loewenstein."

Though both Easton and Oldham had been pushed out of the day-to-day picture, their interest in the Stones had yet to be settled. Klein, Oldham, and the Stones all still faced ongoing lawsuits from Easton. Oldham, in particular, was very nervous. In the three years since his split with Easton, he'd gone to extraordinary lengths to avoid his former partner (and to avoid being served with legal documents), including using a body double and climbing out of an office window. Though Easton apparently found Oldham's behavior nothing more than disheartening or silly, an increasingly paranoid Andrew fretted about testifying in court. He worried Easton's lawyers might have him charged with perjury.

Klein had a totally different view. He was confident that the Stones could dispose of Easton's action by threatening to annul the original agreement by stating they'd been minors when they signed it, something Easton and his solicitors were likely worried they'd do. It was a cinch the man would rather reach a settlement with the Stones himself than let a judge decide.

Still, Easton's attorneys took a harsh tack and may have counted on anti-American and anti-Semitic sentiments when they portrayed Klein as "a predator in the field of pop artists" who'd interfered with Easton's relationships. It was Klein's first but far from his last bloodying in the British courts, and it signaled that the fierce reputation he'd cultivated so effectively in the cloistered world of the music business was crossing over to the general public, where it might be much less advantageous to him, particularly in the UK. That didn't stop him from remaining cocky and punching back. Klein had Peter Howard inform Easton's legal representatives that as Yom Kippur was coming up, Allen wanted to get home to New York. Klein threatened to deduct ten thousand pounds from any offer for each day they went without a settlement. Easton ultimately agreed to drop his claims and disavow any future interests in return for two hundred thousand pounds in back royalties being held by Decca. As part of the settlement, all rights and claims in the original partnership and contracts were vested solely with Oldham. But unbeknownst to Easton, Oldham didn't own them anymore.

During Easton's suit, Oldham had received feelers from executives at Decca Records. They knew he was no longer managing the Stones, or even speaking to them. Would he like to sell his interest in their recordings? The idea of getting a big payday was appealing. The Stones had proven surprisingly resilient, but it had been five years — how much longer could this thing go on? Brian Jones was already dead; God knew who was next. What Andrew didn't like was selling the rights to Decca. The Stones already had no use for him, and if he sold out to Decca, the record company would have no use for him either.

Instead, Andrew told Allen that Decca had offered him $800,000 for his rights but that he preferred to sell them to Klein, as it might give him a measure of protection and opportunity to have his interests pass to someone working with the band rather than to the record company. "Even if you aren't with the act, you kind of are," he later explained. He told Allen he'd be willing to take $750,000 if the deal could be done immediately. It could and was.*

Buying out Oldham in 1968 and settling with Easton would turn out to be the greatest score in Klein's career. For approximately $1.5 million — including what he would have been due out of the £200,000 paid out of the Decca funds — he bought a 50 percent royalty share in everything the Stones recorded through early 1971, beginning with their first recordings and ending with two tracks on the album *Sticky Fingers*. In between, there were eleven studio albums and EPs, two live albums, and numerous compilations. The two-record 1971 hits package *Hot Rocks* sold over six million copies in the United States alone in the first few years after its release.

The deal marked a radical change in Klein's relationships with both Oldham and the Stones. He wasn't just the Stones' adviser, publisher,

---

* Two years later, Klein paid Oldham an additional $250,000 to settle other claims, bringing the total paid to Oldham for his royalty rights to $1 million.

and American record manufacturer anymore; now he was their partner and as such had clearly acquired a conflict of interest. But that was
just business as far as he was concerned. With Klein's relationship to
Oldham, the situation was murkier.

Klein's feelings and actions toward Oldham were complex and contradictory. He could be abusive and insulting to Andrew, especially
when Andrew wanted something. But Klein truly liked him—certainly more than he liked the Stones—and cared what happened to
him, and he sought to give him fair and sound advice. And although
no one, including the Rolling Stones, could imagine that the band
would thrive for at least another forty years, Klein knew that, at the
very least, Andrew had made him an offer he couldn't possibly refuse.
In the coming years, as Oldham had to reconcile himself daily with the
knowledge that he'd given the golden goose to Klein, their relationship
became one of stormy codependency defined on Oldham's side by his
eternal desire for a readjustment and on Klein's side by his need to balance friendship, fairness, business, and his own sense of himself as the
sharpest operator on the scene.

## 9

## THE PRIZE

TO PROMOTE *BEGGARS BANQUET,* Mick Jagger conceived a television special. Dubbed *The Rolling Stones Rock and Roll Circus,* the program was to feature the group atop a bill with numerous other artists including Jethro Tull, Taj Mahal, Marianne Faithfull, the Who, and the debut of John Lennon and Yoko Ono fronting a unique band boasting guitarist Eric Clapton and drummer Mitch Mitchell with Keith Richards on bass. Filmed near London in a twenty-four-hour marathon session in December 1968, the project never aired, reportedly because the Stones feared they'd been upstaged by the Who.*

Klein didn't care whether the program aired or not—that was Jagger's business. He came to the all-night recording session for only one reason: to meet John Lennon. He achieved his goal, but just. The set was hot and cramped, no place for a conversation let alone a full-blown seduction. Allen had to settle for a handshake and hope that he'd finally registered with Lennon as more than just another outstretched palm.

---

* A portion of the Who's performance became the first publicly shown footage from *Rock and Roll Circus* when it was included in the 1979 documentary *The Kids Are Alright.*

Klein was growing frustrated. His obsession with getting the Beatles wasn't new, but since Epstein's death, he'd focused his strategy on
finding a way to see Lennon. In that regard, Klein's relationship with
the Rolling Stones was clearly a positive; though Lennon had heard all
kinds of dark rumors about Allen, he didn't think it was coinciden-
tal that the Stones had become more and more successful throughout their association with him. Even Jagger endorsed Klein in his own
tepid and smarmy fashion, telling the Beatles that he was "all right if
you like that kind of thing." The Beatles had apparently been ready to
accept Klein into their world when they briefly talked about combin-
ing forces with the Stones in a joint venture to include a recording
studio and other creative outlets. Those discussions ultimately came to
nothing, and in January 1968, the Beatles instead opted to form their
own company, Apple Corps, for the same purposes.

As with so much in the world of Allen Klein and his clients, Apple
represented high hopes, lofty goals, and grand illusions but owed its
genesis to the more prosaic challenges posed by Britain's tax laws. Despite the substandard recording, publishing, merchandising, and management arrangements negotiated by Brian Epstein, the extraordinary
success of the Beatles meant they were still taxed at the highest rates.
In 1966, when Epstein arranged a ten-year recording extension with
EMI, the Beatles' royalties increased. Now fearful of losing two million
pounds in taxes, they opted to create a corporation that could both
receive the bulk of payment and, hopefully, someday produce additional revenue they could keep. "The amount of money owed by EMI
was mountainous," said Peter Brown, a former Epstein assistant who
became director of Apple. "Eighty-five percent or more would have
gone to the Exchequer. The structure of Apple was to avoid that."

Its basis was a new partnership, Beatles and Company, into which
the group's earnings, excluding songwriting income, would be placed.
Each musician owned 5 percent of Beatles and Company, while the
new unnamed corporation owned the remaining 80 percent of the
partnership, thus shielding them from the lion's share of taxes. Looking for a business to substantiate the company, Epstein, who'd grown
up working in his family's Liverpool furniture stores, envisioned a re-

tail chain, perhaps something selling greeting cards. The Beatles had no interest in that. Instead, they proposed a creative company, one that might make real use of the band's cultural cachet and become not just a profitable venture but a transformative one. The seed for Apple was planted.

Following Brian Epstein's death, control of his management company, NEMS, passed to his family, most notably his brother, Clive, whose sole goal appeared to be not to blow whatever fortune his brother had made. He was not at all interested in having NEMS take part in Apple.

Left to their own devices, the Beatles announced the new venture with a May 1968 press conference by Lennon and McCartney at New York's Americana Hotel. "It's a business concerning records, films, and electronics," Lennon announced, one aiming to get "artistic freedom within a business structure. . . . We want to set up a system whereby people who just want to make a film about anything don't have to go on their knees in somebody's office. Probably yours." Apple was the prototypical hippie corporation: altruistic, optimistic, off the cuff, and clueless. When McCartney invited people to simply mail their work and proposals to the new company, he unwittingly and fatally cast Apple as a psychedelic sugar daddy. "We really want to help people, but without doing it like a charity or seeming like ordinary patrons of the arts," he said. "We're in the happy position of not really needing any more money. So for the first time, the bosses aren't in it for profit. If you come and see me and say, 'I've had such-and-such a dream,' I'll say, 'Here's so much money. Go away and do it.' We've already bought all our dreams. So now we want to share that possibility with others."

It was a lovely sentiment, and in that regard Apple certainly fit the conception of the Beatles that many fans had, that the group was much more than entertainment, their influence pervasive, wholly positive, and improving the world. What started as pop music now felt like social revolution. Everything was possible as the Beatles invited their fans to make a better world simply by dreaming it.

As a record company, Apple was born with every advantage. Though the Beatles were signed to EMI and its American subsidiary,

Capitol Records, they were able to deliver their own recordings under the Apple logo, and their first release, the enormous worldwide hit single "Hey Jude," couldn't have given Apple Records more visibility. If Apple was intended to be a business that challenged the status quo, the record company certainly did that; the major labels had to be loath to see the biggest pop act in the world striking a blow for artist-owned imprints. If successful, the Beatles' label would be difficult to compete with — what artist wouldn't want to be associated with the Beatles? And Apple Records showed every sign of becoming a quick success with hits by Mary Hopkin and the Iveys (who later changed their name to Badfinger) and clearly could have become a powerhouse. Aside from the Beatles, Apple signed James Taylor and was in the hunt for Crosby, Stills, Nash, and Young.

Yet Apple's description as the unbusinesslike business would prove far too accurate. A series of McCartney-designed ads inviting everyone to submit demos ran in *Rolling Stone* and *New Musical Express* and soon produced a mountain of tapes and queries from around the world that then sat unopened and unheard. Worse, the record company was just one of numerous Apple Corps Ltd. companies and about the only one that the Beatles and the friends they'd selected to run them knew anything about. There was a music publisher, a film company, a recording studio, a design firm, and an electronics lab run as a dream factory/playroom for their protégé "Magic" Alex Mardas, a former TV repairman turned self-styled inventor and visionary. Mardas's gee-whiz projects were said to include a car that changed colors, wallpaper that acted as a stereo speaker, and invisible sound barriers. One of the most concrete projects, an attempt to build a seventy-two-track studio in the basement of Apple's London offices, resulted in a sixteen-track console that was all but useless; the Beatles ripped it out after the first day.

The fatal flaws wired into Apple's DNA were certainly on display at the Baker Street fashion shop known as the Apple Boutique. Magic Alex's plan to unveil an artificial sun at the store's debut came to naught, and the shop, lavishly designed by a Dutch art collective, was opened in December 1967 by Lennon and Harrison and out of business six

months later, largely because employees and potential customers simply helped themselves to the merchandise.

The situation at Apple Corps' Savile Row office was much the same:
a free-for-all. The Beatles had announced that Apple would break the
rules, but in practice, it had no rules. Publicly, the Beatles talked as if
they would continue on that path. When announcing the closing of
the Apple Boutique, McCartney, who was the most hands-on regarding Apple, had taken pains to continue casting the company in a soft
Aquarian light, emphasizing that they were going to give away their remaining stock rather than consign it to a broker, find new jobs for and
provide generous severance pay to the employees who'd helped drive
the store into the ground, and otherwise continue to be groovy. Perhaps he was thinking primarily of the band's reputation. Privately, the
Beatles were coming to see Apple as a giant financial sinkhole, one that
was costing them a fortune and taking all their attention. "I wanted
Apple to run," McCartney said. "I didn't want to run Apple."

Lennon, though less involved in Apple's day-to-day business, was
the first to publicly sound an alarm. "We haven't got half the money
people think we have," he told journalist Ray Coleman in early January 1969. "It's been pie-in-the-sky from the start. . . . We did it all
wrong — you know, Paul and me running to New York saying we'll do
this and encourage this and that. It's got to be business first, we realize
that now. . . . It needs a new broom and a lot of people there will have
to go. . . . If it carries on like this, all of us will be broke in the next six
months."

Lennon's assertions that the Beatles were in imminent financial
danger came as a shock to many when they were published five days
later in *Disc and Music Echo*. They also produced opposite emotions
in two particular quarters. In London, McCartney called Coleman,
who'd covered the Beatles since the earliest stirrings of Beatlemania,
and chided him for publishing the remarks. In New York, Allen Klein
knew his moment had arrived.

Very few people ever earned the unwavering trust of the Beatles. Derek
Taylor did.

An established journalist when the Beatles were on the rise, Taylor was an early and unqualified admirer; he got and loved them right away. As a result, he was invited into the tent, collaborating on an early syndicated column by George Harrison and later ghosting Brian Epstein's autobiography, *A Cellarful of Noise.* By the mid-1960s he was a press agent, first for the Beatles and then on his own in California, where he helped establish the Byrds and worked with the Beach Boys and Paul Revere and the Raiders. After promoting the Monterey Pop Festival, he settled in for a year at A&M Records as the "house hippie."

Difficult to imagine now, the house hippie was an odd, amorphous, not always legal, and important record-industry role in the mid- to late sixties, a position that required its holder to be part go-between, part cultural ambassador, and 100 percent double agent. At the time, record-company executives were unsure how to deal with artists from the underground, and it was the house hippie's job to show them what to do—and to show the artists that the record company "got" them. It was an unusual tightrope walk, and its most admired practitioners—Billy James at Columbia, Andy Wickham at Warner Brothers, and Derek Taylor at A&M—had the rare and valuable ability to keep their footing while astride two worlds. When the Beatles started Apple, Derek agreed to be its press liaison.

Two days after Lennon's worries concerning the Beatles' financial future were published, Andrew Oldham's partner Tony Calder offered to drive Taylor to the office, primarily so he could deliver a message to him from Klein.

"Allen Klein says you are in his way," he told Taylor. "Allen says you are blocking him from meeting the Beatles and doing business with them. He thinks you're sore at him." Taylor was flabbergasted. Nothing could be farther from the truth. A few years earlier, Oldham and Klein had spoken with Taylor about handling press for the Rolling Stones and then nothing had come of it, so while Taylor could certainly see why Klein might imagine he bore him a grudge, his only lasting feeling had been bemusement. He'd found Klein both grating and oddly ingratiating. Allen had offered him sound and thoughtful financial and business advice but only, Derek suspected, as a way to impress him.

"He is an asshole for thinking that," Taylor told Calder, and he offered to do what he could to clear the way for Klein.

"Allen Klein wants to meet the Beatles," Taylor told Apple director Peter Brown.

"Does he ever!" Brown quipped. A former assistant to Brian Epstein at NEMS, Brown remembered Klein's earlier unsuccessful attempt to woo Epstein. He told Taylor that the only impediment to Klein's speaking with the Beatles was the musicians themselves.

Taylor sent a message back to Klein telling him to call. But a few days later Taylor heard from another Klein emissary, Stones' publicist Les Perrin, that Allen still couldn't get Brown to put him through. When Lennon and Harrison came in for lunch that day, Taylor broached the subject directly and learned that Lennon had told Brown he didn't want to take the calls. Derek allowed that Klein was a little strange and that his reputation and tactics engendered strong feelings; he characterized him as "hated by many who have never met him and by some who have only heard of him," to which Harrison deadpanned that Klein sounded really nice. Nonetheless, Taylor said, Klein might be just the person to sort through the Beatles' money woes.

Shortly after nine o'clock on the evening of January 26, just eight days after Lennon's interview appeared in *Disc and Music Echo,* Allen Klein opened the door of his penthouse suite at London's Dorchester Hotel and invited in John and Yoko Ono.

Both men were on their guard, agitated, and anxious. For Allen, this was it — the crucial moment in years of planning and scheming. Could he harness his nerves and put it over?

Klein's public pursuit of the Beatles — particularly the repeated boasts that he would get them, that it was just a matter of time — had spooked Lennon. "He called me once but I never accepted it," Lennon said. "I was too nervous." Still, he was impressed with how well the Rolling Stones had done since pairing with Klein and couldn't square it with the dark rumors he'd heard. "I could never coordinate it with the fact that the Stones seemed to be going on and on with him . . . I started thinking he must be all right." Yet Lennon began to relax only when he realized that Klein was at least as nervous as he was. "You could see it in his face," he said. "When I saw that I felt better." Lennon also liked that Klein had made sure the three of them were alone in the room to establish a rapport, although Allen's assistant Iris was nearby in case they needed anything. Klein offered them a carefully researched and prepared vegetarian meal — exactly the macrobiotic dishes John and Yoko preferred — and his tone was unusually personal and unguarded: *Let's put business aside for a bit and see what we make of each other.* It felt as if Klein had come to them naked with nothing to hide.

It wasn't what Lennon expected. Since Epstein's death, the Beatles had sought out new management and advisers in fits and starts. They knew they were rudderless and courting real financial danger, yet they were skeptical and distrustful of outsiders and had no idea whom to turn to. Along the way, Lennon and McCartney had looked at a number of possibilities. At Paul's suggestion John met with Lord Beeching, the chairman of British Railways. The meeting did nothing except confirm John's suspicions that everyone in the business world was an animal, and he'd be fucked and damned before he'd have anything to do with any of them.

Allen's music-business expertise and take-no-prisoners negotiating style at least fit the job. But more important to Lennon was the feeling he got that Klein was cut from a different cloth than the others he'd met — the same plain, coarse, ordinary cloth that Lennon flew for a flag. John, who had a world-class chip on his shoulder, listened to Allen's stories about the orphanage and the painful indifference of his father and his childhood on the streets of Newark, and he saw himself: the underdog who had proven to be the leader of the pack, the everyman who'd had the temerity to become extraordinary only to be rewarded with the scorn of all the third-rate bastards he'd bettered and beaten.

Allen had spent years preparing for this moment. He didn't make a direct pitch, since they all knew why they were there, and he won points with the couple for doing what few did: speaking to them as partners and equals. And while Klein was the first to admit that not everything the Rolling Stones recorded was for him, his appreciation for the Beatles' genius was boundless. He didn't talk about business; he talked about Lennon's music, correctly picking out which songs were John's and noting where Lennon's contributions and personality could be found in compositions primarily written by McCartney. Lennon was floored. He would later compare Klein to a human jukebox for his awesome ability to recall what felt like every pop lyric written in the last fifty years.

Clearly, Klein's obsessive research had paid off. In Lennon's estimation: "Anybody who knew me that well — without having met me — had to be a guy I could let look after me."

Lennon told Klein that he wanted him to handle his and Yoko's business. He added that the Beatles had recently asked New York attorneys Lee Eastman and his son, John, to look into their affairs. The elder Eastman had a well-established practice that at one time had focused on music publishing but was best known for representing painters, particularly Willem de Kooning. Lee and John were also the father and brother, respectively, of Paul McCartney's girlfriend, photographer Linda Eastman. Klein, continuing to play it cool, didn't ask Lennon to formalize their arrangement. They continued chatting until 3:00 a.m., when John finally asked if Allen didn't need something in writing.

A portable typewriter miraculously appeared from the bedroom. Yoko sat on the floor and typed out brief letters, similar in wording to the one Klein had given Sam Cooke to sign, informing the top executives at EMI, music publisher Northern Songs, the Beatles' accountants at Bryce Hamner, and NEMS that John Lennon had retained Allen Klein to look into his business affairs and to please provide him with any help he required.

Holding a letter — he would later have one framed — Allen was overcome. "At last!" he said. "At last!"

At Allen's insistence, in the morning, John telephoned each executive and alerted him to the about-to-arrive note. When he stopped by the Apple office in Savile Row for lunch, he told the other Beatles and several senior staff members that he'd hired Klein. Taylor, who still wasn't sure how he felt about helping to open the door for Klein, was bemused to see Lennon completely smitten with him. "Don't care about the others, don't give a shit," he said when asked how the other Beatles reacted to the news. "I'm having Klein. He can have all my stuff and get it sorted out."

The following evening a confident Allen met with the four Beatles. After he'd reiterated that he would be looking into Lennon's finances, the topic quickly came around to a plan John Eastman had proposed. NEMS, Brian Epstein's management firm, still had a 25 percent interest in the Beatles' earnings, but the Epstein family was willing to sell their interest to the Beatles for a million pounds; Eastman had arranged to borrow the money from the Beatles' British record company, EMI.

It was a quick and reasonable settlement, but Klein said he didn't like it and that borrowing against royalties was needlessly expensive; he suggested that the Beatles would likely have to earn double the amount just to cover the taxes on the income. More to the point, he said he wouldn't sign off on any deal for Lennon until he'd gotten a complete overview of his financial situation. McCartney, however, spoke up for the deal, reminding the others that Eastman had strongly recommended it and that it was already in the works. Allen wondered if the best idea might be to schedule another meeting with the Eastmans over the weekend. Everyone agreed, and McCartney left soon after that. Harrison, Starr, and Lennon remained behind, and Klein talked in greater depth about what he would be doing for Lennon. George and Ringo asked Allen if he'd do the same for them.

Clearly, Klein impressed them more than the twenty-six-year-old John Eastman had; Ringo would later characterize the young lawyer as "pleasant but harmless," while George thought him unqualified to manage the Beatles. But there was more to it than that; George's and Ringo's votes for Klein were also votes for Lennon — and against Eastman and McCartney.

Whatever Klein thought he knew about the inner dynamics of the Beatles, it's unlikely he understood just how divided and near splintering they were. Lennon, the band's founder and original leader, had abdicated much of that role over the preceding two years, focusing instead on his life with Yoko Ono when not distracted by heroin. McCartney had stepped into the breach, taking greater command of the group's sessions; he was the driving force behind the group's current project, a stripped-down album and TV documentary entitled *Get Back*. Still, tension in the band was running high. Just a few weeks earlier, Harrison had walked out of the sessions and threatened to quit, tired of being condescended to and treated like the eternally junior partner. And a few months before, during the recording of *The Beatles* (a.k.a. *The White Album*), Starr had stormed off to Greece and had to be cajoled into coming back.

McCartney had already assumed a dominant role in the studio; Harrison and Starr were loath to see his girlfriend's family take control of their business. They'd rather follow Lennon. "I thought, well, if that's the choice, I think I'll go with Klein because John's with him," George said.

"We were convinced by him," said Ringo, who got a kick out of Klein's brash attitude and felt at ease with him. He also saw that Klein knew what he was talking about. "I was convinced by him, and John, too. I liked Allen. He was a lot of fun, and he knew the record business. He knew records. He knew acts. He knew music. A lot of people we spoke to were trying to get in with the music crowd but didn't know anything about the music business."

Klein hoped that having three Beatles firmly in his corner would be enough to cement his status as the group's manager, but those hopes quickly evaporated at the Saturday meeting in Klein's Dorchester suite. John Eastman (his father, Lee, was not there) once again made his case for buying NEMS, saying that the company owned 275,000 shares of the Beatles' music publisher, Northern Songs, and that the Beatles should own them, but Klein dismissed that as an insufficient reason to buy the company, adding that any decision should wait until they had a better picture of the Beatles' finances. Eastman got the message right away: Klein wasn't going to like anything he brought to the table, no matter how smart it was.

At that point, with each man feeling that his status and credibility were on the line, Eastman and Klein dropped all pretense of civility. Klein had the clear advantage; Lee Eastman's decision not to fly to London for the meeting meant that all Allen had to do was look and sound more knowledgeable than a young attorney who'd only recently handled his first record negotiation, a revised deal for the group Chicago. Allen suggested that things would go best for the Beatles if he took care of the business and the Eastmans contented themselves with being their lawyers, but John Eastman flatly rejected the idea. "He was trying to subsume me into what he was doing, which I wouldn't do," Eastman said. Going on the offensive, Eastman brought up Cameo-Parkway's unusual saga and ABKCO's ultimate delisting by the American Stock Exchange and questioned Allen's integrity. "It certainly wasn't a friendly thing," Allen said. When Eastman discovered a bottle of suppositories in the bathroom medicine cabinet, he couldn't resist showing them to the room. "Whose are these?" he asked. When Klein said they were his, Eastman grinned. "Why, Allen," he said. "I thought you were the perfect asshole."

A meeting in April between the Beatles, Klein, and John's dapper father, Lee Eastman, was even uglier. Though they were all there to discuss publishing, Allen threw the first verbal roundhouse, announcing with too much relish that he'd done a little research and discovered that the eminent Harvard-trained Lee Eastman was actually Bronx-born Leo Epstein, the son of Russian-Jewish immigrants who'd met at Ellis Island. The obvious implication — that Eastman had buried a past that looked a lot like Klein's — hit a nerve with Lee.

A well-known art collector who'd married a department-store heiress and moved in prestigious Manhattan circles, the elder Eastman had nonetheless been considered something of a hustler while on his way up. As an attorney working with music publishers, Eastman had put together his own music holdings; sometimes, it was reputed, by taking deals away from his own clients and steering them to confederates. Later, as the attorney for several notable painters, including Josef Albers and Willem de Kooning, he amassed a renowned art collection. At his death in 1991, his estate — which included pieces given to him by clients as gifts or in payment — would be valued at $300 million.

Under the pressure of Klein's needling, the elder Eastman quickly lost his composure and began screaming insults at him, calling Allen "the lowest scum on earth." Klein, by contrast, kept his mouth shut and just took it—a strategy that made Eastman look doubly bad.

Lennon loved it. Though he later claimed he had been willing to go with Eastman "if he would have turned out something other than what he was," he never liked him, or the idea that McCartney's in-laws should manage the Beatles.

"Lennon understood power," said attorney Harold Seider, who worked first for Klein and then for Lennon. "He was very astute. And this was critical: Lennon always thought he was the leader. Rightly so or not. The idea of Paul and his family overseeing, advising, whatever, was anathema, pure heresy. So Klein was the alternative. His aura—the New York Jew, the tough guy—this was the theme that created the relationship. Similarly, Ringo and George would not be happy. They'd rather follow John against Paul; they just did not like the idea."

Lennon also had an inferiority complex and a fear of being condescended to, which gave him another reason to rebuff the Eastmans. He had found the attorneys' midtown office, with its Picassos and de Koonings, and Lee's talk of Kafka novels unconvincing.

"Lee was a climber," said Seider. "From Epstein to Eastman. John told me he and Yoko went to Lee's apartment and he was trying to impress them with the paintings on the wall. Whatever Lennon's failings, his perceptions were unbelievable. He learned by experience and really had an understanding when it came to people. It was real world and he understood who the phonies were. And here was Lee trying to impress him with the artwork, because that was the way he sold. Most people would say, 'Oh, this guy is terrific!' Only it had the opposite effect on Lennon. He wanted a guy who was a fighter. So all these things worked in Allen's favor."

Eastman's costliest mistake was mocking Klein's taste; it confirmed Lennon's suspicion that Lee was a snob. "Fuck it!" Lennon said. "I wouldn't let Eastman near me. I wouldn't let a fuckin' animal like that who has a mind like that near me. Who despises me too, despises me because of what I am and what I look like."

It was classic Klein; he had come out on top because he'd done his homework and made an intense study of his quarry while Lee Eastman had not. As much as anything Klein had done himself, Lee Eastman's tantrum sealed his relationship with Lennon. Allen was everything Lee was not and therefore everything Lennon wanted.

A few days later, Eastman and Eastman changed course and agreed to Klein's suggestion that they act as attorneys for the Beatles.

Klein met with Clive Epstein at NEMS and asked him to hold off on any decision about selling the management company until he'd had three more weeks to look into the Beatles' situation and make an informed offer. The next day he went back to New York.

It had been the most successful week of his career, and Allen couldn't wait to tell someone how he'd landed the Beatles. He was pleasantly surprised to discover that he knew the person seated next to him in first class on the flight home: music-publishing executive Freddy Bienstock.

A Viennese immigrant who favored monogrammed shirts and sported a monocle, the unlikely-looking Bienstock knew his way around the music business as well as anyone; he'd been deeply involved in Elvis Presley's music publishing and song selection as an executive with Hill and Range, and his wife, Miriam, was one of Ahmet Ertegun's original partners in Atlantic Records. He'd recently purchased Hill and Range's British subsidiary and made it the basis of his own company, Carlin Music. In the coming years he would succeed where Klein had failed, buying Chappell Music and later selling it to Time Warner.

Bienstock congratulated Allen when he heard the story, but he didn't seem to share Allen's enthusiasm for the Beatles. Indeed, he quickly ticked down what he knew about the band: they didn't tour anymore, British publisher Dick James controlled their music publishing through Northern Songs, and EMI still had them signed worldwide for records. Where, Freddy wondered, did Allen think he could get the Beatles — and himself — paid? It was an excellent question. Klein, ebullient on boarding, was a good deal more sober by the time he landed.

Bienstock was right — he might have the ball but it wasn't a slam dunk. He'd better start looking at the Beatles' audit statements and the two principal American deals, Capitol Records and United Artists Films.

What he saw didn't cheer him; a combination of substandard deals and a 95 percent tax rate had left the Beatles cash poor. On paper they'd made less than a hundred thousand pounds the prior year, and meanwhile they were each drawing cash out of Apple as if it were a bank. But before Klein could really dig into the various business arrangements, he was hit with the first crisis: despite what Clive Epstein had told him before he left London, NEMS had been sold — not to the Beatles, but to a British investment group, Triumph.

Equally frustrating was the discovery that the apparent spur for the sale had been a letter from John Eastman to Clive Epstein saying Klein was going to audit NEMS — something Klein had neither planned nor suggested to Epstein. Regardless of whether Eastman simply misunderstood or was out to make life difficult for Klein — and Allen, of course, suspected the latter — the result was disastrous: Klein found Triumph's chief, Leonard Richenberg, uninterested in selling the Beatles' rights or NEMS's share of their publishing back to them.

If the news that Allen Klein was preparing an audit was Clive Epstein's nightmare scenario, Richenberg looked like a made-to-order solution. He wasn't in the music business, and he wasn't impressed or cowed when Klein suggested that Triumph had just paid £750,000 for a lot of headaches, liabilities, and rights he would soon show it didn't actually have title to. Turning a deaf ear to Klein's overture, Richenberg didn't wait to launch his own offensive. When Allen requested that Beatles' record royalties be paid directly to Apple instead of through NEMS, Triumph sued EMI, and the court froze one million pounds in an escrow account pending the outcome. In a more personal attack, Richenberg commissioned an investigator's report on Klein and then leaked the results to the *Sunday Times,* which roasted him.

The snarky piece, headlined "The Toughest Wheeler-Dealer in the Pop Jungle," knocked the wind out of Klein, who read anti-Semitic, anti-American undertones in its relentlessly personal portrayal of him as an unwashed, grubby lowlife who wore a dirty polo shirt. Harold

Seider, ABKCO's attorney at the time, believed Klein's in-your-face style played particularly poorly with the English establishment.

"The EMI people didn't like him," said Seider, "and the Decca people had to deal with him but they didn't like him. He was essentially a New York Jew. It was that kind of thing and I'll leave it at that. He had that aura about him and he never tried to dissuade people [out] of [believing in] that aura because that was how he got to Lennon, to a certain degree. Ultimately it came back to bite him in the ass."

Attributing Klein's success to a constant hunger for publicity and an ability to "lie like a trooper," the article cast the Cameo-Parkway stock offering in a particularly unflattering light and painted Allen as a tax cheat for having failed to file paperwork on employee-with-holding taxes in a timely manner a decade earlier (although the taxes themselves had been paid). It also intimated that he had swindled the Rolling Stones. Klein threatened to sue the paper for libel but later became friendly with the article's author, John Fielding, and even hired him to work on a film he produced in 1978, *The Greek Tycoon*. Allen was a good deal less forgiving toward the article's catalyst, Richenberg, who relished Allen's discomfort. But there was little for Klein to do, as Richenberg just shrugged and characterized the attack as part of the game. Klein told him he was acting like a child. "I stopped playing in the mud," Allen said.

It took nearly six months, but a settlement with Triumph was finally hammered out. In the end, Klein got the better of Richenberg: the Beatles regained their rights, including NEMS's shares in Northern Songs. Even better, the price was low, with Triumph's only ongoing participation 5 percent of the Beatles' record royalties for a period of four years.

It proved just a warm-up for a fight Lennon and McCartney cared a good deal more about with Northern Songs and its publisher, Dick James.

Just a few years earlier, in December of 1962, Dick James had been a singer turned music publisher with a small startup in Denmark Street. His life and fortunes changed dramatically when Beatles producer George Martin, who had also produced several records featuring James, included his name on a shortlist for Brian Epstein when he was seeking publishers for John Lennon and Paul McCartney. Epstein found James — who'd been advised by his son that the Beatles were unique and worth signing — eager and helpful. When Epstein said he wanted to get the Beatles on TV, the publisher used his contacts to get them booked on *Thank Your Lucky Stars* (where Epstein would meet Andrew Loog Oldham) and was rewarded with the Beatles' publishing, which was incorporated as Northern Songs Ltd. As with other deals he made for the Beatles, Brian had undertaken it with good and earnest intentions but proved unduly and naively trusting.

It was a typical publishing deal of the era. In the UK, Dick James and his financial partner, Charles Silver, got half of any earnings, and Lennon, McCartney, and Epstein split the rest twenty-twenty-ten. In 1966, the publisher's share dropped to 45 percent in return for John and Paul extending the contract through 1973. They also created a tax dodge, Lenmac Ltd., to hold the writers' share of their first fifty-six songs and then sold the company to Northern for £140,000 plus 15 percent of Northern's stock each, which James had taken public. (NEMS received its 275,000 shares of Northern Songs in the same transaction.) It was the kind of deal that Klein frequently recommended to his British clients: exchange highly taxed royalty income for lower-taxed capital gains. A second rights company, Maclen, was set up to house all their compositions going forward.

On the surface, it all sounded good. But James had stacked the deck in his favor in foreign deals, particularly the all-important U.S. market, where the Beatles made the lion's share of their money. When James licensed Northern Songs to a foreign publisher, that publisher received 15 percent of any local income and James split the remaining 85 percent with Epstein and the songwriters; he set up the same arrangement with George Harrison, who began to publish the songs he wrote for the Beatles through his own James-administered company, Harrisongs. However, when James set up his own subpublisher in a foreign market — as he did in America — the split was fifty-fifty rather than fifteen–eighty-five. That meant James and Silver kept half of all publishing income earned in the market and sent the remainder to

England, where they again took 50 percent, thus keeping seventy-five cents on every American dollar. Though far from unusual, it was classic double-dipping. To further muddy the waters, James wrote a letter that appeared to change the U.S. split to fifteen–eighty-five, but he worded it in such a way as to actually confirm the original fifty-fifty agreement.*

Like Clive Epstein, Dick James viewed the arrival of Allen Klein as the worst possible news. Not only was Klein a publisher himself who would likely want to put the Beatles under his own umbrella — the deal he'd given the Rolling Stones was significantly better and fairer than the one Dick James had given the Beatles — but Klein had audited numerous publishing firms around the world and there weren't many hustles he hadn't seen. Klein was particularly down on the practices of wholly owned foreign subpublishers, whose actions he compared to "slicing cheese" because the publisher kept carving off another slice for itself in each successive market, and so he was sure to object to James's arrangements. When Allen Klein started working with the Beatles, it could only mean the beginning of the end for Dick James.

"Dick James had seen the writing on the wall; it was written in Allen Klein's handwriting," said Peter Brown, the Apple director and former assistant to Brian Epstein. "And James was determined to pull out." But not by offering to sell the company to the Beatles or to Lennon and McCartney, who'd written all its songs and already owned 30 percent of the shares. Indeed, he never even told them he was selling Northern Songs — that would have necessitated opening the door to a tough adversarial negotiation with Klein or the Eastmans or both. Instead, he found a friendly buyer in Lord Lew Grade, the powerful British entertainment mogul with whom he'd worked as a singer.

The news that Dick James had sold their songs to Grade without telling them or offering them the opportunity to buy infuriated McCartney and devastated Lennon. To make matters worse, they didn't like or trust Grade. Brian Epstein had once declined to have Grade's

---

* Years later, in 1986, another Dick James writer, Elton John, finally succeeded in having a similar contract voided by the British courts.

brother Leslie act as the Beatles' booking agent, and Brian and the Beatles subsequently came to believe the Grades had used their considerable power and connections to slow the group's career and punish them; now the enemy would have their publishing. During a meeting with Harrison at Apple, a condescending James was full of excuses when answering George's questions about the deal. Speaking as if to a child, James said that he'd been worried about the future value of his own shares in Northern Songs and that he'd had to move quickly before the price fell, adding that it was a serious matter. Harrison, who knew very well that James was selling the Beatles' assets out from under them, went ballistic. "It's fucking serious to John and Paul is what it is!" he yelled.

Lennon and McCartney both telephoned Klein, who was on vacation in Puerto Rico, and insisted he return to London immediately and do something to counter the sale to Grade's company, ATV. Klein huddled with executives of the English merchant bank Ansbacher and Company and proposed that Apple make an offer to shareholders to purchase a million shares of Northern Songs, enough to give them 51 percent. Where ATV had bid £1.85 per share — a modest price that produced a lukewarm response — the Beatles' limited bid was significantly higher, £2.13. It was also a more complex deal than ATV's, and the arrangement with Ansbacher required Apple to put up half the money. That meant the Beatles pledging their individual Northern Songs shares as security. While Lennon readily accepted, McCartney, who had agreed to the Ansbacher proposal, declined, apparently on advice from Eastman that it was too risky. When it looked like McCartney's hedge would sink the deal with Ansbacher, Klein offered to put up 45,000 shares of MGM stock held by ABKCO and valued at £750,000. Klein would later say he did it solely to save the deal, but it's hard to imagine he was being completely altruistic or that he would have relinquished ABKCO's interest back to the Beatles.

With the competing bids from ATV and Ansbacher and the Beatles in the market, Klein and Lennon made an unsettling discovery: McCartney had been using Peter Brown at Apple to secretly buy shares in Northern Songs and now had 751,000 shares; Lennon had only

644,000. Lennon, believing he and McCartney had agreed to have equal shares in Northern Songs, felt betrayed and characterized it as the first time a member of the band had gone behind the others' backs to gain an advantage.

Looking for money and allies, Klein tried to get the Beatles' record companies, EMI in Britain and Capitol in the United States, to buy an interest in Northern Songs or lend the Beatles money. Neither label would help, apparently unwilling to anger Grade. To allay people's fears that he would personally take over Northern Songs and either kick out or ride roughshod over its directors, Allen put forward the established and respected music publisher David Platz, who headed Essex Music, to run the company. However, Essex was the British sub-publisher for Klein and the Rolling Stones, and there was little doubt who Platz would be loyal to.

Though Klein met frequently with Grade, the mogul clearly preferred a deal without the Beatles — or Allen. He would later characterize the meetings as tedious and unproductive; Klein, as he typically did, dragged out negotiations, fearful of overlooking something and constantly churning through the fine print for additional advantages. Grade was worried. He "didn't like the way it was going."

A group of three London brokers holding a combined 15 percent of Northern Songs' shares banded together, and it was clear they could make or break either the Beatles' or ATV's bid. What they wanted most was a cash deal, something ATV was loath to do, preferring a swap for its own stock. That reluctance gave Klein an opening. The consortium, as the London brokers were known, liked the offered price but also demanded an independent management in which neither they nor the Beatles would have a vote.

That may have made intuitive sense for the brokers — after all, why would they want to oversee a publishing business they weren't qualified to run? — but the notion that he would have nothing to say about his songs was unacceptable to Lennon, who continued to find the whole Dick James fiasco very upsetting. "I'm sick of being fucked about by men in suits sitting on their fat arses in the City," he blurted to a reporter. Reading Lennon's outburst, the consortium quickly opted to make a deal with ATV that gave Grade 54 percent of Northern Songs.

Realizing he'd just lost the war, Klein congratulated Grade and sued for peace, still hoping to get the best deal he could for the Beatles. Allen was ready to sell Grade enough of the Beatles' shares for the same terms as the consortium if ATV made the deal with the Beatles instead. He also dangled an attractive carrot: the Beatles would re-sign and extend their deal with Northern Songs if John and Paul could buy back Lenmac and if Apple got the rights to be the American subpublisher. It was a good deal for ATV, the Beatles, and ABKCO, which almost certainly would have administered the American publisher.

To everyone's surprise, John Eastman sent a letter to ATV saying Klein had no authority to speak for McCartney. Paul had in fact discussed the proposal several times with Klein and the other Beatles, and though he still had not committed his own shares, he was not against it. During a five-hour meeting that night at Klein's apartment, McCartney made it clear that he'd known nothing about the letter and telephoned Eastman several times to discuss it. Ultimately, McCartney called Grade personally to apologize and back the proposal. "Allen Klein is coming over and he speaks for me," McCartney said. But it was too late. Grade informed Klein the next day that ATV had voted to accept the consortium agreement. Once again the infighting between the Beatles and their own representatives had scared off an advantageous deal. The best they could do was simply sell, with no chance of negotiating for more rights. (In 1985, McCartney would try to buy ATV Music — and the rights to the Lennon/McCartney songs — himself. He made the mistake of mentioning his opportunity to Michael Jackson, who then jumped into the negotiations and outbid him, buying ATV Music for $47.5 million.)

The Northern Songs debacle underscored two problems. First, the Beatles were saddled with contracts and relationships over which they did not have nearly enough control. Second, the rift in the band was widening. Whether the Eastmans and Klein were abetting it — each was clearly at pains to paint the other as darkly as possible — it was becoming increasingly clear that the Beatles were coming apart.

By May, Allen had been working with the Beatles for over three months without a management agreement. Pointing out that he had already spent considerable time and sixty thousand dollars of his own money, he pressed them for a formal contract. The deal they agreed to on May 8 was informal and unusually straightforward: Klein was exclusive business manager for the Beatles with a three-year contact that could be canceled with three months' notice at the end of each year. He was to be paid 20 percent of gross income received from any source during that term and 20 percent of all income on deals he negotiated for as long as they ran, whether he was still the manager or not — with a few big stipulations. In particular, he was to receive a percentage of any increases he negotiated on contracts, but he was not entitled to a percentage of royalties on preexisting contracts that he did not improve.

When he took the document to the studio where the Beatles were working on *Abbey Road,* Lennon surprised Klein by momentarily hedging. John said he wanted to run the note past their lawyers and use it as the basis for a more formal and structured agreement. Allen told him he shouldn't have to wait anymore — he'd been doing the job for months. Plus, there was a simple annual escape clause built in if they were ever unhappy. McCartney, after earlier suggesting to the others that he might agree to have Klein as the manager if his fee was lowered, now said he didn't want to sign with Klein under any conditions. He did, however, agree to pose with Klein and the others for a press photo when they signed the agreement so they would at least present a harmonious image for the public.

Although disappointed by McCartney's decision, Klein wasn't surprised, and he said he understood why McCartney would rather be represented by family. In any case, he didn't really see it as a problem; Lennon, Harrison, and Starr had signed as representatives of "Apple Corps Ltd. on behalf of the Beatles Group of Companies." The foursome was incorporated as the Beatles and Company, with Apple as its successor; he had the signature of three of the four, and that made him officially and legally the business manager. Allen had won his long-sought prize. Besides, Lennon and Harrison, concluding that the Eastmans wanted only to obstruct and frustrate Klein, had dismissed Eastman and Eastman as the Beatles' attorneys. Allen was firmly in control.

## 10

---

# WITH THE BEATLES

IN 1966 A HUNGRY Allen Klein had been casting about for acts and opportunities. He and Marty Machat hatched a plan to poach a promising London band, the Small Faces, from the unpredictable and much-feared English manager Don Arden. Not wanting to launch a broadside against Arden, they quietly dispatched Eric Kronfeld, a junior attorney in Marty's office, to England with instructions to meet the band and sign them. They didn't tell Kronfeld about Arden or his thuggish reputation.

Though the band was doing well, touring steadily and enjoying hits, its members had made a dreadful deal with Arden, who paid them each just twenty pounds per week. Meeting with them in a basement apartment in Pimlico, Kronfeld found the group interested in going with Klein and Machat but unaccountably nervous.

"A noise would be heard outside the door and they would literally jump and flinch," he recalled. "I said, 'What are you afraid of?' and they said, 'You don't understand. Arden has this guy working for him, Mad Tom.'"

Suspecting the band had seen too many bad movies, Kronfeld rolled his eyes and spent the next five hours selling Klein and Machat to them. Convinced he had a deal, Kronfeld went back to his hotel to relax. Before long there was a knock at the door.

"Are you the kid?" His visitor was rough-looking and wore a grimy overcoat. "You the one who met with the Small Faces?" When Kronfeld said he was, Mad Tom opened his overcoat just enough to reveal a sawed-off shotgun. "It's not a good idea for you to see them again."

Kronfeld thanked him for the advice and took the first morning flight back to New York.

In 1969, a few months after Klein signed the Beatles, his associate Iris Keitel came back from a recording session run by Mickie Most with some very good news. The successor band to the Small Faces — now called just the Faces — didn't have a manager and wanted Allen. Their new singer, Rod Stewart, was a Sam Cooke fanatic and excited by the idea of having his idol's manager as his manager. Klein just shook his head. There was no way he could manage anyone else. Besides, why would he bother?

Indeed, Klein now occupied a position of power in the entertainment business that dwarfed any other person's before or after: he was the manager of the Beatles *and* the Rolling Stones. But problems were becoming obvious. First, untangling and rebuilding the Beatles' business was going to be an all-consuming task. He was just starting on the record companies and trying to figure out how to get money out of their film deal with United Artists, and cutting Apple down to a manageable and sensible operation was sure to be an ugly job. He was determined to do everything right; he would prove their great champion and construct the kind of lucrative, far-reaching deals that confirmed his mastery and brilliance. "He did want to enhance their monetary position and their career," said Harold Seider.

The second problem was just as thorny. Mick Jagger and Keith Richards weren't going to play second fiddle to anyone — especially not the Beatles. Klein and Jagger clearly weren't made for each other, and their mutual antipathy was a constant and increasing current sparking the relationship.

Marty Machat's son Steven recalled Jagger telephoning his family's house in Roslyn, New York, when Klein was visiting there. "Is Allen there with your father?" Mick asked.

Steven excitedly ran to Klein and told him that Jagger was on the phone for him. But fifteen minutes later, the teenager noticed one of the phone lines blinking, and he picked it up to discover Jagger still waiting for Klein.

When Steven reminded Klein that Jagger was on the phone, Klein waved him off. "Tell him I'll be there," he said.

"I think he's upset."

"He'll wait."

Looking back, Machat still shakes his head over the obvious snub. "My dad said Allen lost all interest in the Rolling Stones. All he wants is the Beatles."

"He's only been here three months and he's sorted out seven years of crap," Lennon enthused to *Time*. "This guy talks our language. He just says, 'Where is it?' and 'When do I get it?' and 'How much do the tax boys take?' It's as simple as that."

Klein's brass-tacks knowledge of the business and take-no-prisoners tactics appealed to Yoko Ono, who insisted Lennon have a dedicated protector. "Yoko told me that when she and John came to me, they were looking for a real shark—someone to keep the other sharks away," Klein told *Playboy*. "Now she says sometimes I'm *too* moral."

"There was a hierarchy," said Al Steckler, who handled creative affairs at ABKCO, working with the musicians and overseeing the artwork and packaging on their albums. Klein was eager to find opportunities and enhance Harrison's and Starr's careers, but it was Lennon's light that drew him, personally and professionally. They bonded. "Allen was there for John. They had the same sense of humor—John was so insightful, so wickedly funny. And Allen loved John's songs," Steckler said.

Klein was fully aware that he'd broken the hustler's cardinal rule, but he couldn't help himself. "I fell in love with Lennon," he admitted.

As did everyone at ABKCO, who marveled at the three Beatles' extraordinary abilities to retain their humanity while living in the world's most closely observed fishbowl. Though prone to mood swings and tirades born of pressures and frustrations, Lennon clearly relished his celebrity — he'd earned it — but he also nursed a horror of succumbing to pretension. It was immensely important to him to remain just a guy named John. He was remarkably successful in that quest. One of attorney Peter Howard's fondest memories in his nearly fifty years of working for Klein would be ducking out of the London office to shoot games of snooker in a nearby pub with Lennon. In New York, Paul Mozian had replaced Schneider as Allen's assistant and now found himself accompanying the Beatles as they explored Manhattan.

"They liked to just walk around New York and tried to live unencumbered," he said. "Especially Lennon. He loved talking to people on the streets and signing things." Indeed, John's casual just-folks attitude sometimes made Mozian nervous. The New Yorker was horrified when a trusting Lennon paid for a newspaper at a corner kiosk by holding out a wad of bills and inviting the vendor to take whatever was needed; Mozian put a quick stop to the practice. Harrison also enjoyed exploring New York, but he preferred to blend in and avoid attention. While George was eating at a Nathan's hot-dog stand with a friend of his, the journalist Al Aronowitz, a stranger noticed them. "Gee," he said, "you look just like George Harrison!" The Beatle gave him a quizzical look. "Really?" he asked. When another person made the same remark a few minutes later as they walked down the street, Harrison replied, "Gee, that's so funny! You're the second guy to say that."

Lennon's ability to visit New York had not been a given, particularly at the beginning of the group's association with Klein. As part of their honeymoon in March, John and Yoko had greeted the press in their suite at the Amsterdam Hilton dressed only in pajamas for what they dubbed the bed-in for peace. The weeklong conceptual-art event, intended to bolster the peace movement, proved a worldwide media sensation, and the couple wanted to stage a second bed-in in America in May. But the United States would not issue John a visa because he had been arrested in England the previous year for possession of hashish, a charge to which he'd pleaded guilty and paid a fine of a hundred and fifty pounds. Turned away by the U.S., John and Yoko instead held the bed-in in Montreal.

That fall, Lennon returned to Canada after concert promoter John Brower made a cold call and invited him to come as a guest to an all-day show in Toronto at which his idols Chuck Berry, Bo Diddley, Little Richard, and Jerry Lee Lewis would be performing. Lennon stunned Brower by saying he wasn't royalty and couldn't imagine himself sitting in the reviewing box. "I wouldn't feel right," he said. "I'd want to play. Can I play?" Lennon didn't even want any money — just a chance to play with his new group, the Plastic Ono Band, which featured Eric Clapton, bassist Klaus Voormann, drummer Alan White, and Yoko. Klein, however, insisted that Brower grant Lennon all rights to record and film his performance, and he hired the noted documentarian D. A. Pennebaker to shoot the show.

Meeting Lennon in Toronto, Klein found him extremely nervous about performing a concert for the first time in three years — so nervous that he threw up backstage. More unnerving to Allen was the news John had for him: he was quitting the Beatles.

Klein begged Lennon not to say anything in public about his intention to quit the band. Allen was in the midst of renegotiating the Beatles' recording agreements and the last thing he wanted the record companies to hear was that the band was coming to an end. Though John informed the other Beatles of his plans a few days later at the Apple office in London, he agreed to keep mum in public for the sake of the negotiations.

The recording contracts were substandard. Aside from the fact that they paid the Beatles a fraction of their true value, the primary agreement was an exceptionally ambiguous contract that Epstein had signed with EMI in Britain in 1967 after the band's initial five-year contract ended. It yoked the Beatles to EMI for ten years *and* obliged them to deliver a total of sixty-eight tracks. The Beatles had already given EMI sixty-eight tracks, and Klein maintained in his discussions with EMI chairman Sir Joseph Lockwood that they'd fulfilled their obligation and should get a new and vastly improved deal. Not surprisingly, Lockwood read the contract differently — they had to deliver a *minimum* of sixty-eight tracks and he had the right to sell whatever the Beatles recorded over ten years at an already-agreed-to price.

Klein was in no hurry to challenge Lockwood in court, as he expected he'd lose. Instead, he took a page out of his own playbook in hopes of prying a concession out of EMI. Forgetting about Britain for the moment, he suggested that Lockwood let the Beatles and Apple make a new and fairer deal in North America with EMI's subsidiary there, Capitol Records, where they received just forty cents an album. Lockwood, perhaps sensing that he needed to keep the relationship positive — or maybe just eager for Klein to be someone else's headache — agreed.

It was a good win. North America was by far the Beatles' biggest market. And nearly as important, the worldwide sublicensing rights to the Beatles' recordings were administered through Capitol, not EMI. That meant Allen could improve the price on every record the Beatles sold outside of EMI's home territory.

Klein and the Beatles had a big ace up their collective sleeve when they sat down with Capitol: they had just delivered *Abbey Road,* which the label expected to be huge and wanted to release at a dollar more than the normal list price. And though there had been recent years when the singer Glen Campbell had sold more records for Capitol than the Beatles, *Abbey Road* was clearly its crucial moneymaker for the year. Klein suggested there were more good titles to come, including a compilation of singles not found on other albums, *Hey Jude.* The last thing he wanted Capitol to hear was that John Lennon wasn't interested in the Beatles anymore.

Instead, he said that the group records were likely to be complemented by solo projects. There had already been a few decidedly noncommercial releases by individual Beatles, including Apple's first title, Harrison's instrumental soundtrack album, *Wonderwall Music,* as well as several albums by Lennon and Ono, among them *Unfinished Music No. 1: The Two Virgins,* with its outrageous and unmarketable cover portrait of them naked.

It was unlikely that the prospect of similar solo projects excited the Capitol executives. Instead, Klein got them to agree to a unique system. The Beatles would restart their current ten-year agreement with Capitol in 1969. Klein didn't want an advance — the Beatles weren't *that* cash poor — but he did want a better royalty rate. Provided the albums sold at least five hundred thousand copies, the group would receive fifty-six cents per album for the first two years, then seventy-two cents after that — a big improvement. Though John Eastman had written to Capitol saying Klein didn't speak for McCartney and suggesting there should be a separate contract for each of the Beatles, everyone was pleased with the terms Klein negotiated and all four Beatles signed. "If you're screwing us," the skeptical McCartney quipped, "I don't see how." In an unusual wrinkle, Capitol would also release any solo project by the Beatles during that period, but the label would have to make a choice: it could consider the album one of the Beatles records the company was owed and pay the fifty-six-cent royalty rate, or it could refuse to count it as a Beatles album and pay a much higher royalty rate of two dollars.

Obviously, no record executive would have traded *The Two Virgins* for a chance to get *Abbey Road*. But Capitol declined to count the soon-to-be-released Plastic Ono Band album *Live Peace in Toronto* against the Beatles cap, which proved an expensive blunder — and another indication of Klein's creativity. The album was a hit and the company paid $1.5 million in royalties right out of the box — about what Capitol would have paid on three million Beatles albums.

Once again, Klein set up the contract as a buy/sell agreement that inserted Apple and ABKCO into the equation as the manufacturers. Instead of Capitol pressing Beatles records, ABKCO would do that for Apple, and Capitol would buy them from ABKCO and sell them to record stores. Along with providing an additional revenue stream on the records, the arrangement had other advantages for both Klein and the Beatles: they didn't have to worry if the manufacturing numbers Capitol gave them were real, and they were paid monthly rather than twice a year.

• • •

When Capitol agreed to the contract for the Beatles, it had no idea that *Abbey Road* was the band's final statement and that they would never record again. But there was an abandoned project sitting in the can that Klein, for a variety of reasons, thought the band should take another look at.

Proposed and championed by McCartney, *Get Back* was conceived as both a television documentary and a back-to-basics album built on live in-studio performances. Coming on the heels of *The Beatles,* an exhausting five-month project that made extensive use of overdubs and frequently found the musicians working as individuals rather than in a group, *Get Back* was McCartney's attempt to respark the band. But the others were never more than listless and halfhearted about it, treating it more like Paul's project than a Beatles album. The constant presence of Yoko Ono, whom Lennon insisted on having by his side in the studio at all times, was another uncomfortable new wrinkle. *Get Back* might have been undertaken to revitalize the Beatles, but that wasn't evident in the bare-bones tracks recorded by producer/engineer Glyn Johns. Much of the footage shot by director Michael Lindsay-Hogg didn't show the Beatles coming back together, just drifting farther apart.

Allen, however, wondered if it couldn't be salvaged and put to good use. The Beatles still owed United Artists a third picture on the deal that had included *A Hard Day's Night* and *Help!* Plus, Ringo was eager to pursue an acting career, and United Artists had raised objections when he'd signed to appear in *The Magic Christian,* saying *they* were owed his next movie. Maybe the unfinished documentary could be blown up into a theatrical release to satisfy UA. Klein showed the footage to Saul Swimmer, the director he had worked with on *Mrs. Brown, You've Got a Lovely Daughter* and other films. Swimmer saw no technical reason the footage couldn't be transferred from 16- to 32-millimeter film and released as a movie.

In November, Klein screened some of the footage in London for McCartney, Harrison, Starr, and their wives, and he sold them on the idea. Since the song "Get Back" had already been released as a single six months earlier, he suggested to McCartney that the film needed a new name, and they considered *The Long and Winding Road* before agreeing on *Let It Be.* Over dinner that evening Allen reminded Paul, George, and Ringo that UA was also entitled to the soundtrack album and said producer Phil Spector had unexpectedly come by ABKCO's office in New York to pitch his services to the Beatles. Klein, at Eastman's request, had had lunch in New York with another producer, Jim Guercio, best known for his work with Chicago, whom Eastman had represented. When Klein told Lennon of the two approaches, John wanted Spector. Now, over dinner, the others agreed to meet him as well. That dinner proved to be the last time Klein ever met face to face with McCartney.

Six weeks later, Klein flew from New York to London with Spector. The high-strung producer was so nervous about meeting the Beatles that he spent much of the flight lying in the middle of the first-class aisle. But he pulled himself together by the time they reached Apple's Savile Row offices, and that evening he was in EMI's studio with Lennon and Harrison cutting "Instant Karma." The match was made.

Klein, meanwhile, turned to resolving the problem that had initially brought Lennon to his hotel door. Apple desperately needed to be cleaned up and cleaned out. Allen was just the bulldozer for the job.

Perhaps a more introspective or diplomatic man could have foreseen the traps lurking in the task ahead. The Beatles, after all, were the sun at the center of an exciting new universe—who would willingly leave their orbit? But if the thought even occurred to Klein, he didn't care; he had a job to do, promises to keep and clients to impress. If that meant worlds would collide, well, he could guarantee how that would end: with a lot of unhappy former employees, friends, and hangers-on. He just couldn't imagine the enormous impact it would have on his reputation.

At the core of Apple was a quartet of dedicated Beatles intimates who functioned as directors and oversaw the day-to-day business: publicist Derek Taylor, former Epstein assistant Peter Brown, and ex-road managers and aides Mal Evans and Neil Aspinall. Working with them were department and operation heads, some appropriate to their jobs, some not: Apple Records president Ron Kass was an experienced record executive while Terry Doran, the head of Apple Music Publishing, was a former car dealer who had sold luxury vehicles to Harrison and later became his pal and gofer. At the end of the day, Klein concluded, no one was getting the job done and Apple needed a clean sweep. "Ron Kass was a good frontman but in over his head," said Harold Seider. "It was a disaster."

The company's employees certainly loved the Beatles — not to mention the incomparable perk of having the world's hippest job — but the Beatles were no longer loving them back. "People were robbing us and living on us," Lennon said bitterly, "to the tune of 18 or 20 thousand pounds a week." The money "was rolling out of Apple and nobody was doing anything about it. All our buddies that worked for us for 50 years were all just living and drinking and eating like fuckin' Rome." The Beatles were hardly blameless. Though frequently in the office, they simply did not or could not provide thoughtful hands-on leadership as to how time and money should be spent, sometimes to the detriment of loyal friends and employees. While Apple wasted thousands of pounds every month, Mal Evans, who had been with the Beatles since their days at Liverpool's Cavern Club, was still being paid a surprisingly modest thirty-seven pounds a week. Apple had become an unsupervised playground. When the Grateful Dead's manager Rock Scully dropped in unexpectedly for an extended visit, he brought a crew that included several Hells Angels. They added insult to injury by not only brawling at an office party but charging Apple the cost of flying their motorcycles to London. On another occasion, a family wandered in and announced they'd come to carry John and Yoko off with them to Fiji. Since John and Yoko weren't around, they set up camp and lived in the office, the mother taking to wandering the halls naked, her fifteen-year-old daughter pestering assistant Chris O'Dell to help her bed George Harrison.* Magic Alex, the TV repairman

---

* Chris O'Dell's excellent and moving memoir *Miss O'Dell: My Hard Days and Long Nights with the Beatles, the Stones, Bob Dylan, Eric Clapton, and the Women They Loved* includes some of the best and most insightful reporting I found on Apple and is the source of several anecdotes in this chapter.

turned resident inventor, was outfitted with a laboratory from which he sent out approximately one hundred half-baked patent applications through EMI's attorneys, none of which were ever approved. Klein estimated that Alex had cost Apple over £180,000 all told. Klein also discovered that Apple had bought a building for reasons no one could remember, that two company cars had disappeared, and that a series of payments on Apple's books marked "erections and demolitions" had gone to prostitutes.

The real money drain, however, was daily expenses; the Apple offices were the best press club and hangout in London. Despite a personal plea from McCartney, who'd called the staff together and begged them to stop wasting money, Apple continued to run an open bar for the world, employees and visitors going through several cases of scotch and cartons of cigarettes every week. There were also tabs run for journalists at a nearby restaurant and telephones available to anyone for worldwide calling. Any box of new records that arrived in the office disappeared immediately. Kass tried to limit the employees to one free record each, insisting that they pay wholesale prices for any more, but it didn't stop the thievery. Anything not nailed down was likely to walk out the door, as it had at the Apple Boutique.

Klein's job was to be the Beatles' hatchet man, to bring order to the chaos and an end to the rampant expenses. Everyone at Apple knew what that meant: the bastard was going to tear the playhouse down, and he was hated and feared. For his part, Klein, though never able to personally fire anyone, had no qualms about the job and set about cutting Apple down to seeds and stem. For the actual dirty work of face-to-face dismissals, his attorney and aide Peter Howard wielded the hatchet.

Tony Bramwell, a Beatles gofer who'd grown up with them in Liverpool, managed to survive Klein's purges but expressed nothing but contempt for him. To Bramwell, Klein was a greasy, dirty American, a usurper and crook who had no right to be paid for what he did. "He wanted to get rid of everybody so he could cook the books and milk the company dry," said Bramwell. "He spent his days conspiring about how to get rid of us, whispering about everybody behind their backs to John and George, who thought he was some kind of New York financial genius. Klein's tentacles were long. He tore everything apart. Within a few months of him taking over, I was the only member of the old staff left in the company." Still, Bramwell managed to hold his nose long enough to accompany Klein to the Capitol Records convention in Hawaii, "before it became so touristy." There, he and Jack Oliver, who'd become head of Apple Records when Klein fired Kass, camped out by the pool, drank cocktails from pineapples, and traded witticisms as they watched "that fat bastard" working the executives from Capitol and, as Bramwell put it, "playing tennis with the Italian crowd from New York."

Singer Mary Hopkin, a protégée of McCartney who enjoyed one of Apple's biggest hits with "Those Were the Days," also detested Klein.

"Everyone hated him," she said. "A creep. A real creep." She added, "I was never directly involved with him financially, thank God. I just didn't like the man. I don't like people that try and patronize me. . . . He'd say, 'Do this and that.' I remember walking away from him in the middle of a meal once. I like to think I'm a good judge of character. Maybe I'm not. Maybe that's why I'm divorced now."

When Klein fired Kass, Kass and an assistant, Ken Mansfield, were quickly hired by MGM Records. But Allen hadn't fired Mansfield and didn't like it when someone quit his employ or rejected a job offer. He decided he had to get him back and offered to triple Mansfield's salary if he would come to ABKCO and oversee Apple Records in the United States.

Though a Kass loyalist, Mansfield confessed to his mentor that he found the money very tempting and wasn't sure he should say no. "You lay down with pigs and you get up dirty," the angry executive replied. More to the point, though, Mansfield feared that working for Klein would make him a pariah in the business. Allen's in-your-face manner had always made enemies, but his hard-charging style and aggressive cost-cutting for the Beatles had stirred so much ill will and jealousy that there was now a Klein brush, and Mansfield didn't want to be tarred with it. Meeting with Klein at the Beverly Hills Hotel, he realized he had underrated him — especially as a salesman. Allen's relent-less pursuit was both flattering and confusing. "He had derailed me and a lot of other people's worlds by upsetting the Apple cart," Mans-field said. "And here I was being beguiled. You couldn't help being taken in by this guy. He was charming and disarming in some obtuse, off-the-wall way. . . . I didn't like anything about him, but I was enjoy-ing listening to him and I liked what he was saying to me."

Mansfield didn't want to say yes, but Klein was so unwilling to ac-cept no that he offered to expand Mansfield's responsibilities to include working with the Rolling Stones and Donovan. Fearing he was about to give in, Mansfield hit on what he assumed was a foolproof plan to get himself off the hook and away from Klein's increasingly tempting offer. An outstanding tennis player who had won club tournaments in California, Mansfield knew he could destroy the older, portly Klein handily, and so he offered him a sucker's bet: If you beat me at tennis, he told him, I'll take the job; if I win, I stay with Kass at MGM.

When Mansfield caught a glimpse of Klein on the court the next day he felt a little guilty; in tennis whites, Klein looked like "an egg on rejected drumsticks." Mansfield was going to trounce him with-out breaking a sweat. Then they started playing, and Mansfield, to his eternal shock, discovered he couldn't get a ball past Klein. "He couldn't have looked worse yet couldn't have been more formidable," he said. "I thought I'd gone to tennis hell." Most unnerving was the realiza-tion that Klein wasn't near the tennis player Mansfield was; the man played on will alone, the sheer refusal to knuckle under to someone else. "This was not really a tennis match — it was a negotiation, and Al-len Klein was virtually unbeatable in negotiations and was not about to lose this one no matter what form it had taken. I was in over my head."

It took hours but Mansfield eventually outlasted the older man, fi-nally putting Klein away, 15–13. Shaking hands with Allen at the net, Mansfield saw Klein's intensity evaporate. The game and the player had already been forgotten, and Mansfield imagined Allen was con-sidering whom to offer the job to next. He never saw or spoke to Klein again.

· · ·

As directors of Apple, Peter Brown and Derek Taylor had front-row seats to Klein's wholesale firings and massive restructuring. Well aware of Apple's problems, they nonetheless had very different reactions — both to Klein and to the firings.

Brown saw Klein as a lout bent only on achieving his own ends, believing, for example, that the sole reason Klein had fired Kass — whom Brown liked — was so he could move into the townhouse Apple and Brown had rented for Kass in Mayfair. If that was the case, Brown foiled him by signing over the house's lease to Kass. "I got supreme pleasure in seeing Kass get that town house," he said, adding that he strove to soften what he thought of as Klein's callous and impersonal assaults on the staff, sometimes at the expense of his own reputation. "Some of the dirty work was left to me. I have been criticized for serving Allen Klein in this task but I unhappily agreed to do the job only because I hoped the news could be delivered with kindness and dignity, instead of from Klein's mouth." After leaving the Beatles, Brown launched and chaired the public relations firm BLJ Worldwide, where he continued his dedication to kindness and dignity as publicist for Muammar Qaddafi.

Taylor, the most admired and beloved employee at Apple, was likely also its most thoughtful. It pained him to see Apple in convulsions and his friends fired. Yet he understood Apple could exist only if it was run like a business, and he was philosophic. "Money is pouring into Apple and the only extra overheads are Klein's transportation and accommodations so I guess you could say that Allen Klein straightened out Apple as the Beatles wanted it," he said. "The only thing is . . . where is Apple and where are the Beatles?" Indeed, Taylor was one of the few people at Apple able to summon a little sympathy for the devil. "It's not the same Apple at all when he is there," he said of Klein. "It is so much heavier, so much more serious, so much more interesting. I think we need him more than we know. He is the Man We Love to Hate and I am not sure we are fair to him."

Taylor's young protégée Chris O'Dell was among those fired. Although she continued to socialize and work in the Beatles' circle afterward, her first reaction was pain and anger at Klein and Peter Howard for dismissing her; she initially spoke of them with unusual rancor.

Years later, after O'Dell had worked for the Rolling Stones and as a tour manager for Crosby, Stills, Nash, and Young, she saw things in another light. "The most important piece is that the Beatles were running the whole show and wanted it to be different," she said. "We had fun, and the sky was the limit for creativity and possibilities. Sadly, however, it cost them a lot of money. The party just had to come to an end." Perhaps most clear-eyed and sensible was Peter Asher. The head of A&R for Apple Records, Asher understood the players and the business as well as anyone. A former recording artist with the duo Peter and Gordon, Asher was married to the publicist Betty Doster, who had worked with Klein, and Asher's sister, Jane, had been engaged to McCartney. He believed Apple Records could be a successful artist-oriented label like A&M in America if it took care of business and dispensed with silliness like Magic Alex and the Apple Boutique, so in that regard, the cutbacks were essential. But he also immediately and correctly recognized that Klein's hiring would widen rather than bridge the gulf between McCartney and Lennon. The existence of warring camps was evident to Apple's employees, some of whom at first declined to cooperate with Klein or provide him with the documents he needed. Lennon and Harrison had to personally insist that people help Allen.

"The fact that John was completely convinced that Allen was the right person for the job and Paul was convinced with equal tenacity and determination that he *wasn't* meant that Allen Klein's arrival drove a giant wedge between two people who already were having quite a number of arguments," Asher said. "So it seemed to me that the future looked very bleak with Allen Klein at the helm." Asher had other concerns as well. He had signed and produced James Taylor for Apple, which released his first album, and Taylor, after a brief meeting with Klein, knew the company would change drastically and wasn't keen on staying. After resigning his position at Apple, Asher became Taylor's manager and continued to produce him for Warner Brothers Records. When James Taylor's Warner Brothers debut, *Sweet Baby James*, proved an enormous hit, Klein was criticized for having lost Apple a major artist.

• • •

Klein's most provocative act at Apple was directed not at an employee, but at an owner. During a staff meeting at Savile Row, the receptionist buzzed Allen. Everyone in his office heard the message: Paul McCartney was on the line for him.

"Tell him I'm in a meeting and I'll call him back later," he said.

After a few seconds, the receptionist stuck her head in the door. Paul was insistent; Klein would talk to him now — or never. The Beatle clearly knew he was being snubbed in front of a roomful of his employees. Klein shrugged. "I can't talk to him now."

Paul McCartney kept his word. He never spoke to Allen Klein again.

Klein nonetheless worked tirelessly to set the Beatles' financial house in order. If McCartney objected to any of his cost-cutting decisions at Apple, he never said so. Just as important to the group's financial picture, Klein's decision to negotiate with United Artists for the release of *Let It Be* proved a very savvy and lucrative move for the Beatles. Between the film and its soundtrack album, Klein could claim that Apple made six million dollars in just the first month following its May 1970 release — at a time when the Beatles were grateful for a real payday. The best thing may have been that it was found money, a project McCartney had shelved and the others hadn't cared about.

Yet although it contained several memorable tunes, *Let It Be* wasn't an artistic success. Coming on the heels of the miraculous ending that was *Abbey Road*, the album and film were a flat and disappointingly inconsequential coda to the age's most brilliant career. *Let It Be* could never quite become more than it was: a collection of tapes missing the Beatles' spark.

The original "live" session tapes engineered and produced by Glyn Johns certainly felt as if they were missing something. Before "Let It Be" was released as a single, it was given to George Martin, and the producer fleshed it out with horns and backup vocals and replaced Lennon's original bass part with an overdub by McCartney. To make the album, the rest of the tapes were given to Spector, who worked on them with Harrison and Starr. McCartney spent much of this period on his farm in Scotland recording the music that would become his first solo album, *McCartney*. Lennon was not involved. "Paul and I were too bored with the project to give him any help at all," John said.

The soundtrack to *Let It Be* was supposed to be released a month or two after the film's April 28 New York premiere. But when Spector announced that work had proceeded quicker than expected and that he could deliver the album for simultaneous release, that seemed good news; the album could be in stores at the height of interest. There was just one glitch: Paul's solo album was also slated to debut in mid-April.

To maximize their success, the Beatles had always tried to schedule new releases when they had a reasonably clear field; they shared information on upcoming records with the Rolling Stones so the bands could avoid competing with each other. The market was already crowded, particularly in America, where a compilation of Beatles singles, *Hey Jude*, had been released at the end of February and Ringo's first solo album, *Sentimental Journey*, was to come out in early April. Klein and the other Beatles worried that the additional titles would hurt the sales of *Let It Be* and told Capitol to push back the release date of *McCartney*. Since Ringo's album was also being released, he agreed to go and give Paul the letters about the postponement.

"I thought I would take the letters around to Paul myself," Ringo said, "expecting Paul might be disappointed and thinking it was right that one of the Beatles personally should tell him." To Starr's dismay, McCartney flew into a rage, pushing him and making threats. "I'll finish you all now," Ringo recalled Paul saying. "You'll pay." When Starr asked McCartney to at least consider postponing the release of his album, Paul threw him out. Shaken, Ringo convinced the others to alter their plans and push *Sentimental Journey* up to late March and the soundtrack-album and film premiere of *Let It Be* back to May 8, letting McCartney have his original release date of April 20. "I felt since he was our friend and the date was of such immense significance to him, we should let him have his own way."

The new arrangement didn't mollify Paul. Having already stopped speaking with Klein on the phone, he now pointedly refused to attend any meetings that included Klein, sending solicitor Charles Corman in his stead. Though taken aback, the other Beatles teasingly asked the attorney where his bass was. Still, Ringo said he wished Paul had come and judged Klein's abilities for himself.

McCartney also took exception to seeing credits on the back of an American copy of his album describing Apple Records as "an ABKCO Company." He insisted that ABKCO had nothing to do with his career or his work and that the company's name had no business being on his record. ABKCO was in fact pressing and administering the records in the United States, but Klein did as McCartney asked and removed the line.

More significant, Klein and McCartney were soon at daggers drawn over Phil Spector's postproduction and mixes for *Let It Be,* particularly over the song "The Long and Winding Road." The overblown arrangement — with a huge string section, ringing horns; harp, and a choir — surprised George Martin, who considered it so uncharacteristic that it sounded at odds with the group's body of work. He could also have called it silly, which it was. Spector, who had no great love for McCartney, later suggested he had added the arrangement to cover a sloppy bass part by Lennon, although why he didn't just erase it as Martin had done on "Let It Be" is a mystery.*

Incensed to hear his song buried under Spector's wall of bombast, McCartney indignantly said no one had the right to alter his work without his approval — although whether that was actually what happened is debatable. Both Harrison and Starr would later publicly say that all the Beatles had received acetates of the Spector mixes and that McCartney had okayed them. But if he had ever been satisfied, that was certainly not the case as the album came to market. "We heard no more about it from him until it was too late to do anything," Ringo said.

Regardless, Paul was now livid. Michael Kramer recalls seeing a nasty note from McCartney to his uncle Allen concerning the track. "It

---

* Lennon's bass part is so poorly played that at least one Beatles historian, Ian MacDonald, has wondered if it wasn't an act of out-and-out sabotage. See Ian MacDonald, *Revolution in the Head: The Beatles Records in the Sixties* (London: Fourth Estate, 1994).

was addressed '*Dear Fuck Klein,*'" he said. For his part, Klein twisted
the knife by having "The Long and Winding Road" released as the
Beatles' next single, guaranteeing it would be omnipresent. It became
the band's final number-one hit in America, where it spent ten weeks
on the charts. The track stood as it was — or at least it did for thirty-
three years until *Let It Be . . . Naked* was released with the original,
nonorchestrated performance used in the film.

While McCartney railed that Klein and Spector had perpetrated
"the shittiest thing that anyone's done to me," the other Beatles were
displeased by what they viewed as a betrayal perpetrated by Paul: in
a mock interview included as an insert in the first copies of *McCartney* sent to the press, Paul announced that he had quit the band and
that the Beatles were no more. The others remembered when Lennon
had privately told them he was done with the Beatles and had agreed
to keep it quiet for financial and promotional reasons. Declaring his
independence while promoting his solo record, McCartney seemed
to be separating himself from their shared interests — a substantive
change. Indeed, McCartney now wanted to change the way income
from their solo projects was divvied up.

Under the original plan for Beatles and Company, the corporate
predecessor to Apple, all Beatles' income paid into the company was
ultimately split four ways — and that included earnings on solo projects. That was fine with the others. Lennon didn't care when the $1.5
million windfall from *Live Peace in Toronto* went into the general
kitty; Harrison was happy to split the sizable royalties on his best-sell-
ing box set *All Things Must Pass* with his former band mates. But Mc-
Cartney took a different view. He may simply have been ready to bet
on himself, believing his own career going forward would be worth
more than a quarter share in an ongoing partnership with Lennon,
Harrison, and Starr, and his secret purchase of Northern Songs shares
suggested he had been thinking of himself as a separate agent for some
time. But one thing was certain: Paul did not trust Allen Klein and
didn't want him anywhere near his work, assets, or money. He made
that abundantly clear in the interview sent out with review copies of
*McCartney.*

*Q: Is it true that neither Allen Klein nor ABKCO have been nor will be in any way involved with the production, manufacturing, distribution or promotion of this new album?*
*A: Not if I can help it.*

Behind the scenes, John Eastman hoped for a quick and amicable resolution. Though the Eastmans had repeatedly tried to frustrate Klein's plans with Northern Songs, Capitol Records, and United Artists, John now struck a conciliatory tone, essentially saying, *Let McCartney go his way and you can go yours.* "My sole purpose was to make sure my client gets his twenty-five percent," John Eastman said. "I talked to Allen and said, 'We can resolve this.' We would have made a deal at any time to disgorge Paul's twenty-five percent. Paul had no qualms about letting Allen handle the others—let them do as they please. Klein was incapable of making a deal."

Though it would have been close to impossible to bring a quick and legal end to the Beatles' partnership, Eastman's remarks suggest a workaround agreement likely would have satisfied McCartney (although precisely how Paul could informally separate himself from ABKCO's relationship with Apple is unclear). In any event, Klein wouldn't budge; he was managing the Beatles' affairs by majority consent of the Apple principals and he was going to follow the agreements. Whether McCartney liked it or not, it was Klein's position that he had signed on to those agreements and he couldn't just change his mind now. Clearly there was never going to be a rapprochement.

To manage the Beatles had been the great crusade of Allen's career, the act that would vindicate him personally and professionally. And while he'd achieved the holy land, he hadn't quite conquered Jerusalem. Yes, he had a contract to manage the affairs of the Beatles. Unfortunately, there were no longer any Beatles to manage. He was John Lennon's regent in a now unavoidable divorce.

## 11

## MR. POPULARITY

IN THE SPRING OF 1970, the Rolling Stones' contract with Decca Records — the deal that had changed their fortunes and ushered in Allen Klein as their business manager — was about to come to an end. They began searching for a new record company.

Now deeply immersed in the business of the Beatles, Klein discussed the Stones' impending availability with executives at RCA, EMI, and Capitol, but it was Jagger who personally handled the discussions with the executives and labels the band seemed most interested in, Ahmet Ertegun at Atlantic Records and Clive Davis at Columbia. In mid-July, Allen accompanied Mick Jagger to a meeting with executives from Capitol Records, but the odds were slim the Stones would sign there. Capitol already had the Beatles and Apple — why would the Stones go into any deal where they weren't the biggest act?

Of course, they already knew they were seen as smaller than the Beatles, not just by the world at large, but by Allen Klein in particular. "The moment Klein got the Beatles he began to ignore and spend less time on the Stones business," said Harold Seider. So it shouldn't have surprised Klein when, less than two weeks after he visited Capitol with Jagger, a letter arrived from the Rolling Stones' lawyers informing him that ABKCO would not be negotiating the band's new record deal and that Prince Rupert Loewenstein would henceforth handle all financial affairs.

Yet Klein was surprised.

"Allen lives by denial," said Seider, adding that Klein believed he could ultimately overcome any obstacle, even the unnecessary ones he had created. Now suddenly eager to hang on to the Stones, Klein launched a charm offensive, inviting Jagger to a sit-down in his suite at the Dorchester Hotel. Jagger was happy to oblige and used the meeting to pry an advance out of Klein. "He knows he's going to leave and he just wants to get cash out of Allen," said Seider, who was at the meeting. "It was that kind of thing."

Klein's surprise and dismay at finding the Stones, and Jagger in particular, unhappy is perplexing. He had given them short shrift in favor of the Beatles, and there were several other issues as well. Allen had recognized early on that Oldham's financial overreach and lack of support during the drug arrest and trial had contributed to the end of that relationship with the Stones, and Allen's own financial interests in the band were similar to Oldham's; in fact, they were deeper, more valuable, and more complicated.

In his earliest days with them, Allen truly cost the Stones nothing; his 20 percent commission was paid out of Easton and Oldham's cut. However, after Klein bought out Oldham's interest in the Stones and settled the various lawsuits brought by Eric Easton against the band and their representatives, ABKCO emerged as the owner of all recording rights previously held by Easton and Oldham—which is to say that ABKCO now received 50 percent of all royalties on every Rolling Stones record released on Decca or London. Jagger hadn't liked Oldham and Easton making five times as much as he did on his own records, and he couldn't have been pleased to have Klein replacing them.

When asked why he didn't sell his interest in the records to the Rolling Stones, Andrew Loog Oldham said he didn't believe they'd be willing to pay for them. Whether that means he thought the band had come to view their original management agreement as unconscionable and indefensible or that there was just too much bad blood for them to make a deal with him — or both — he knew that Klein had the money and the desire to acquire the rights. And as Oldham said, he believed making a deal with Klein would also preserve some of his leverage in the business.

The questions in Klein's case are just as fraught. He could fairly say that his legal obligation to the Rolling Stones had limits; he was not a CPA and did not have a contract to advise the band. Yet when Oldham departed, he and Jagger had clearly come to an agreement for Klein to look after the Stones' interests, particularly in America. If Klein himself wanted the suddenly available 50 percent interest in the Stones' recordings, didn't he have an obligation as their business manager to recommend the same deal to them? Oldham may very well have been right in believing that Jagger and company would not be willing to pay for something that they felt shouldn't have been taken from them to begin with, but there's nothing to indicate Klein ever asked them, let alone advised them of the wisdom of buying out Oldham and Easton.

Once Klein acquired them himself, there was a clear conflict of interest. "You can't manage on one hand and have the artist signed to you on the other," said Michael Kramer. "When [Allen] bought the rights to the Stones' masters from Andrew, he became an owner as well as the business manager. It can't end well. That becomes part of the Stones' dissatisfaction later. 'Hey, Allen Klein — you were our business manager. Why didn't you buy it for *us*?'"

Klein's conflict wasn't unique; if anything, it was typical of the record business. A record contract made the company the owner of a performer's recordings, and often the publishing rights as well, and paid the artist the lowest royalty possible, which meant that the vast majority of any money earned on a hit and all its asset value remained with the company. The artist's manager could be expected to create career-long ties to the artist, either by becoming a partner in ventures such as publishing or production companies or by retaining an interest in any contract he negotiated even if the artist ceased to be his client.

A manager who came early to a rapidly developing commercial music scene or who was able to negotiate better deals than other managers — and Klein was both the first and sharpest of the managers of the

modern rock era—could demand the biggest fees and the best percentages. Before Klein, in the 1950s, Elvis Presley's manager, Colonel
Tom Parker, had been a fifty-fifty partner with his client. After Klein,
the next major businessman in the record industry, David Geffen,
grew enormously wealthy and powerful by being even bolder; he acted
as agent, publisher, and record company for the artists he managed,
and the obvious question—who is looking out for the artist's interests
when the manager owns the record company and the publisher?—was
never asked. Or at least, it wasn't asked until the artists became successful and those rights valuable. Until then, Geffen's clients were happy to
have him help them produce records, play concerts, find an audience,
and make money.

The situation was much the same in the concert business. The contemporary whose professional practices and career most resembled
Klein's was Bill Graham, the impresario who owned the Fillmore East
and West and who did more than anyone else to invent the modern
rock concert.* Like Klein, Graham was the first hardball player in what
had been, until then, a slow-pitch league. Graham created an appropriate format for presenting bands and then helped make rock concerts
a real industry. And while he treated concertgoers well by providing a
professional show at a fair price, woe to the band or manager who did
not recognize that Graham was in business; bad contracts and ficti-
tious ticket counts were the usual result. Nor was he averse to using
his leverage to block bands from taking gigs with rival promoters or
bullying them to sign their merchandising rights to his Winterland
company. The band Santana owed much to Graham, who insisted that
the then unknowns be given their career-making slot at Woodstock.
But they split with Graham after he made himself both their booking
agent and their manager, which was illegal. The Grateful Dead spent
decades going back and forth between collaborating and fighting with
Graham, and the promoter was ultimately supplanted at the top of his

---

* The promoter's life and work have been examined in several books, including his
own *Bill Graham Presents: My Life Inside Rock and Out* and Dean Budnick and Josh
Baron's *Ticket Masters*.

industry in 1989 when the Rolling Stones spurned him for the more financially inventive Canadian promoter Michael Cohl, a one-time manager of Ontario strip clubs, at least in part because Mick Jagger was said to have tired of Graham's funny ticket counts.

Like Graham, Klein didn't change with the times. In the early days, when each was ahead of the pack, they created the market and dictated the terms. Later, when others saw how it was done and the artists began to better appreciate the financial value of their own work, they didn't make appropriate adjustments. Or maybe Klein just didn't care if the Rolling Stones became unhappy. Though he never said as much, he could have concluded that owning a piece of the Rolling Stones was a far better and more lucrative approach than trying to stay in their good graces for the rest of his life.

Whatever Klein's motives, his decisions would lead to nearly two decades of litigation with the Rolling Stones marked by few real financial victories for the band. In public, Jagger was at first cordial and politic, telling a reporter three weeks after breaking with ABKCO that he was "grateful to Allen for what he has done for us" and volunteering that the split had nothing to do with the Beatles. "His involvement with Apple was not what worried me," he said. Yet behind closed doors, Mick was seething. According to Prince Rupert Loewenstein, Jagger believed Klein had made him look like a fool. "He felt very aggrieved," said Loewenstein, adding that Jagger had to be physically restrained from attacking Klein in a meeting. Nor was the 50 percent interest in the Rolling Stones' royalties the only annoyance. Aside from being Jagger and Richards's music publisher for all songs written through 1971, ABKCO was the sole controller of the Rolling Stones' master recordings in America, meaning it oversaw manufacturing. Though the records couldn't be moved from London Records or its successors, first PolyGram and then Universal Music Group, there was still money to be made and it was to become a flash point for both sides in their subsequent battles.

Under the original management agreement, Easton and Oldham owned the Rolling Stones' master recordings and leased them to Decca.

In the United States, those rights were leased to Decca's American subsidiary, London Records. When Klein came into the picture, he created an American company, Nanker Phelge Music, to house those rights, which were then leased by Nanker Phelge to London Records for the term of the contract. The American company was supposed to allow the Stones to repatriate their U.S. income without paying the ruinous British taxes on foreign income by taking it out through a similarly named extant British company, Nanker Phelge Ltd.—although that company had a completely different function and nothing to do with master recordings. Ultimately, Klein's scheme failed to impress the Inland Revenue, who said it would still tax the money at the foreign rate of approximately 90 percent—disastrous for the band, since they were guaranteed at least $1.25 million from London Records. Klein came up with paying the musicians' American guarantee through Nanker Phelge in twenty annual installments in order to reduce the taxes. As he had done with Sam Cooke, Klein explained to Oldham and the Stones that this would be recognized as a legitimate arrangement only if it was an outside corporation; if it wasn't, they would be taxed at once. Though the Stones would later claim they had no idea that they didn't own the company, this doesn't appear to be the case. In a 1968 letter to a record company, Jagger referred to Nanker Phelge Music as a firm owned by Allen Klein.*

Having the rights to assign the master recordings made it easy for ABKCO to manufacture the records and then sell them to London, which the company did. That was valuable and made money for ABKCO—but not as much as 50 percent of the royalties from Easton and Oldham brought in. Yet despite the fact that none of the rights controlled by Nanker Phelge Music would ever be available for re-lease or sale—a subsequent deal negotiated by Klein between London and the Stones had already guaranteed that London would keep the records "in perpetuity"—Nanker Phelge Music became a potent symbol to the Stones of how Klein had burrowed his way permanently into their

---

* In their subsequent suits against Klein and ABKCO, the Rolling Stones would attempt to void this letter—unsuccessfully.

business. The idea that they could never completely separate from him came as a shock. Allen Klein wasn't their business manager — he was their partner. *Forever.*

"What did he want from us?" Jagger would later ask rhetorically after spending over a decade trying to separate the Stones from Klein. "Apart from the moon, I don't know. He wanted everything. He wanted a hold on us, on our futures."

How quickly Jagger and the others came to this realization is unclear. But the Stones' recording contract with Decca ended August 31, 1970, as did Easton and Oldham's original production deal with the band. Unless the band extended the contract, the Rolling Stones were sole owners of anything they recorded in the future. The last week in July, they informed Klein that they were breaking with him.

Klein had lost the Rolling Stones, but he was eager to impress and take care of the three former Beatles who were still talking to him. John had long been his focus; now he sought to improve the fortunes of Ringo and George as well.

For Ringo, who wanted to expand his acting career, there was a feature role in *Blindman,* the first of three spaghetti Westerns Klein produced with his friend and longtime associate actor Tony Anthony. In the movie, filmed in Spain, Klein made a tongue-in-cheek cameo as a gruff-looking outlaw dynamited into oblivion in the production's opening sequence.

Harrison presented a more complex and idiosyncratic challenge for Klein. The Beatles had left George with issues. The youngest member, he'd been brought into the band specifically as lead guitarist, and John and Paul had never treated him as an equal. In the ensuing years, as he grew as a musician and sought to expand his role to include more vocal features and then his own compositions, he found Lennon and McCartney uninterested. His junior status and their continuing condescension had touched off the incident during the *Get Back* sessions in which he'd walked out and threatened to quit the band. That had been fine with Lennon — he seemed inclined to hire Eric Clapton rather than placate Harrison. When George was treated as an icon and superstar during a stint as a sideman with the American group Delaney and Bonnie, it only reinforced his sense that he didn't have to take any abuse from Paul or John.

Klein was sympathetic to Harrison. As a rule, Lennon and McCartney split singles; if one was the primary author of the A-side, a song by the other became the B-side. Listening to the just-completed *Abbey Road,* Allen found his favorite song on the album was a Harrison composition, "Something." He pushed Lennon to make it the B-side to the album's single "Come Together," and Lennon did; it was only the third Harrison song to appear on a Beatles single. The record was a two-sided hit — "Come Together" reached number one on the U.S. charts and "Something" got to number three — and it became George's only hit as a Beatle.*

Looking forward, Klein was eager for Harrison to succeed as a solo artist. "Allen always gave George a lot of attention," said former ABKCO executive Paul Mozian. Klein was particularly aggressive in negotiating a big promotional budget and a lavish packaging allowance for George's three-record solo album, *All Things Must Pass.* He also recognized that he shouldn't interfere or impose arbitrary cost restrictions on the work. Al Steckler, ABKCO's creative director, functioned as an in-house advocate for the artists and made it a point to turn a blind eye to costs.

Ultimately, the album proved an enormous success for Harrison; its

---

* Breaking with tradition and picking a Harrison song may have been Klein's way of getting under McCartney's skin. If that's what he was trying to do, it apparently worked; some years later, during an appearance on the American television show *Larry King Live,* McCartney repeatedly referred to the Harrison song as "Something in the Way She Moves." The opening line of Harrison's "Something," it was also the title of a song on James Taylor's debut album for Apple, which — whether McCartney intended to do this or not — reinforced suspicions that Harrison had filched at least the inspiration for the song if not the song itself. But then, there was a lot of that going around; the A-side, "Come Together," led to charges that Lennon had lifted that song from Chuck Berry's "You Can't Catch Me." Klein would later say that Lennon, in conversation, was frank about using other people's songs as a jump-off point for compositions and reminisced about how Dick James had even offered him pointers when he was a young songwriter on how to avoid stepping over the line into plagiarism.

lead single, "My Sweet Lord," became a worldwide hit. Most important, it liberated him once and for all from the shadow of Lennon and
McCartney, both in the public eye and his own. When George first
played *All Things Must Pass* for Steckler, the executive was effusive,
predicting it would produce at least three bona fide hits — an assessment that surprised and pleased the musician. "Really? You think so?"
he asked. "They never let me release anything."

Such an improvement in Harrison's self-image pleased Klein. Not
only did it augur well for George's future career, but it fed Allen's own
ego. He liked to think of himself as the Beatles' great defender and
facilitator, believing that he was finding opportunities for them and
helping them in ways no one else could, freeing them to expand their
work and creativity. No doubt they would recognize this and be grateful. But despite the honeymoon his financial know-how provided, that
would not prove to be the case. And Harrison certainly wasn't display-
ing any gratitude.

As Klein recalled, "George once said to me, 'If you think John is
difficult, give me one hit and you'll see what difficult is.' And he was
right."

Despite the handholding he was obliged to do, Klein basked in
his role as Beatles manager, taking a star turn with an expansive and
boastful interview about his intimate relationship with them and his
business acumen in *Playboy*. And while he considered it a matter of
course and validation that he had critics and enemies, he seemed to
have no sense of how precarious his position was. If he remembered
from time to time that there was another man in New York taking responsibility for a Beatle's business, he didn't give it much thought.

John Eastman told his father that something needed to be done if Paul
McCartney was to gain control over his career and financial future.
But the elder attorney wanted no part of a war with Allen Klein. "This
is going to be a dirty battle and you're probably going to lose," he said.

It was a frightening proposition, but Eastman saw little recourse.
He'd talked to Klein about trying to separate McCartney's business,
insisting Paul would be happy to just go his way, but gotten nowhere.

Klein viewed the legal partnership among the four musicians as an insurmountable wall that would take years to dissolve before the assets could be distributed. In the interim, Eastman knew he had a problem. He and Klein had gone at it pretty hard when both were wooing the Beatles, and there was no love or trust between them. Now that Klein was in control, Eastman worried that McCartney would suffer. He also worried about what he didn't know about finances, fearing in particular that Paul might find himself in a lifelong tax hole.

With no chance that Klein would simply let Paul walk away with his 25 percent, Eastman began thinking about a legal remedy. Before long, he hit on a good common-sense argument: the Beatles had had a partnership and its sole purpose was to exploit the Beatles. Now that they'd broken up, the partnership had no purpose.

Eastman began scouting around London for legal representation. What he found didn't cheer him. There were only about twenty-five hundred barristers who could argue in British courts at the time, and the Chancery, where a challenge to the Beatles' partnership would be heard, was rarefied air. With no idea whom to engage, he came up with a very clever strategy: he'd let the British banking establishment tell him whom to hire.

McCartney's accountant, Geoffrey Maitland Smith, opened a checking account for Paul at N. M. Rothschild and Sons with an initial deposit of fifty thousand pounds. When McCartney added an additional hundred thousand, it was enough to catch the eye of Rothschild partner Philip Sherburne, who called John to ask where McCartney wanted his checks sent. Eastman thanked the banker, who was also a tax attorney, and said they were interested in having McCartney's loan stock from Northern Songs handled by the bank. He also wondered if Sherburne wouldn't mind giving them a little advice.

Meeting Sherburne in New York, Eastman outlined McCartney's situation and his own fruitless search for top-notch legal representation in London. Sherburne offered to introduce him to solicitor Martin Lampard. A senior partner at the City powerhouse Ashurst, Morris, Crisp, and Company, Lampard had a style and reputation not unlike Klein's; he was considered a cunning and brilliant strategist and a brawling, unorthodox fighter with a taste for confrontation. He was also Rothschild's go-to lawyer for takeovers.

Huddling with Lampard, Eastman quickly realized that the partnership laws weren't on his side; the Beatles were a corporation and three of the four directors had voted to make Allen Klein their business manager. All Klein had to do to win a case, he feared, was keep the court's focus on that. Since corporate law wasn't with him, McCartney could win only by making a case for equity, the English legal tradition of granting discretionary rulings in the service of a broader justice. That meant only one strategy: painting Klein as an imminent and obvious danger to McCartney's career and financial future and insisting that a court-appointed receiver had to replace Klein in order to protect Paul's interests.

Lampard steered Eastman to barrister David Hirst. Though he'd never tried a commercial case, Hirst had just the kind of background that made him perfect for going after Klein: he specialized in libel suits. Hirst and two junior associates spent six weeks with Eastman in New York, getting a handle on the ins and outs of the music industry and planning their case. Confident the team was ready, Eastman had one more call to make.

Since the public outcry that had met McCartney's announcement that he had quit the Beatles, Paul and Linda had largely been holed up on his farm in Scotland. John Eastman, accompanied by his wife, joined them for a week. Though he'd kept McCartney in the loop, he now had to convince him that the only way to target and hopefully separate himself from Klein was to sue the other Beatles and Apple, demanding that the Beatles' partnership be dissolved. It was a huge step—and enough to give McCartney pause. He'd already been knocked about in the press for breaking up the Beatles; did he really want to sue them?

"Are you sure?" McCartney asked.

"If we don't sue," Eastman told him, "I worry about your partners bankrupting you."

McCartney agreed, but he was nervous. He insisted Eastman go back to London for a week and review the plans again before he made a final decision.

But there was little left to review. McCartney's team knew what to do and how to do it. Klein was going down — and Eastman couldn't wait.

A business meeting of the four Beatles had been slated for January in London, so the others were stunned to receive a letter during Christmas week from McCartney alerting them that he was about to serve papers to dissolve the partnership. The writ itself arrived on New Year's Eve.

"I still cannot understand why Paul acted as he did," a flabbergasted Harrison would tell the Chancery court two months later. Harrison and McCartney had met in New York in November and discussed Paul's continuing unhappiness over Klein's appointment and his own desire to dissolve the Beatles' partnership. George thought the conversation had been amicable and that they'd agreed to discuss the issue with the other ex-Beatles in January. Harrison felt strongly that he, John, and Ringo had the right to appoint Klein as the manager for the Beatles over McCartney's objections. "The reality is we're a partnership," he'd told an interviewer the previous spring. "Like in any other business or group you have a vote and he was outvoted three to one and if he doesn't like it, it's really a pity. We're trying to do what's best for the Beatles as a group or Apple as a company. We're not trying to do what's best for Paul and his in-laws." Harrison also believed that nothing was written in stone — if McCartney was unhappy, they should work something out. But George worried that a hasty dissolution of the partnership could cause large financial problems. "He seemed to think all we had to do was sign a piece of paper." Harrison suggested that all four should discuss it with financial advisers when they got together in January. Since Paul seemed to agree, George "just could not believe it when instead — just before Christmas — I received the letter from Paul's lawyers." Ringo, equally upset at being sued by McCartney, saw the suit as willful and incendiary. "Paul is the greatest bass guitar player in the world," he told the court. "But he is also very determined; he goes on and on to see if he can get his own way . . . I am as shocked and dismayed as George that, after Paul's promises about all of us meeting in January, the solicitor's letter should have been sent on the twenty-first of December and the writ issued on the thirty-first of December. Nothing happened to my knowledge which would have provided Paul with a good reason for going back on the arrangements for the January meeting. My own personal view is that all four of us together, having the opportunity to consult our separate advisers if necessary, could even yet work something out satisfactorily."

In an affidavit filed along with the writ, McCartney cited four motives for his actions: the Beatles had ceased to perform as a group; an unacceptable manager — Klein — had been imposed on him by the others; he feared a continuing business partnership would impinge on his artistic freedom; and financial accounts were not being properly handled. Until the partnership could be dissolved, the action sought the appointment of a receiver. Though Klein was not named as a defendant, he was clearly the impetus for the lawsuit and its primary target.

He was also the person who would have to craft and oversee the response. Few in the music business relished a court case as much as Klein — Keith Richards accurately pegged Allen as a "lawyer manqué" — and he would have taken on the role under any circumstances. But since Eastman and McCartney were clearly building a case on impugning his reputation, he was doubly motivated. In fact, the McCartney team's strategy would prove brilliant.

Anticipating McCartney's barristers would wave the *Sunday Times* article planted by Triumph that portrayed him as "The Toughest Wheeler-Dealer in the Pop Jungle" — an article that had upset Klein enough to make him sue for a retraction — and expecting a rehash of the Cameo-Parkway stock issues that Eastman had previously used to tar him with the other Beatles, Klein focused on defending himself. But his weapons were limited. He wasn't a named defendant so he couldn't give testimony, be cross-examined, or provide direct answers to anything McCartney's representatives said in court. His only tools were an affidavit — and he offered an exhaustive, 142-paragraph filing that attempted to anticipate every avenue of personal and professional attack — and the overall defense strategy mounted by the Beatles' attorneys. Klein was determined to counter what he perceived as slander and give the Chancery judge voluminous proof that he had rescued the Beatles from financial disaster.

It was a mistake born of pride.

McCartney and Eastman's lawyers had recognized that corporate law was not on their side; Harrison had accurately observed that Apple was a partnership and McCartney was just an aggrieved minority voter and should get over it. The proper response was far simpler than the one Klein gave; the Beatles' team should offer as little information to McCartney as possible and bludgeon him over and over again with the law on corporate partnerships until the judge would be hard-pressed to rule any other way.

Instead, Klein offered a personal and professional defense so vigorous and wide-ranging that it covered virtually every aspect of the Beatles' business. Indeed, Eastman would later admit that one of the chief complaints offered in court by McCartney's barrister, David Hirst — that Klein's commission had been revised and adjusted by the others without McCartney's knowledge or consent — wasn't even known to McCartney's team before it was found as a footnote in an accountant's report that Klein gave them. Said Eastman: "I wouldn't have even replied to our complaint except to say, 'Seventy-five percent in the partnership want this arrangement — so this is ridiculous!'"

McCartney and Klein attended all eleven days of the March trial; the three Beatles who were the actual defendants weren't there. But their affidavits gave credence to McCartney's claims by answering them — he'd touched some nerves. Lennon, in particular, was angry at McCartney's contention that the Beatles' partnership hampered his artistic freedom. "We always thought of ourselves as Beatles whether we recorded singly or in twos or threes . . . I have always thought of the partnership agreement as an organization of our business affairs drawn up by lawyers and accountants. I have never thought of it as a document which tells us 'You have got to do this, that or the other kind of work as a group.'"

As to McCartney's charge that financial accounts weren't being handled in a proper or timely manner, Lennon suggested that Eastman's continuous objections and obstructions were actually the culprit. And as far as Lennon was concerned, McCartney had accepted Klein, even if he didn't like him; the proof was that he'd asked Allen to come to London and sort out the Northern Songs situation. Besides, there were already controls in place — as McCartney knew, Klein's deal could be terminated annually with a month's notice. The whole case was just more of what Lennon termed "the Eastmans-Klein power struggle."

McCartney's other complaints were both general and specific. He reiterated in his affidavit how his work had been abused and altered against his will with Spector's production on "The Long and Winding Road" and how Klein and the others had tried to sabotage the release of his first solo album.* But mostly he was worried about Klein co-opting his career and his future through self-serving and shoddy management. As proof of how worried he was, he had instructed EMI Records not to pay his royalties through Apple but to hold them until a way could be found for the money not to pass through Klein's hands. Klein, aggressively maintaining that McCartney had no right to ignore his own relationship with Apple, took a commission on the record anyhow from other EMI payments.

Being portrayed as untrustworthy and unprofessional pressed all of Klein's buttons. He prepared a defense based on showing just the opposite, that he had done an exceptional job of sorting through a disastrous financial mess. "Mr. Epstein was not a businessman," Morris Finer, the representative for the three Beatles, told the court. "They inherited a mass of trouble when he died, and that trouble increased over the following two years. It is plain from the evidence, and no one disputes it, that their situation in 1969 was desperate. They were in-

---

* In subsequent years he would back off this charge and say he had been upset and "a little silly."

solvent. All that vast sum of money had flowed through their hands
like sand. That was the position in 1969. That is not Mr. Klein's fault,
whatever one says about Mr. Klein. This is why my clients are fighting
so hard to make sure that he is not thrown out. He has rescued them."
To bolster the case, Finer submitted extensive documentation meant
to demonstrate that Klein had greatly improved the Beatles' financial
strength and solvency. Yet it was quickly apparent that none of that
mattered. On the first morning of testimony, Hirst surprised Klein and
Finer by submitting a copy of a U.S. federal court's recent conviction of
Klein — handed up by a New York jury only the previous month — on
ten counts of failing to file tax forms in a timely manner.

The U.S. court case proved a huge embarrassment for Klein, and
it was his own fault. It had grown out of the incident years earlier in
which Klein had petulantly kept an IRS auditor waiting outside his office for hours and then refused to see him. It was nothing more than
Klein being willful and intransigent; what should have been settled in
a fifteen-minute meeting instead became a senseless and years-long
battle of wills between the U.S. government and Klein, who'd already
paid the taxes and appeared to take umbrage at the notion that the IRS
could break his chops and fine him over late paperwork. It was strange
behavior for an accountant but vintage Klein: challenged over virtually anything, he'd rather fight than settle, certain he'd figure out how
to get his way eventually. Attorneys who worked with him frequently
found that Klein was more eager to try cases than they were and that
he would ignore warnings against wasting money on litigation. "Allen
did a lot of things based on principle," said attorney Donald Zakarin,
who represented him in several cases. "He didn't necessarily do things
based on pure dollars and cents. Also, he liked litigation. He liked the
sport of it." That sport was about to cost Klein his reputation.

Hirst was extremely well prepared, and he knew the tics of the judge,
the Right Honorable Lord Justice Stamp, including that he was a man
of habit who recessed for lunch every day at precisely 1:00 p.m. Hirst
introduced news of Klein's recent conviction, along with documentation, at 12:55. The Beatles' counsel, unaware of Klein's American case,

had no immediate rejoinder. Since Finer couldn't explain that it resulted from a silly skirmish over paperwork and that painting Klein as a tax cheat was inaccurate, Stamp had his entire lunch hour to consider whether he could afford to ignore McCartney's plea that the court use its equity to protect him from a toothy New York shark. If Hirst had made a mountain out of a molehill, Klein had only himself to blame for kicking up dirt in the first place.

The impact of this legal ambush was obvious to Eastman.

"Did we just win this case?" he asked Hirst over lunch.

The barrister smiled. "There's about three weeks left," he replied. "But you can go home now if you'd like."

Over the course of the next two weeks, Justice Stamp would prove consistently unmoved by the mountain of documentation offered on the defendants' behalf. It didn't seem to matter how much Klein had improved the Beatles' finances or that the only financial issues McCartney's attorneys could raise had to do with preexisting tax problems. Stamp seemed particularly keen on Hirst's testimony regarding how Klein's commission arrangement had been revised and the attendant and unsubstantiated suggestion that Klein had been more concerned with his own fee than with the Beatles' taxes; it was immaterial that McCartney had voluntarily declined to deal with Klein.

Tipping his hand on the final day of testimony, Stamp wondered aloud if appointing a receiver might satisfy both sides: McCartney could hire a submanager to report to the receiver while the other Beatles could continue to employ Klein in the same capacity. The subsequent ruling, although seemingly Solomonic in its suggestion of a compromise, was actually a complete victory for McCartney: all the Beatles' business would be handled by the receiver, their finances tied up and held in his care until they came to some agreement among themselves regarding the dissolution of the partnership. Klein's work with Lennon, Harrison, and Starr would now encompass only their post-Beatles careers. In his remarks from the bench, Justice Stamp repeatedly said he passed no judgment on Klein's character — words that stood in stark contrast to his actions.

It was a public shellacking. The great irony was that Klein *had* bailed the Beatles out of a financial hole at Apple and had improved the contracts and futures of all of them, McCartney included. Call it cosmic payback; if Klein appeared guilty of anything, it was of bringing Allen Klein's formidable, messy reputation into the Beatles — of being the advocate that John Lennon wanted and the devil that Paul McCartney wouldn't abide.

The only positive was that Klein's three Beatles remained steadfast in their support. If anything, they were angrier than ever at McCartney. They saw his action as vengeful and unnecessary, the court's decision a repudiation of common sense and corporate law. They hadn't heard anything to change their opinion about Klein and wanted to move forward with him.

Across the aisle it proved a career-making victory for John Eastman. No one in the music business, including his own father, had given him odds against Klein. "The idea of John Eastman going up against Allen — it was a baby against a tumulter," said Seider. In the coming years Eastman would count David Bowie, Tennessee Williams, Andrew Lloyd Webber, and Billy Joel among his clients. But none would prove more important than Paul McCartney, who, with the help of Eastman and Eastman, built a significant music-publishing company, MPL Communications. Along with Paul's own post-Beatles compositions, the company bought a broad range of valuable work by Buddy Holly, Harold Arlen, Frank Loesser, Jelly Roll Morton, Hoagy Carmichael, Carl Perkins, and Louis Jordan, among others. It also administers songs from numerous Broadway shows, including *Hello, Dolly!, Annie, Grease,* and *A Chorus Line.* In the future, McCartney would emerge as the most financially successful of the former Beatles.

Whatever credit he deserved for his own intelligence and success in beating Klein, John Eastman knew he'd gotten lucky. Some years later, he ran into Allen in the first-class cabin of a flight, and John made it a point to show his one-time adversary that he bore him no lingering personal animosity. Quite the contrary. "You made my whole career," Eastman told Klein. "It was like bringing down a blimp with a twenty-two."

McCartney would not be as happy or gracious a winner. Three years after the Chancery ruled in his favor, McCartney was asked about Klein. "Even a murderer has a great line in his own defense," he said. "But he's nothing more than a trained New York crook. My back was against the wall. I'm not proud of it. But it had to be done." Nearly forty years later, he was still battling Klein, at least in his mind. Asked about Klein in a television interview with David Frost, he mimicked delivering a roundhouse punch. The winner by knockout.

## 12

## SOME TIME IN NEW YORK CITY

IN THE SPRING OF 1971 George Harrison was spending much of his time in Los Angeles, partly to work on the soundtrack to a film about his friend and mentor the legendary Bengali musician Ravi Shankar. During the sessions, Ravi told George of his concerns over what was shaping up to be a catastrophe in the newly declared country of Bangladesh, where the rebellion against Pakistan had unleashed wholesale slaughter and privations throughout an area already ravaged by a deadly cyclone and subsequent widespread migrations. When Shankar said he hoped to raise funds and awareness through a concert, Harrison volunteered not just to participate but to spearhead it and use his celebrity as a former Beatle to attract publicity and support.

Hiring Jonathan Taplin, the former road manager for Dylan and the Band, as his stage manager and relying on Klein for help with nearly everything else, Harrison organized what would come to be called the Concert for Bangladesh virtually overnight. Steve Leber, at the William Morris Agency, booked New York's Madison Square Garden for afternoon and evening shows on July 31. With an eye to alleviating the human catastrophe, they moved quickly; the concert was held five weeks after Harrison spoke with Shankar.

Writing and recording the song "Bangladesh" in Los Angeles, Harrison assembled a backing group including Leon Russell, Jim Keltner, Klaus Voormann, Billy Preston, and Jim Horn that would later provide the nucleus for the concert, which would be given by, simply, "George Harrison and Friends."

Whom those friends would encompass and whether they would include the other Beatles became that summer's hot topic among fans. Though mum in public, Harrison had already invited the then-reclusive Bob Dylan, who had performed only a handful of shows in the preceding five years and none since the Isle of Wight Festival in 1969. Klein was convinced Dylan wouldn't appear, but Harrison was confident that he would. Ringo Starr, Eric Clapton, and the group Badfinger were also added to the band, but Harrison rebuffed calls from other artists looking to perform at the show, including the Rolling Stones and Crosby, Stills, and Nash. Invitations were, however, extended to both McCartney and Lennon. "He wanted the Beatles and he wanted Dylan and he figured, 'What more do you need?'" said ABKCO's Al Steckler. While McCartney demurred, Lennon — then in New York — initially agreed and watched a rehearsal session with Klein, who had developed bursitis in his heel and was hobbling around the hall on crutches. But when Lennon realized Harrison didn't want Yoko Ono in his show, he knew he couldn't perform. John's decision not to insist on including her reportedly infuriated Ono, who very much wanted to be part of the event, and led to a bitter fight between them punctuated by the sound of breaking furniture. Lennon ended the fight by leaving unexpectedly for Paris.

Klein, who appreciated that Harrison was angling to have the Beatles, not just John and Yoko, steered clear of the whole controversy: "That was also the beginning of the end for me with Yoko," with whom he'd gotten along well until then, he said. He added with a laugh, "I just didn't push for her." Klein believed that Lennon expected Ono to come after him in Paris to settle their differences. Instead, she remained in New York, and he came back to her. "That's when I realized that he needed her more than she needed him."

With the question of a Beatles reunion answered with an emphatic no, the biggest artistic question marks became Clapton and Dylan. The impenetrable Dylan appeared to be unsure as to whether he would really go through with the show, while the English guitarist was just a mess, so strung out on heroin that he missed his flight to New York. Once Clapton actually arrived, he could barely play. Klein's nephew Michael Kramer was dispatched to a rock 'n' roll–friendly doctor to score enough methadone to get the guitarist through the shows.

High and tired, Kramer got back to the rehearsal at 3:00 a.m. in time to see Harrison and Dylan running through tunes, first one playing a song, then the other. Watching long-haired laborers in overalls hustling to complete the stage, the stoned Kramer had a cosmic epiphany about how much the Beatles had changed the world. He couldn't resist sharing it.

"Look at their *hair*," he said to Harrison. "Look at the *clothes*. Everybody dresses like this because of *you*, man! Doesn't that flip you out?"

"No."

Michael's uncle Allen seemed to be having his own epiphany — albeit of a more grounded and lucrative variety — and this one had to do with Bob Dylan. Surprised to see him building up to a public return, Klein found himself wondering if the man couldn't use a new manager, and he urged Phil Spector, who was supervising the recording of the concert for release as an album, to buttonhole Dylan and encourage the singer to let Klein handle his affairs. Believing that Dylan's caustic song "Positively Fourth Street" was about his last manager, Albert Grossman, Allen pressed Dylan to include the song in his set list — seemingly in hopes of having Dylan publicly rebuke Grossman or draw his own positive comparison between the two handlers. When Dylan said he didn't want to play the song, Klein instructed his promotion man, Pete Bennett, to suggest it again later when he drove Dylan home. But if Dylan even registered Klein's efforts to entice him, he never rose to the bait.

The two Madison Square Garden shows were guaranteed sellouts and at ten dollars a ticket would net a gate of $243,418.50, all of which would be donated to the U.S. Fund for UNICEF within two weeks of the concerts. In keeping with the goal of fundraising, ABKCO was unusually stingy with free tickets; a hundred tickets were given to Bennett to distribute to radio stations and there was a small consignment for William Morris, but everyone else had to pay. Harrison had higher ambitions than giving a concert; he wanted to raise more money and awareness by filming the show for theatrical release and recording it for an album. Klein had to hustle to make those things happen.

Naturally, the record would go through Capitol in the United States, where Harrison, the Beatles, and Apple Records were contracted. But Klein told Capitol chairman Bhaskar Menon that since all artist royalties were going to charity, he expected the record company to bite the bullet and give them an extraordinary cut. For *The Concert for Bangladesh,* a multi-record set that would list for $12.98, Klein insisted Harrison and his charity had to have 50 percent of the ten-dollar wholesale price — an unheard-of royalty of five dollars an album. The Indian-born Menon may have been particularly sensitive to the pressing need for aid to Bangladesh; in any event, he agreed. Though few albums would have the charitable aims of *The Concert for Bangladesh,* Klein's success in getting such a high rate sent a message that was heard loud and clear by artists and other managers: there was a lot more room to negotiate on price than record companies wanted to admit. Over the next decade, artists' royalty rates would rise steeply.

The only seeming hitch for clearing the album was that Dylan was signed to Columbia, not Capitol, and that label wasn't about to let him go without recompense — Beatle charity and starving Bangladeshis notwithstanding. Ultimately, Klein arranged for Columbia to manufacture the cassette-tape version of the album in return for its clearing Dylan's participation.

*The Concert for Bangladesh* proved an enormous success, critically and artistically. Along with raising funds and awareness about the desperate human crisis, it became a benchmark and model for future popular-arts events of charity and conscience. The concert — coupled with the success of Harrison's *All Things Must Pass* — made George the most commercially and artistically successful of the solo Beatles at that point.

While the artists donated their time and performances, not every-thing and everybody was free. Ravi Shankar, the impetus for Harri-son's involvement, insisted on being paid for his appearance, and song-writers did not donate their royalties. "I try so hard to be the person I'm not," an evidently torn Harrison told Steckler. "I'm keeping the publishing on 'Bangladesh.'" Phil Spector, who produced the concert album with Harrison, was paid $50,000.

The film version, owned by Apple and distributed by Twentieth Century Fox, would prove a success — although a somewhat unlikely one. Acting as coproducer, Klein once again hired his go-to director Saul Swimmer, who had handled *Let It Be* and *Mrs. Brown, You've Got a Lovely Daughter.* Swimmer delivered mixed results. Though failing to turn the camera on the audience — necessitating the subsequent photographing of the crowd at an unrelated Madison Square Garden concert — Swimmer did a very good job of shooting the performances themselves. The sound, however, was mismanaged. For the first show, in the afternoon, the stage was miked for filming. As a result, the sound quality for the audience and the recording suffered. For the evening, the situation was reversed, meaning the second audio recording would become the concert album and the film would subsequently need to be synced to that soundtrack, a laborious job.

When Dylan seemed unsure about granting approval for the inclu-sion of his performance in the movie, Klein saw it as an opportunity to impress him. He ordered a special 70-millimeter print of the film and hired the Ziegfeld Theater in Manhattan for a private screening. Dylan liked what he saw and signed on.

From start to finish, *The Concert for Bangladesh* was an on-the-fly triumph, going from conception to performance to worldwide recog-nition in a few months. Or, rather, it was a triumph with one glaring exception: though the film and album raised more than fifteen million dollars through sales, it would take over a decade for the lion's share of that money to be disbursed.

Harrison didn't pick a charitable organization to receive the funds until after the concert. And though he then made his choice promptly, selecting the U.S. Fund for UNICEF over the Red Cross and other organizations in a matter of days, the fact that the project wasn't initially constituted as a dedicated charity, that UNICEF wasn't involved in the staging of the show and that the money was funneled through Apple, led the IRS to insist the funds were actually taxable income. As a result, more than ten million dollars was held back while the issue was argued.

As an artist, Harrison couldn't reasonably have been expected to anticipate this problem. The finer points of tax liability, however, is precisely the kind of knowledge a business manager is expected to have — or acquire. Yet Klein would prove surprisingly unprepared.

A month after the Concert for Bangladesh, John Lennon and Yoko Ono moved to New York City. Living at first at the St. Regis Hotel, the couple jumped into America with both feet: Lennon released what would prove his most successful solo album, *Imagine,* just ten days after arriving.

Coming so closely on the heels of the spring defeat in the McCartney case, the success of both Harrison's Madison Square Garden concerts and *Imagine,* which sold two million copies in the U.S., were much-needed boosts for Klein. To hell with McCartney. "My Sweet Lord," released as a single by Harrison nine months earlier, was an enormous worldwide hit, well on its way to being the most performed song of 1971, and now Lennon was about to top the American charts. Klein had the Beatles that mattered.

He also had what he most desired: the imprimatur and validation of John Lennon. As far as John was concerned, Klein was real—"Allen's human, whereas Eastman and all them other people are automatons," he told an interviewer the week he arrived in New York—and Klein reinforced John's sense of their camaraderie by ferrying him and Yoko out to Newark in a limousine to show them the orphanage and the streets and playgrounds where he'd grown up.

John, Yoko, and Allen were an unlikely trio. Whatever affinity Lennon felt for Klein's working-class roots, they lived in very different worlds. "There were fundamental levels on which they couldn't communicate," said Dan Richter, who worked for John and Yoko and dealt frequently with ABKCO. He recalled visiting the office with John and Yoko to discuss a proposal from Jonas Mekas to mount a festival of their films only to have Klein unable to talk about anything other than the expensive custom molding a carpenter had just installed in his office. Still, if Klein sometimes left John and Yoko at a loss, they were delighted to have found him. "John and Yoko were not money people at all and he was very excited about Allen for the first year or two. Allen was a hard hitter who played hardball and I never felt he was dishonest."

Allen was pleased that his opinion mattered to John, and he made a habit of speaking plainly and without deference to him. A few months before Lennon moved to New York, Klein had visited John's hotel room and listened as Lennon sat in bed with Ono and strummed an unrecorded older composition, "On the Road to Marrakesh," that he'd written in India in 1966. When John sang the song's second line, "I was dreaming more or less," Klein made a face.

"That's just terrible," he said bluntly. He called the line tacky and dated and suggested it wasn't up to John's current standards.

"Well," Lennon shot back, "maybe you can give it to Bobby Vinton."

But the next day when Klein visited the couple again, Lennon showed that he'd taken his advice. "I was dreaming of the past," he sang, "and my heart was beating very fast." Overnight he had updated the idea and completely rewritten the song as "Jealous Guy."

As he had from the beginning, Klein remained attentive to Ono, showing her respect as both an artist and Lennon's full partner. Yoko was locked in a bizarre and emotionally taxing custody battle for her young daughter, Kyoko, with her previous husband, photographer and aspiring filmmaker Tony Cox. Klein had traveled with the couple as they pursued Kyoko to the Spanish island of Majorca, where Cox was studying mysticism; more recently, Ono and Lennon had gone to the Virgin Islands where a judge had awarded Yoko custody of the girl, whereupon Cox disappeared with her. Later, Cox and his current wife, Melinda Kendall, were found to be living in Houston, and Michael

Kramer would accompany John and Yoko in a vain pursuit through Texas. At that point, Cox, Kendall, and Kyoko simply vanished, leaving Yoko distraught.*

Ono was an enigma to Beatles fans — what, for example, were those who came to see John perform with the Plastic Ono Band in Toronto supposed to make of Yoko caterwauling from inside a white body bag? But that was precisely the point to Ono, who was a central figure in the neo-Dada Fluxus movement begun by composer John Cage, her friend and mentor. And although Fluxus existed on the avant-garde fringe a million miles from Beatlemania, she was established and well regarded in that world before she met Lennon. "The Beatles were fantastic," said the cellist and performance artist Charlotte Moorman, who had been Ono's roommate and the performer in Yoko's controversial *Cut Piece*, in which the audience was invited to scissor away her clothing, and had gained notoriety herself as "the topless cellist" arrested for performing Nam June Paik's *Opera Sextronique* at New York's Film-Makers Ciné-mathèque in 1967. "But a hundred years from now, it's Yoko Ono the world's going to remember, and not John Lennon or the Beatles."

Professionally, Yoko was eager to have her work seen. Jim Harithas, director of the Everson Museum of Art in Syracuse, New York, met Ono and Lennon at a gallery in New York and offered to turn the entire museum over to her for a monthlong show. "Very few women were getting shows and I thought she was a significant member of a very important movement," he said. Dubbed *This Is Not Here*, the show was punctuated by Ono's subtle and self-deprecating sense of humor (tagged a conceptual artist, she preferred the shortened term *con artist*). The exhibit featured her installations and pieces as well as screenings of her films, many codirected with Lennon, such as *Fly*, a twenty-five-minute short depicting the film's star crawling on a naked

---

* Fourteen years later, Cox finally surfaced and said that he and his family had joined a charismatic Christian cult in Los Angeles, the Church of the Living Word. He added that Kyoko had changed her name to guard her privacy and did not wish to have a relationship with her mother. For details, see Jim Calio, "Yoko Ono's Ex-Husband, Tony Cox, Reveals His Strange Life Since Fleeing with Their Daughter 14 Years Ago," *People*, February 3, 1986.

woman; *Erection,* a punning time-lapse record of a construction site; and *Up Your Legs Forever,* a collection of bare-legged portraits panning from the toes to the waists of approximately three hundred well-known men, including composer Cage, author Tom Wolfe, folksinger Utah Phillips, actor George Segal, music journalist Al Aronowitz, TV host Dick Cavett, filmmakers Jonas Mekas and D. A. Pennebaker, *Village Voice* columnist Howard Smith, painters Larry Rivers, Peter Max, Robert Rauschenberg, and Jasper Johns, *Rolling Stone* publisher Jann Wenner, and Allen Klein. Also featured in the exhibit was a gallery of pieces solicited from like-minded artists; Andy Warhol contributed a video, Frank Zappa displayed the Volkswagen that Ono had filled with water, and Phil Spector donated a Beatles souvenir cup on which Paul McCartney's image had been crossed out.

Although the Everson wasn't exactly the Prado, it was a major event for Syracuse — and for Ono and Lennon. The show opened on October 9, John's thirty-first birthday, and the couple reportedly harbored hopes that a private preshow birthday party might be the occasion of a Beatles reunion, which, if nothing else, signaled that Ono wasn't a factor in their dissolution. "Definitely, the idea was there," Harithas said. "I think they tried to get them all." In the end, Ringo was the only other Beatle to make the trip, and he joined Lennon and Ono at the Syracuse Hotel for a birthday party that also included Phil Spector, Allen Ginsberg, and Abbie Hoffman. Hoping to tie the event to their bed-ins and agitation for peace, Lennon had ABKCO create souvenirs with the slogan *War Is Over!* "John said, 'We need to bring things to Syracuse we can sell,'" recalled Steckler. "'Make up T-shirts and towels — best quality you can get.' So thousands were made — and hundreds sold. The rest were just dumped." It wasn't unusual for Ono and Lennon to spend money on projects they never finished. As part of the move to New York, Lennon had the recording studio at his English home in Ascot disassembled and shipped to him. It sat unclaimed and ultimately rusted at Kennedy Airport.

Back in Manhattan, Klein continued to show his support and woo Ono. When art dealer Ivan Karp at the OK Harris gallery in SoHo mounted an auction of Yoko's work, Allen sent his assistant Paul Mozian with instructions to bid up the prices. "I bid so high we had to buy some things," Mozian said. At first, Klein was annoyed—"I didn't tell you to *buy* things!" he thundered—but when Yoko later saw her pieces hanging in ABKCO's offices, she was very pleased, and Paul was off the hook.

Lennon's intense relationship with his wife—they were virtually inseparable—was a subject of fascination around the office. And because John was open and candid, people felt they could ask him very personal questions. On one occasion, Jackie Kennedy, her sister Lee Radziwill, and John and Caroline Kennedy had come by to watch a recording session, and Yoko had subsequently left with them, so Al Steckler found himself alone in the studio with Lennon. He couldn't resist the opportunity.

"You're with Yoko twenty-four/seven," Steckler said. "How do you manage that?"

"She makes me think," Lennon said. "I'm always thinking when she's with me."

When John and Yoko moved out of the St. Regis Hotel and into an apartment on Bank Street in the West Village that they'd sublet from Joe Butler, the drummer for the Lovin' Spoonful, Michael Kramer was a frequent guest.

"I always had really good pot," Kramer said, "and I'd get a call around four p.m. from Yoko, which was about when they woke up, asking me to come down to the house to see them. Meaning, 'Come get us high.'" Arriving one afternoon, he was surprised to find Yoko on her way out.

As Kramer sat on the bed and smoked dope with Lennon, his curiosity got the better of him. "I had to ask the Barbara Walters question," he said. "'Why Yoko?'"

Lennon was surprised. "What do you mean?" he asked.

"John," Michael said, "you could have any woman in the world. Why her?"

Lennon shook his head. "Once," he said. "I can have any woman once. After you fuck them you're not a Beatle anymore."

Nonetheless, Lennon didn't always acquiesce to Ono's wishes, as his

# Something's New

- This unit is shipped in an Energy Saver mode per government regulations.
- ***The unit will turn off when the set temperature is reached and will then automatically cycle on and off to maintain the desired room temperature.***
- This will save you energy and also money!
- We recommend leaving the unit in the Energy Saver mode, however please select the "mode" button to change the setting.
- <u>Consult the use and care guide for a complete description of the air conditioner's features.</u>

refusal to appear with her at the Concert for Bangladesh had shown. One afternoon when Yoko and Lennon were at the ABKCO offices, Harrison appeared, and the two former band mates were pleasantly surprised by the coincidence and glad to see each other. Noticing Harrison had a guitar with him, Lennon grabbed one of the instruments he kept in the office, and the two began to play together. When Yoko tried to join in and sing along, John asked her to stop. When she didn't, he picked her up bodily and carried her out of the room.

Lennon and Ono's private life could be unorthodox (during a period when John and Yoko were living apart, an ABKCO receptionist, May Pang, became Lennon's Ono-sanctioned concubine), but Klein's private life might have had even Lennon and Ono scratching their heads. Though married and unwilling to get a divorce, Klein was obviously romantically involved with one of his employees, Iris Keitel. The two couples were frequently together for both business and socializing. One evening they went out to dinner, then returned to Keitel's apartment in midtown. After a few minutes, there was a knock at the door; it was Allen's wife, Betty. Sensing a scene they wanted no part of, John and Yoko excused themselves, went into Iris's bedroom, and closed the door. But Allen did them one better: he simply left, leaving his wife and mistress to yell at each other with John and Yoko trapped in the bedroom.

One Saturday night Kramer took Lennon to the Elgin Theater for the midnight screening of *El Topo,* an underground psychedelic spaghetti Western from South America. Lennon loved it and raved about the film to Klein. Allen decided to buy the film and put it in general distribution.

"Why is Klein interested?" asked ABKCO attorney Harold Seider. "Because John loved it. Klein is a great panderer to the artist. A terrific salesman. When we were negotiating [for the film], Allen said, 'I want to pay top dollar.' So we overpaid."

Klein did more than that; he produced and financed Chilean director Alejandro Jodorowsky's next film, *The Holy Mountain.* A drugged-out Dadaist fantasy revolving around a Christ-like figure whose excrement could be turned into gold, the visually overloaded picture cemented Jodorowsky's reputation as the enfant terrible of the cinematic avant-garde.

Klein, always interested in being in the movie business, began to look at arthouse films. In 1973, he would acquire the American rights to *La Grande Bouffe,* a scatological farce concerning four friends who eat themselves to death.* Initially, Jodorowsky and Klein got along famously. ABKCO sent the director a plane ticket so he could come to New York and attend the Concert for Bangladesh. When Jodorowsky arrived at Kennedy Airport, there was a limousine waiting, and, he recalled, a beautiful sari-wrapped woman in the back seat. "Of course I fucked her," the octogenarian surrealist said wistfully. But the relationship with Klein turned acrimonious with the next project. Klein wanted him to film the sadomasochistic bestseller *The Story of O.* Jodorowsky took Klein's money, then announced he wasn't a pornographer and wouldn't make the movie. Furious at being played, Klein yanked both *El Topo* and *The Holy Mountain* from distribution. Neither film would be shown again for over twenty years.

Though he was eager to spend ABKCO's money on *El Topo* and other projects to impress Lennon, Klein worried about the three Beatles' finances. With the appointment of a receiver by the British court, Apple's income from the Beatles no longer passed through ABKCO. Until a settlement on the dissolution of the partnership could be reached, the Beatles received a limited monthly stipend. In the interim, Klein advanced the three Beatles large sums of money — ultimately more than a million dollars — as loans. He was particularly concerned about Lennon and Ono. "I don't know what I'm going to do," he told Steckler. "Yoko's spending a fortune on these projects and John doesn't really have it."

The ABKCO creative director was well aware of Ono's artistic and financial habits. In the last week of November, he'd received an angry call from a director at the Museum of Modern Art.

---

* Klein duplicated the dishes from the film's feast at an opening-night party at the Four Seasons restaurant.

"What's wrong with you people?" the incensed official asked.

"What are you talking about?" Steckler said.

"There's an ad in today's *New York Times* for a Yoko Ono exhibit at MoMA. Only there isn't any."

Steckler quickly dialed Yoko, who told him that there was, indeed, a MoMA show. "It's in my head," she said.

"Well," Steckler said, "MoMA is pretty upset."

"They shouldn't be. It's just a conceptual act."

Steckler called the museum to explain. "Well," the director said, "what about the calendar? People are asking us for it." The newspaper ad had said a one-dollar calendar "filled with photographs from the event itself" was for sale in conjunction with the exhibit.

Steckler headed over to the Bank Street apartment and found Yoko eager to make good on the ad. "We'll make a calendar," she said. Throwing herself into the project, she hired a London fashion photographer and had ABKCO fly him to New York on a first-class ticket and put him up at the Plaza Hotel. Two weeks later, when Steckler received the results, he discovered the photographer had spent the entire time in New York taking pictures of door locks — perhaps a sly comment by Ono on the museum's inaccessibility to her as a venue. The photos were taken to Queens Litho, the printer ABKCO used for record jackets. Each one-dollar calendar cost eight dollars to produce.

In his single-minded pursuit of the Beatles, Klein had given the Rolling Stones short shrift. Whether it was irony or payback, his split with the Stones was proving as time-consuming as managing them.

Initially frosty to each other — the Stones had simply informed ABKCO by letter in the summer of 1970 that they would no longer be working with the company — Klein and the band had nonetheless continued to deal with business issues as they came up. Most notably, the band still owed at least one album to London Records, even though Jagger had already made a deal sans Klein for their own label through Atlantic. ABKCO's creative director, Al Steckler, suggested they fulfill the old contract with a two-record anthology. "I wanted to put together something that was a history, not just singles," he said, "and Allen said, 'Speak to Jagger.'" The result, *Hot Rocks,* would become one of the Stones' bestsellers.

It would also turn out to be a bone of contention. *Hot Rocks* was released by London for Christmas 1971, more than six months after Rolling Stones Records debuted with *Sticky Fingers,* and ABKCO soon found it had unexpected competition when the Stones, via Atlantic, pressed up their own copies of *Hot Rocks.* ABKCO quickly sought a preliminary injunction barring Atlantic from selling the album.

Over the previous months, the Stones had grown far more aggrieved and aggressive regarding Klein. Nearly a year after terminating their relationship with him, they sued Klein over the Nanker Phelge agreements. Three months later, in October 1971, they also sought to break their publishing contracts with ABKCO. "There was no rancor before that," said Kramer. "They signed with Atlantic and then started questioning the validity of the old artist agreement with Andrew Oldham that Allen bought."

Though the Rolling Stones were not a party to ABKCO's *Hot Rocks* suit against Atlantic Records, the same lawyers who were representing the group against ABKCO, Allen Arrow and his litigation specialist, Peter Parcher, were defending Atlantic. In this case, Klein's selection of attorney Max Freund to represent ABKCO proved fortuitous: he and the trial judge, Jacob Markowitz, had attended Harvard Law School together.

The hearings were brief and almost comical. During oral arguments on extending the temporary order restraining the Stones from selling their illicit version of *Hot Rocks,* Markowitz ruled that Atlantic was enjoined from manufacturing until a final decision was made, at which point a junior associate working on the case for Atlantic asked if that meant the company could sell what it had already manufactured. The judge promptly slammed that door shut: Atlantic was not to manufacture, sell, or distribute the record.

A few weeks later, Klein happened to run into Arrow at a Manhattan movie theater. "You know, Allen," the Stones' attorney said, "one good settlement is worth a thousand lawsuits." The *Hot Rocks* case was quickly dispatched — ABKCO got to purchase at cost whatever Atlantic had manufactured — and discussions to settle the suit brought against ABKCO by the Stones began in February in bungalow 6 of the Beverly Hills Hotel. On one side of the table, the Rolling Stones were represented by Prince Rupert Loewenstein and Arrow; on the other, attorney Alan Kahn had just replaced Harold Seider as ABKCO's in-house attorney, and he was assisted by Kramer, who was still in law school. Unbeknownst to the Stones' team, Klein was actually in the bedroom of the bungalow, listening through the door. He quickly realized Loewenstein was still trying to ascertain the extent of ABKCO's relationship with the Stones; the banker clearly feared making a settlement and finding out later that he'd been unaware of the full scope of material and rights involved.

As discussions continued throughout the spring it also became apparent that whatever the Stones had said and would later say regarding Nanker Phelge and the notion that they'd been hoodwinked, Loewenstein was simply on a mission to get as much money out of Klein as he could, as soon as he could. The real issue was that the Stones had already earned $2 million in royalties *over* the $1.2 million guarantee, but Klein was entitled to hold the money back for another fifteen years, ostensibly for tax purposes but also because it gave him the chance to play with someone else's money. The Stones had decided to move to France and take advantage of the drop-out year available under British tax law, and they were eager to collect as much income during that time as they could. By deducting money Klein had already advanced to the Stones as "loans," both sides soon agreed that the band would receive $1.2 million as a settlement of all American record royalties earned up to that point. Jagger and Richards dropped the challenge to ABKCO's publishing rights, and the band pledged not to rerecord any songs they'd cut for Decca for at least five years, essentially a ban on live albums, so as not to dilute the value of the Stones albums ABKCO manufactured. In May, a deal was signed at the Manhattan offices of the Stones' lawyers and celebrated with a party filmed by Robert Frank, who was making the documentary *Cocksucker Blues*. Both Loewenstein and Kramer characterized the celebration as wild and orgiastic. All was settled.

But not for long.

George Harrison's success produced two surprising and unwelcome results for Klein. Convinced he'd been an effective and eager advocate for Harrison—the formerly junior Beatle was now a huge artistic and commercial power in his own right—Klein was shocked to discover that Harrison wasn't going to shower him with gratitude. As spiritually attuned as he was, the musician had a skeptical, flinty side. The echo of Harrison's earlier warning—"Give me one hit and you'll see what difficult is"—frequently sounded in Klein's ears. When George was sued for plagiarism in early 1971 by publisher Bright Tunes, which claimed "My Sweet Lord" had infringed on "He's So Fine," a hit for the Chiffons in 1963, Klein jumped into the case, planning the musician's defense and opening negotiations with the company. Still, he was starting to sour on Harrison, seeing him as an ingrate.

The other surprise was Lennon, who hated the idea that George Harrison was suddenly the most popular and successful Beatle. While accompanying Yoko to Majorca to see her daughter, Kyoko, John and Allen had been walking past a country club when they heard "My Sweet Lord" being played. "Can't I go *anywhere* in the world without hearing that song?" Lennon grumbled.

Back in New York, John felt the need to mount his own Madison Square Garden benefit concert. When a series of television reports by New York journalist Geraldo Rivera exposed the horrific warehousing of the mentally handicapped in large institutions like Staten Island's Willowbrook, a new group-home and community-based-housing movement took hold. Lennon telephoned Rivera and offered to headline a pair of fundraising shows at Madison Square Garden to benefit the charity One to One. Tickets for an afternoon and evening show both sold out, although Lennon himself bought and distributed $59,000 worth of tickets to One to One volunteers. Television and radio rights sold to ABC and the King Biscuit Flour Hour, respectively, and Lennon's performances alone raised over $500,000 for the charity.

That would have to satisfy Lennon, who, if he was looking to eclipse Harrison and put his former junior back in his place, didn't come close. Backed by the New York band Elephant's Memory, with whom he and Ono had recently recorded the album *Some Time in New York City*, and the drummer Jim Keltner, Lennon and the show received mixed reviews, perhaps owing to Lennon's decision to alternate songs and vocals with Ono, and the set lists being heavily weighted toward newer material. The only Beatles song performed at either show was "Come Together."

While the One to One concerts were less than they might have been, the public response to *Some Time in New York City* threw Lennon for a loop. Peaking at number forty-eight in the U.S. — his previous album, *Imagine*, had gone to number one — the record was the first bona fide bomb of his career and sold far worse than McCartney's disappointing debut album with Wings, *Wildlife*. Lennon was being actively harassed by the Nixon administration's Justice Department, which had initially refused to grant him a permanent visa and was now seeking to have him deported as an undesirable, so he and Ono had embraced America's new left, and the overtly political album featured songs about black activist Angela Davis, the imprisoning of Detroit poet, political activist, and MC5 manager John Sinclair for possession of two joints, women's rights, and the riots at New York's Attica prison. The title of the album's single, "Woman Is the Nigger of the World," was obviously meant to outrage and didn't disappoint on that score; it created a media stir, particularly in the black community. The ultimate commentary, however, was the indifference of record buyers; it was the worst-selling single of Lennon's solo career. Of the album as a whole, *Rolling Stone* reviewer Stephen Holden, likely picked by the magazine's editors because he had a reputation for being even-tempered and open-minded, had a hard time finding anything kind to say in his review. While commending John and Yoko for their daring, he characterized the results as smug, shallow, and "artistic suicide."

Plans to make the Madison Square Garden shows the start of an American tour were scrapped. Lennon's artistic misfires consumed a great deal of Klein's attention in New York, but a bigger problem

was festering in London. Since the British court's appointment of a
receiver, the Beatles' business hung in limbo. Yes, each member could
move forward with his own career, but their shared business and the
fate of the Apple partnership remained as big a question mark as ever.
On a practical level, that meant millions of dollars accruing to the Beatles could not be divided and disbursed to them.

With the court behind them, the Eastmans pushed for a resolution.
"There was a settlement to be made," said Kramer, who met with Lee
Eastman and found him bright, courteous, and ready to deal. The impediment was Klein; he couldn't bring himself to admit that he had
lost and that he needed to reach a settlement for the benefit of his clients. "This was always Allen's problem," Kramer said. "He was a victim
of his own success as a negotiator. It *killed* him to give anything up, to
think he wasn't ultimately going to be victorious."

Instead of admitting defeat, Klein was lending money to the three
Beatles, confident he would get it back when the receivership was terminated. Unwilling to discuss a settlement, he seemed to think that
the problem of McCartney, the Eastmans, and the receivership would
somehow disappear or resolve itself.

His clients, however, thought differently.

Klein's management contract came up for renewal every year. John,
George, and Ringo had happily continued with Klein in the two years
after McCartney's suit, but they had since grown impatient, realizing
Klein wouldn't make the settlement they needed. By early 1973, Klein
could sense that, though they'd recently signed a short three-month
management extension, he'd lost them. Heading into a meeting with
Klein and Kramer one afternoon, attorney Alan Kahn tried to bring
his boss up to speed, but Allen's mind was elsewhere. "I've got bigger
worries," he said. "I haven't spoken with John Lennon in two months."
Indeed, just a few weeks later, Harrison ruefully told Steckler that a
Beatles settlement "will never happen with Allen." Two days after that,
Klein was informed via an attorney's letter that the Beatles would not
be renewing his contract when it expired in March. To save face, Allen
was allowed to say he had declined an extension offer.

## 13

# A SPORT AND A PASTIME

HIS INABILITY TO REACH a settlement with McCartney and the East-mans had proven disastrous for Klein. Ironically, ABKCO enjoyed a few financial bright spots in the period, courtesy of the Rolling Stones.

As part of the deal with Klein, the Stones had affirmed the valid-ity of their publishing contract with ABKCO, which ended in 1970, and agreed not to record anything that Klein controlled until 1975. But when the group released a new album in 1972, *Exile on Main Street,* some of the songs sounded familiar to executives at ABKCO. Klein had his assistant Paul Mozian spend a night in the studio comparing the cuts on the new album with unreleased tapes of tunes the Stones had worked on in the earlier years. Mozian came to the conclusion that the band had definitely written and worked on numerous songs on the new album when they were with ABKCO. Since the songs had never been released, the Stones were free to record them and put them out now on Rolling Stones Records. But as Klein pointed out, they'd been written when Jagger and Richards were signed to ABKCO's publishing company, Gideon Music. Klein, not Mick and Keith's current publisher, EMI, was therefore the legal owner of the rights. Not surprisingly, the Stones and their attorneys disagreed. In response, Klein ratcheted the argument up several notches with a claim that the Stones' breach of settlement entitled him to put out another album of their music. He even had a title in mind; what did they think of *Necrophilia*? In short order, Klein and the Rolling Stones were back in court.

When the smoke cleared, ABKCO had the publishing rights to five additional songs: "Sweet Virginia," "Loving Cup," "All Down the Line," "Shine a Light," and "Stop Breaking Down,"* which meant Klein received a portion of royalties on *Exile on Main Street*. Additionally, ABKCO got to release another album, although cooler heads prevailed regarding the title; the album, coproduced by Andrew Loog Oldham, was eventually sold as *More Hot Rocks (Big Hits and Fazed Cookies)*.

Of all Klein's relationships with his clients, the one with Oldham was the most complex. Like Allen, Andrew could undertake a course of action with more than one aim in mind, and neither man could seem to shake an abiding affection for the other, even as he tried to outmaneuver and get the better of him. It was, ultimately, a battle of two kindred souls, each brilliant but forever hustling his way through the world. It was love; it was hate; it was commerce; it was codependency.

For Oldham, who had been too young and crazy to grow with the Stones and hold on to his claim, the dreadful mistake he had made in underestimating the staying power of the Stones became an enduring fact of his life. He was the hip version of Esau, the man who had sold his birthright for a bowl of cocaine. If Allen Klein was proving his Jacob, Andrew wasn't going to let him get away without periodic adjustments. After forcing an improvement on the original sale of his rights by suing Klein, Andrew and Allen settled into the unusual and sometimes antagonizing friendship that characterized the rest of their lives. Over the coming years, any time ABKCO had a project to which Oldham could lay claim—however central or tangential—a negotia-

---

* "Stop Breaking Down," recorded and copyrighted by bluesman Robert Johnson in 1937 as "Stop Breaking Down Blues," would later be part of a lawsuit between the Johnson estate and Klein that included a second Johnson song covered and claimed by the Stones, "Love in Vain."

tion always ensued. The game would never be over, and whenever Allen needed his help, Andrew sought to make the most of it.

For Allen, it was much the same. Andrew's firsthand knowledge of the Stones and their recordings was valuable and worth the money and aggravation of dealing with him. And in his treatment of Oldham, Klein was often at his best and worst. He'd come away from the relationship with the assets — although, like Andrew, he hadn't initially recognized the Rolling Stones for the cultural institution and dynasty they'd prove to be, he'd known they were damn valuable and he wasn't about to let go — and Oldham, eternally in need of money, was never allowed to forget who had them now.

At the same time, Klein genuinely liked Oldham and gave him solid advice and direction, and he paid the legal costs of a lawsuit against the original British publisher of "As Tears Go By" that resulted in Oldham being recognized as a co-author. When, at a particularly needy juncture, Andrew had come to Klein and offered to sell his continuing interest in the Rolling Stones' music publishing, Allen declined to buy it. Instead, he chided Andrew for undervaluing a lifetime annuity. "If I buy your publishing, you'll be my ward for the rest of your life," he told him. When Klein negotiated a new recording contract for Donovan with Epic Records in the early seventies, he got Oldham a payday by making him the singer's producer for the album *Essence to Essence*.

The two men, when not fighting, were apt to be socializing. Incapable of being alone, always needing to pick up the tab or spend more money than he should in order to call the tune, Allen played the willing patsy, glad to pay for Andrew's company so as to be able to expound to him on various topics endlessly. For as long as Klein lived, Oldham came in and out of his life as the need arose.

The Beatles' quiet, impersonal departure from Klein was not indicative of their relationship and would prove an aberration, the lull before an appropriately stormy divorce. To reach a final settlement of their accounts, Klein sued the Beatles and Apple in New York; they sued him in London. "We went into war mode and went to the mattresses," said Kramer.

To be their new representatives, Lennon and Ono selected someone already intimately familiar with their work and business, ABKCO's former in-house attorney Harold Seider. Harrison, now having his business interests overseen by Denis James O'Brien, the former manager of Monty Python and Harrison's partner in HandMade Films, retained Bob Dylan's attorney David Braun. Starr began what would be a decades-long relationship with Los Angeles attorney Bruce Grakal.

Klein, whose unwillingness to concede defeat was both his strength and his greatest vulnerability, would move through the ensuing four years of legal wrangling like a man trying to serve two masters. He knew his run was over and that it was incumbent upon him to make the most advantageous settlement possible, and for that he needed no counsel, representative, or unwavering voice whispering in his ear that this was business. Yet managing the Beatles had satisfied his personal need for validation like nothing else, and he would never voluntarily let that go. Until the day John Lennon was murdered, Klein never stopped believing they would eventually return to him.

"If Allen was behind the eight ball, he always thought it was going to get better," said Seider. "In his relationship afterward with John and Yoko, in the back of his mind I'm sure he always thought, *I'm going to get them back*. This was Allen. He lived by denial." Added Michael Kramer: "Allen loved being the Beatles' manager. And hindsight being twenty-twenty, they could have gotten him for whatever price they named. They had no idea how much they could have gotten him to do for how little. We'll never know what the emotional impact of losing the Beatles was. He suppressed those kind of emotions — you never show anyone you're worried. He could have used a few decades of therapy."

Instead, his chosen balm would be a few decades of litigation. Typically, Klein was impelled by a variety of motives, sometimes all at once. Nowhere was his unique and confounding ability to undertake an action for a twisting confluence of reasons more evident than in the plagiarism suit over "My Sweet Lord."

In February 1971 a small publisher, Bright Tunes Music, claimed the song was substantially copied from its song "He's So Fine" and filed the suit after the Harrison record had spent five weeks at the top of the *Billboard* singles chart. Klein, still Harrison's manager at the time, publicly shrugged it off, telling an interviewer that the tunes weren't at all alike. Behind the scenes he tried to make the suit go away by telling Bright Tunes that Harrison was willing to buy the company. Seymour Barash, Bright Tunes president and majority owner, countered by suggesting Harrison give the copyright ownership of "My Sweet Lord" to Bright Tunes and split the royalties. Klein and Harrison decided to go forward with the case, hiring attorneys and an expert witness who could testify that the song was unique. The case was still waiting to go to court when Klein and the three Beatles parted company two years later.

In the interim, Bright Tunes had been struggling with its finances and was placed in receivership. It wasn't until five years later, in 1976, that the suit was resumed. At that point, Harrison made Bright Tunes a settlement offer in which he would retain ownership of the copyright and pay them $148,000, equivalent to 40 percent of the American songwriter and publisher royalties. But unbeknownst to Harrison, at about the time Klein was losing the Beatles he had been talking with Bright Tunes about buying the rights to "He's So Fine"—for approximately double what Harrison was offering.

Klein, in conversation with associates, often said he wanted to buy the copyright and settle the case for Harrison as a show of goodwill and to demonstrate that the ex-Beatle had made a mistake in leaving him. There may have been some truth to that, but he also told one friend, Leonard Leibman, an attorney who spent a great deal of time with Klein during much of the "My Sweet Lord" dispute, that the song had been a big earner around the world and that a settlement in favor of "He's So Fine" was worth a lot of money. Whatever his reasons, Klein was clearly interested in buying the song, which reportedly convinced Barash that Klein, Harrison's former manager, had knowledge of the true worth of "My Sweet Lord" and that it was far more than Harrison was offering. The publisher countered Harrison's settlement offer by asking for a much bigger chunk of earnings as well as transfer of the copyright. Rejecting that—and not knowing of Klein's inquiries — Harrison and his attorneys took the case to court. The trial was set in two parts, the first to determine whether plagiarism had taken place and, if it had, the second to determine damages. Though Harrison testified on his own behalf and denied any conscious attempt to rework the earlier song, the judge eventually found for the plaintiffs and the ruling was upheld on appeal.

Then, to the shock of Harrison and his attorneys, they received notice just prior to the start of the trial's penalty phase that the Bright Tunes attorney was being replaced by Alan Kahn, the staff attorney at ABKCO. Klein had purchased Bright Tunes lock, stock, and "He's So Fine" for $587,000. Suspecting the worst, Harrison's lawyers had Kahn disqualified, pointing out to the judge that he had been involved in setting the case in motion for Harrison and couldn't possibly now represent the plaintiff — which was suddenly Allen Klein. Attorney Gideon Cashman, who had initially represented Bright Tunes and then been dismissed by Klein, who believed that he would have no trouble reaching a friendly settlement on his own with Harrison, was hastily called and begged to come back. "Allen so completely misjudged the pulse of Harrison as to be talking about the man in the moon," Cashman said. If Klein had ever meant to demonstrate his largesse, Harrison clearly wasn't buying it. With the waters already churned by the simultaneous and rancorous settlement discussions over ABKCO's management of the Beatles — who were not pleased to discover that it was going to cost them millions of dollars to finally be done with Klein — Harrison had no trouble believing Allen had interfered with George's chance to settle the plagiarism suit for his own benefit. "The thing that really disappoints me is when you have a relationship with one person and they turn out to betray you," he said. "He was the one who put out 'My Sweet Lord' and collected 20 percent commission on the record. And he was the one who got the lawyers to defend me . . . He, on one hand, was defending me, then he switched sides and continued the lawsuit." Others, however, wondered if Klein wasn't simply amusing himself and exacting a bit of revenge. In Seider's opinion, "that was Allen being mischievous."

At first, mischief was its own reward. After looking over the sales of "My Sweet Lord," the judge determined that its huge success had played a large role in driving the sales of both *All Things Must Pass* and a subsequent album of Harrison's hits, and his first assessment was that the song had cleared $2,133,316 for the artist. But after making a few subjective adjustments, the judge reduced the liability to $1,599,987 — all of which Harrison would have to pay to Klein as the owner of "He's So Fine." Ultimately, however, the judge heard Harrison's objections and decided that Klein's fiduciary duty to Harrison continued even after he'd ceased to be his manager and that he wasn't entitled to profit from his subsequent actions. Under the 1981 ruling, Klein was ordered to hold "He's So Fine" in trust for Harrison with the proviso that his former client reimburse him the $587,000 it had cost him to buy Bright Tunes.

Attorney Don Zakarin, who replaced Cashman as ABKCO's attorney in the case, considered the whole affair — which was unsuccessfully appealed and went on well into the 1990s — extraordinary. He could think of no other case where a songwriter had been found guilty of copyright infringement and ended up owning the song he'd infringed. As the lawyer for the side that won its claim but lost the judgment, he was pleasantly surprised to discover that the man he'd represented had no regrets.

"Unlike most clients, Allen didn't point fingers and say, 'You guys should have done better.' His reaction was that it was his fault, he made a mistake. And it was not a great situation — it cost him a lot of money to litigate."

Harrison, after eighteen years of arguing about it in court, was less sanguine, claiming Klein still owed him "three or four hundred thousand dollars" in earnings on the two songs. "It's really a joke," he complained. "It's a total joke."

Harrison and Starr were also unhappy over their settlement of the Beatles' business with ABKCO. In typical Klein fashion, he'd kept negotiations going, and they'd stretched on until 1977, two years after the Beatles themselves had settled their own partnership agreement with McCartney.

Ultimately, Klein disavowed any continuing interest in the Beatles' business or properties, with the sole and notable exception of publishing administration on "My Sweet Lord." In return, he received a lump payment of approximately five million dollars. The settlement, made in lieu of Klein's future share of Beatles' royalties and to cover loans ABKCO made to them, was straightforward. Yet it still left the three ex-Beatles with a sour taste. Sadly, Harrison's choice of Denis O'Brien to succeed Klein as his business manager would produce bigger problems and greater regrets; in 1995 Harrison filed a twenty-five-million-dollar lawsuit against O'Brien, alleging financial mismanagement and deception. The court awarded him $11.7 million, but O'Brien declared bankruptcy and Harrison never collected.

Klein's negotiations with John Lennon and Yoko Ono were just as contentious. On his 1974 album *Walls and Bridges,* a livid Lennon included a vituperative song about Klein, "Steel and Glass." The title, seemingly referring to 1700 Broadway, the office building where ABKCO was headquartered, was John at his nastiest; he simultaneously threatened Klein and portrayed him as inconsequential. As a final kick in the balls, Lennon sneered at Klein's painful childhood, particularly his mother's death, adding "but you're gonna wish you wasn't born at all."

That was what Lennon sang in public—yet behind closed doors, he concluded the settlement on a decidedly different note. More than any of the other principals, Ono was the one who hung on through the months-long negotiating process and helped hammer out the details of the final agreement, and Klein later told reporters that the settlement was a result of her "tireless efforts and Kissinger-like negotiating brilliance." But just as it seemed the deal was concluded, after the two sides had taken suites on the twelfth floor of the Plaza Hotel in New York and were sending their last proposals back and forth at the end of a marathon, five-day session, Klein threw a final wrench in the works.

"I have one last demand and it's nonnegotiable," he told his attorneys. "John has to have dinner with me tonight."

Kramer, after weeks of work, saw the settlement collapsing under another one of his uncle's caprices. "Oh, for God's sake!" he exploded. "That's not going to happen!"

Allen was unmoved. "No dinner, no deal. Just go tell him."

Sighing and shaking his head, Michael went down the hall. Knocking on the door of the Beatles' suite, he took a deep breath and got ready to make a fool of himself.

He didn't have the chance.

"Tell Allen," Lennon said when he opened the door, "that I want to have dinner with him tonight."

In deciding to continue their friendship with Klein, Lennon and Ono may simply have viewed Klein as a fact of life, someone to be reconciled with and dealt with, treated as a friend and an asset instead of an enemy and a liability. But one thing was clear: intense talents and shortcomings — particularly the inability to separate personal and professional desires — ruled both men. In a lifetime of searching for love and validation, the closest Allen Klein had ever come to a soulmate was John Lennon.

What do you do after you've lost the Beatles?

The road that opened before Klein was not promising. He had the extraordinary distinction of having been the manager of both the Rolling Stones and the Beatles — and the infamy of having been repudiated by both, becoming an object of derision and a symbol of villainy to many of the groups' fans. It certainly didn't help when McCartney continued to portray himself as having won a titanic battle to keep Klein from seizing and destroying the Beatles' work — despite the fact that Klein had never done that. "The choice was: lose everything you've ever earned — and with the Beatles that was quite a substantial amount: rights, royalties, monies, assets and everything," McCartney said years later of his decision to sue for the breakup of the partnership. "Lose all of that, or sue and pray that you win, because if you lose you'll lose it all anyway."

Allen's continuing legal wrangles with the Stones had become a sport and a pastime. In July of '74, the Stones and Klein concluded another round of arduous negotiations over royalties, this one resulting in a payment of $375,000 to the Stones and the granting of another album to ABKCO. The subsequent collection, *Metamorphosis*, was composed largely of oddities, demos, and alternate takes; it was hardly compelling. But at least part of its value to Klein appeared to be that it gave him something to release just as the Stones were starting a new tour, and he got it in stores on the same day as Rolling Stones Records' package of recent hits, *Made in the Shade.*

"Allen liked to futz around with Jagger," said Cashman, who handled much of Klein's continuing litigation with the Stones well into the eighties. Some of the motivation was economic, but some of it was personal and ludicrous; at one point, Allen said he was angry with Jagger for making a face at his daughter.

Nonetheless, Klein was ferocious about guarding the integrity of the Rolling Stones' back catalog. At a time when late-night television was rife with ads for cheap albums of repackaged hits by established artists offered through schlocky mail-order licensees like K-Tel, ABKCO had no interest in exploiting the Stones' recordings. Indeed, the only license granted during the period was a greatest-hits package limited to Germany for which the band and ABKCO received two million dollars. ABKCO wouldn't even license the band's recordings for multiple-artists collections or for soundtrack albums. Though other performers had rejected similar offers in the past — both the Band and Bob Dylan had declined to license the original recordings of "The Weight" and "It's Alright Ma (I'm Only Bleeding)" for the *Easy Rider* soundtrack album in 1969 — Klein was one of the few managers who continued to adhere to that standard. In 1983, he granted the producers of *The Big Chill* the right to use "You Can't Always Get What You Want" in the film but not on the soundtrack album. If someone wanted a copy of the song for his record collection, he would have to buy *Let It Bleed.*

He was similarly tough in his negotiations with record companies. Under distribution contracts with Universal and Sony, ABKCO continues to this day to manufacture records by Sam Cooke, the Rolling Stones, Herman's Hermits, the Animals, and others. And in striking contrast to industry practices, those companies must pay on receipt — meaning anything they hold in inventory, they've already paid for and can't return to ABKCO. "We've got skin in the game with anything from ABKCO," a Universal executive said. ABKCO's tight rein on the music maintained top-shelf prices for the Rolling Stones albums.

It wasn't just the business of the Stones that kept Klein in court. If he thought there was an advantage to be gained by ABKCO or an associated artist, he was more than willing to take it to court; he relished the opportunity. Klein spent so much time and money in court that his own attorneys would try to talk him out of litigating.

"I once asked him, 'Is this really worth it?'" recalled Zakarin. "Allen said, 'You don't worry about whether it's worth it. *I* worry about whether it's worth it.' And it was his decision. But it made you nuts sometimes — he spent a lot of money on litigation."

Klein's biggest legal expenses, however, didn't come from disputing a contract or suing on behalf of a client. It was from fighting a federal tax case against him. As always, he knew exactly how he wanted to proceed and what he did and didn't want his attorneys to do. And this time, it would cost nearly all of what remained of his reputation.

As ABKCO's head of promotion, Pete Bennett had to get records played on the radio however he could.

An industry veteran who'd promoted records by Nat "King" Cole before joining ABKCO, Bennett made the industry leap to rock 'n' roll and pushed whatever record the company was involved with at the moment, whether it was by Herman's Hermits, Lulu, the Plastic Ono Band, Donovan, or the Rolling Stones. He was entertaining, streetwise, and likable — well suited to that segment of the music business where payola lived on via favors, friendship, and expense accounts, the industry hewing to the letter of the law but not its spirit. His primary job was to curry favor with disk jockeys and program directors, and he relished the role. When Bennett traveled on American tours with the Stones, they clearly got a kick out of him, introducing him as "our Mafia promotion man."

"Pete was a character," said Michael Kramer. "He'd say, 'Dis reckid is gonna be a monster in Detroit.' I remember he and his wife, Annette, inviting people from the ABKCO office up to their house for dinner. She sent Pete downstairs to bring up some wine but when he came back up and she saw what he had, she said, 'Not that! Bring up the good stuff!' Pete said, 'Annette! When did you become a cock-a-sure of wine?' That was Pete Bennett."

Emily Barrata Quinn, who was Bennett's secretary and later an assistant to Klein, wasn't as amused by Pete. Having worked at New York radio station WABC-FM, Quinn was used to promo men being hustlers of a certain ilk but found Bennett to be "ilkier than the ones I met at WABC. Those promo guys seemed decent," she said. "After you talked to Pete Bennett, you needed a shower." She had trouble imagining an easier job than getting a radio station to play a Beatles record. "Being the promotion man for the Beatles — that's like Chris Rock's line: Crack sells itself. I was never clear what he actually did."

Nonetheless, ABKCO had a potentially rich promotional budget for the Beatles. Klein's renegotiation of the group's contract with Capitol Records included the kind of free-goods clause contained in most recording deals: ABKCO received five thousand copies of any single or album to use for "promotional purposes."* Some were clearly marked as such and couldn't be confused with salable records; others, known in industry parlance as *cleans,* were identical to the records sold in stores.

Historically, cleans had been given to wholesalers and retailers as inducements to buy a title, and they lingered on as a little-discussed part of the business — an old, bad habit that, like smoking, was hard to quit. It was one of the record business's dirty little secrets that companies sometimes used cleans to create slush funds or gain favor with radio stations and retailers, ostensibly for the ultimate benefit of the artist and his record. But the biggest problem was the recordings' obvious susceptibility to abuse: cleans were untraceable and valuable, and anyone who had cheap copies of hit records could easily find a buyer. Cleans were cash masquerading as vinyl, and executives sometimes made their own clandestine deals and pocketed the money.

---

*  At the time, most record companies sought a free-goods allowance of 10 to 15 percent — meaning the artists weren't paid for 10 to 15 percent of the records the label manufactured.

Despite initially refusing to furnish the items, Capitol ultimately gave ABKCO clean promotional records of the Beatles and their solo projects — including *The Concert for Bangladesh*, despite the fact that five dollars from each copy sold was meant to go to UNICEF. Thomas Engel, the former assistant U.S. attorney who ultimately prosecuted Klein, recalled that the IRS heard that Bennett had been selling Beatles records to distributors out of the trunk of his car — for cash, at least at first. It became considerably easier to bring a case when agents discovered Bennett had let a Long Island wholesaler pay for the records by writing a check to a nonexistent corporation so the buyer could declare the cost of the clandestine sale a business expense. Engel, who was unsure whether the IRS had always intended to target Klein, said he was eager to trade up. "Bennett was a little guy," he said, "and Klein was not."

Though the IRS sent agents to ABKCO to investigate, Klein wasn't worried. He was preoccupied with making a film he expected would be his big commercial breakthrough as a producer, an Aristotle Onassis and Jacqueline Kennedy–based roman à clef entitled *The Greek Tycoon*. Initially, the project had belonged to Klein's friend Laurence Myers and Nico Mastorakis, a producer of soft-core porn films who had conceived the idea and pitched it to Anthony Quinn. When Klein, in search of projects to make in partnership with the respected American producer Ely Landau, learned Quinn had committed to playing Onassis and that the female lead was Jacqueline Bisset, he was eager to be involved. Myers, his affection for Klein notwithstanding, knew what that meant: Allen would take over his project and he'd be reduced to an associate producer. Myers politely declined. But after spending seventy-five thousand pounds he didn't have on a shipping-tycoon-size yacht party at Cannes that successfully drummed up interest among American studios, Myers had no money for a screenplay or a director. Klein bailed him out, and he and Landau became the producers.

With filming in Greece, England, and the United States, Klein reveled in the role, whether he was taking private jets around Europe and the Mediterranean, overseeing the production, or playing chess on the set with Quinn. When they needed a Rolls-Royce for a scene, Klein didn't want to rent one and instead insisted on using the white Rolls he'd bought from John Lennon and kept in London. He had his English driver, Alf Weaver, bring it to Greece.* Klein might have enjoyed his role as producer, but he was also taking a substantial risk: he had guaranteed the film's seven-million-dollar budget—almost certainly more money than he really had—without the backing of a studio. Eventually a deal was made with Universal, one that reserved control over the film's final cut for Klein.

Klein, Iris Keitel, and a friend of his, the film executive Julian Schlossberg, moved into a bungalow at the Beverly Hills Hotel and spent several months overseeing the editing. But when they presented their cut to studio heads Sid Sheinberg and Ned Tanen, neither liked it. They convinced Allen to let legendary film editor Verna Fields, who'd worked with everyone from Fritz Lang to George Lucas and Steven Spielberg, take a whack at it. Not surprisingly, Allen thought his edit better than hers and it was ultimately agreed they would test both cuts and release the one audiences preferred. Klein's version won. Though not well reviewed—the *New York Times* called it "as witless as it is gutless" and "the literature of vultures who have no interest in tearing into something of the first freshness"—the film proved a moneymaker.

Throughout this whole period, the IRS was keeping close tabs on Klein, but he didn't realize it until he and several employees were on a business trip to London, likely on behalf of the Who's Pete Townshend. In 1975 the guitarist and songwriter had complained to Klein that he wasn't getting paid by his American music publisher and had asked him to look into it (Allen would ultimately get Townshend paid and renegotiate his U.S. publishing deals). After arriving on the red-eye, Klein checked into his usual suite at the Dorchester while the others went to another hotel, the Inn on the Park. At that point, two of

---

* Klein also had another Rolls-Royce of Lennon's, this one painted with psychedelic designs by the Dutch art collective the Fool. It sat in Klein's garage in the Bronx, rarely driven and used primarily by Klein's children and their friends for make-out sessions. In 1977, Klein gave the car back to the Lennons, who donated it to the Smithsonian Institution as a tax write-off. After John's death, the Smithsonian auctioned the car for $2.3 million.

them — Michael Kramer and Ken Salinsky — decided to gamble at the Playboy Club, located in a nearby townhouse.

"It was between noon and one when Ken and I walked in," said Kramer. "And the two special IRS agents who'd visited the office were in the vestibule. I think they wanted to see if Allen was a gambler." Kramer wondered if the government had bugged ABKCO's phones, but in any event, it was obvious that Klein was being closely watched. Indeed, when the case went to trial in 1977, the IRS's lead investigator on it, Sid Connor, would testify that he'd trailed Klein around the world for five years.

Charged as coconspirators, Klein and Bennett each faced a six-count indictment: a felony charge of attempted income tax evasion for 1970, 1971, and 1972, and a related misdemeanor charge of making false statements on income tax returns for each of those same years. According to the government, the defendants failed to account for substantial cash received from the sale of Beatles promotional records. Klein was alleged to have received over two hundred thousand dollars in proceeds over the three-year period.

Saying he had no knowledge of Bennett's activities, Klein pleaded not guilty to all charges. Bennett pleaded guilty to a single misdemeanor charge and became a cooperating witness for the government against Klein.

For civil litigation, Klein relied chiefly on Max Freund, a senior partner at Rosenman and Colin. Considered one of the preeminent Jewish law firms in the country, it had long represented CBS and, as a result, had become a powerhouse in the music business; two former Rosenman attorneys, Clive Davis and Walter Yetnikoff, would go on to head CBS Records. Faced now with a criminal case, Freund recommended Klein use Gerald Walpin, a former assistant U.S. attorney who headed Rosenman and Colin's litigation department and who was considered one of the top white-collar-crime lawyers in New York.

It looked at first to be a troubled match. Klein, used to devising strategies and theories in his civil cases and then giving marching orders to his attorneys, came in believing it would be the same story in criminal court. Seeing Allen immediately at loggerheads with his attorney, a prescient Betty Klein stepped out of the meeting, phoned attorney Leonard Leibman, and begged him to come down and referee. Leibman, who would go on to serve as Klein's confidant, sounding board, and daily companion throughout the case ("It took a year out of my life," he said), was able to restore order and convince Klein that he couldn't deal the cards himself if he expected to win this game.

Despite the rough start, Walpin would come to view Klein as one of his best and brightest clients. "I held back no realistic appraisals of the evidence and difficulties," he said. "I did not have to mince words. In the end, Allen gave me full head in litigating it, unlike in his civil cases." In return, Klein demanded Walpin's full attention — and demonstrated that he was willing to pay for it. "Allen was an enormous consumer of time," said Leibman. "He got Walpin a suite at the Plaza and [Walpin] only went home to Long Island on the weekends."

Klein clearly got his money's worth. Before the government could even indict him, Walpin stymied them for a year by bringing an injunction against the grand jury claiming that attempts to subpoena an investigator working for Klein interfered with Allen's right to counsel. When Walpin lost, he appealed to the Second Circuit Court and bought more time. He frustrated Engel, who had to litigate for a year just to get indictments handed up. "Gerry and I have subsequently become friendly, but we were at dagger points," he said. "He was a very tough, sinewy kind of lawyer who would seize any advantage." The person Engel truly did not like was Allen Klein. "He was a sly guy; somewhat oily, in my view. When he took the stand there was something lubricious about him."

When the case finally went to trial, Walpin focused on undermining the testimony of Bennett, not an ideal witness to build a case on. Bennett had initially told prosecutors that he'd received only 10 percent of the money from the record sales and had passed the rest to Klein, but it wasn't difficult to find receipts and bank transactions suggesting Bennett kept a good deal more. Klein testified that, yes, ABKCO had received promotional Beatles records; no, he had not instructed Bennett to sell them; and yes, Bennett had given him money, but it had nothing to do with selling records and represented the repayment of cash advances.

And how did Klein feel about the trial? He didn't like being charged with a crime and professed his innocence — he and others at ABKCO suspected the U.S. Attorney was pursuing the case in hopes of finding that records had been sold to buy drugs for the Beatles — but he couldn't get enough of the action.

"He absolutely loved it," said Leibman, who at that point was being picked up at his Connecticut home by a limousine every morning and driven to meet Allen at the federal courthouse. After spending the day in court, the men would have the transcript of the day's proceedings delivered to ABKCO and then pore over them for the rest of the evening in a quest for openings. "He was totally focused on the case. This was a dream for Allen, because it was a case built on numbers."

Unable to rely on Bennett's testimony alone, the government questioned other ABKCO employees. Allen's former assistant Paul Mozian was brought to the FBI's Manhattan offices along with his lawyer and questioned at length. "They asked me about money," he said. "Money in the safe, money in bags, mink coats, jewelry." Mozian told the FBI he knew there was a safe with money in it because he'd been sent to get the combination from the desk of an ABKCO accountant, Joel Silver, so Klein could give $5,000 in expense money to the musicians rehearsing for the Concert for Bangladesh. Beyond that, there was nothing he could tell them about the safe or cash expenditures. Paul was grateful when Klein later insisted on paying the legal expenses associated with his questioning.

Among the ABKCO employees who did testify were Silver, who confirmed that Bennett had given cash to Klein, and former ABKCO in-house counsel Harold Seider, who likewise testified that he had seen Bennett counting cash and giving it to Klein.

In the absence of uncontested proof that Klein had received proceeds specifically from the sale of records, the IRS sought to build a case by showing Klein had spent more money than his tax returns could explain and must therefore have unrevealed sources of income — a standard tactic in tax investigations known as the net-worth method. But that was a tall order considering the target; Klein, an accountant, seasoned business manager, head of a public corporation, and salesman and strategist par excellence likely knew as much or more than the prosecutors about making money appear and disappear. But government investigators had followed Klein long enough for them to know he was a womanizer and had a steady mistress in his employ in Keitel. Married men with girlfriends always needed money — preferably money that no one knew about. The prosecution's case soon came to include testimony regarding Klein's jewelry purchases at Tiffany and Company.

After a seventeen-day trial, the jury deliberated six days before saying it was deadlocked, and Judge Charles Metzner declared a mistrial. Knowing the federal prosecutor would want to retry the case, Walpin once again sought to derail the prosecution with a variety of challenges and appeals, including arguing that Metzner should have charged the jury to continue seeking a verdict and that a retrial amounted to double jeopardy. "Gerry didn't want to risk another chance of a guilty verdict," said Engel.

By the time Klein finally exhausted his challenges and the second trial began, there was a new judge, Vincent Broderick, and a new prosecutor, Steve Schatz. Engel, who had simultaneously prosecuted a tense, high-profile bombing case involving the radical Puerto Rican group FALN, left the U.S. Attorney's office for private practice and soon bought a home in Hardenburgh, New York, a tiny Catskill hamlet with a reputation of being a hotbed of tax resisters; the majority of residents had become mail-order-ordained ministers in a bid to get off the tax rolls. They elected Engel their town justice.

Whatever had been lacking in the government's case in the first trial was corrected in the second — just barely. At the conclusion of the latter trial, the jury found Klein innocent on all three felony charges and guilty on just one of the misdemeanors — specifically, making false statements on his 1972 income tax return. Whether by design or coincidence, the jury returned a verdict on Klein that matched the plea the government had allowed Bennett to offer. Leibman believed the conviction made no sense and would be overturned on appeal; how could

Klein have been found innocent of the underlying crime — failure to report income — but guilty of filing a misleading return?

But Klein opted to accept the verdict. He may have been counseled to consider himself lucky: Judge Broderick, a well-respected and sympathetic judge, said from the bench that he did not think Klein had testified truthfully, and that was sure to be seized upon if Klein chose to appeal. "Considering the evidence, we were all very pleased," said Walpin. "Including Allen." Additionally, the case had taken years and consumed a lot of money. "Allen had already paid a million dollars in legal fees which were not coming out of the company," said Leibman. Though Judge Broderick apparently believed that the jury had erred and that Klein was guilty of the felony charges, he followed their verdict at sentencing: Allen was fined $5,000 and given two months in jail.

Some in the record business saw it as a miscarriage of justice — or at least a case of extremely selective prosecution. Eric Kronfeld, Marty Machat's one-time junior associate, had risen to become a powerful music-industry attorney and then the president of a major record company, PolyGram. He described Klein's prosecution as sui generis. "Allen got punished for doing nothing different than all the record companies have done since time immemorial," he said.

Eschewing a minimum-security facility for white-collar criminals in order to stay in New York City, Klein began serving his time on July 14, 1980, at the Metropolitan Correctional Center on Park Row. It was a maximum-security prison, but he was pleasantly surprised to discover he didn't have to be cuffed when he turned himself in and that he had his own cell on a floor without convicted murderers. Though initially nervous — *I can do this,* he told himself as they led him into the cell, *I was in an orphanage; I've been alone* — he would later joke that he quickly adjusted. "I was there by myself and I sat down and said, 'Oh! Finally! Peace at last!' It was an interesting experience," he added with evident relief.

Leibman visited Klein virtually daily — forty-eight times, by Leibman's count. As an attorney, he was able to meet privately with Allen for hours on end in the counsel's office. "I'd go in and we'd talk

and then we'd play rummy," Leibman said. Even better for a man who
hated solitude and couldn't abide silence, the office had a telephone.

Beverly Winston, Klein's assistant in ABKCO's London office, was
flabbergasted when Allen went to jail. "He never thought he'd be found
guilty because he didn't believe he was, so it was all rather shocking,"
she said. Still, Winston was used to spending hours on the phone with
him—"I was the one taking dictation and having the long conversations about the profound ethics of life"—and she and her office mates
indulged in a bit of gallows humor, joking that at least they'd get a
few months of peace with Allen in jail. "But no!" she said. "They gave
him phone privileges! It felt like he was on the phone to us in London
all day!"

Through Julian Schlossberg, Allen was able to get films for the inmates to watch, and he acted as the projectionist. As an entertainment-
industry big shot, Allen became something of a jailhouse celebrity.
That meant pleading ignorance when asked for business advice by
wiseguys and taking a ribbing from the guards. "How the hell did they
ever get a guy like you?" they'd ask. "Couldn't you buy your way out?"

The time was easy but killingly slow, a maddening, smothering tor-
ture of enforced vacuity on a hectic mind. He was glad to be released
on September 12, a few days early in recognition of good behavior, and
eager to return to his world.

Allen did not, however, go back to living with Betty in Riverdale. She
had long known and been unhappy over his dalliances, but when the
government literally made a public case out of his relationship with
Iris, it was one humiliation too many. Still, Allen didn't want a divorce
and steadfastly refused to consider it even though Betty was willing
to give him one and Iris was eager to marry him. His friends and colleagues couldn't comprehend what he was thinking. It was as if Allen
had his own rules and code, his own mystifying one-man religion in
which the *shonda*—the public scandal—was the divorce itself rather
than the underlying and all-too-evident acts of pain and betrayal behind it. After his years in the orphanage and a lifetime of obsessing
over his father's indifference, Allen was incapable of splitting from

his family — or at least from the idea of his family. As a father, he was unfailingly loving and just as needy as an infant himself, holding his children in bear-hug embraces that were both heartfelt and stifling. He moved into the Plaza Hotel and then, with Iris, into one of the two apartments ABKCO had bought on the Upper East Side. But on the Jewish High Holy Days, Allen Klein went back to Riverdale and sat at the head of the table with Betty and their children. It didn't have to make sense to anyone but him.

Klein was just as enigmatic in the office. Joel Silver, compelled to testify against him at the trial, was now viewed guardedly — but he didn't lose his job. At such moments, it was impossible to tell whether Klein, the man capable of having several motives for any action, was pondering his morality or his popularity. Perhaps Silver knew too much to be let go, or perhaps Klein, who could be jaw-droppingly insulting in a business meeting or negotiation but hated doing anything unpleasant personally, was simply trying to avoid dealing with the situation. When Al Steckler, ABKCO's ex–creative director, dropped in to visit his former coworkers, the two men ran into each other in the lobby of 1700 Broadway; Klein welcomed him warmly and they chatted amiably on the elevator ride up to the office. Steckler sat down with the first person he saw, and thirty seconds later, the telephone on that desk rang. It was Klein, telling his employee to get rid of Al. On another occasion, Klein flew on the Concorde to England and rented his usual penthouse suite at the Dorchester, taking it for two weeks in order to guarantee its availability for the two nights he actually needed it, just so he could be in the London office when a secretary was fired. He didn't actually tell her personally — though the woman had to know that Klein was in the office, he wasn't even in the room when she was given notice — he just had to be there, and it didn't matter to him if his presence cost more than he paid the woman in a year. More than he wanted money, he wanted what he wanted.

On the evening of December 8, 1980, three months after Allen Klein's release from jail, John Lennon was murdered outside his apartment building, the Dakota. Allen was unable to attend the public memorial in Central Park the following Sunday because he had to be at a wedding, but during the reception, he and his elder daughter, Robin, stepped outside, stood together in the cold, and silently lit a candle.

Eager to pay his respects to Yoko Ono and find out if he could help her in any way, Allen was told to come by the recording studio where she was already assembling the album *Season of Glass,* her anguished response to Lennon's senseless death. Ono looked at Klein, who was on his way to an awards dinner and dressed in a tuxedo.

"He had so much to live for," she told him. "You should have died instead of him."

## 14

---

# NO SYMPATHY FOR THE DEVIL

BY 1980, PEOPLE KNEW three things about Allen Klein: he'd been released by the Beatles, released by the Rolling Stones, and released from
prison. The decade ahead hardly seemed promising.

Seemingly finished in the music business, Allen found his career as
a film producer was also stalled. After *The Greek Tycoon,* he and Ely
Landau had tried and failed to develop several other projects, including two films that would eventually get made by others, *That Champi-
onship Season* and *The Stunt Man.* He passed on a chance to produce
Monty Python's *Life of Brian,* its humor eluding him, and instead acquired the film rights to a book that had captivated Keitel: natural-
ist Gerald Durrell's memoir of growing up on Corfu, *My Family and
Other Animals.* Never satisfactorily developed, the project languished
before moving to the BBC, where it became first a ten-part television
series and then a feature film. Klein stepped in briefly as an uncred-
ited producer for Robert Towne's *Personal Best* when Towne got into a
wrenching battle with his backer David Geffen.

He tried his hand at producing theater. Julian Schlossberg took
Allen to a showcase by the husband-and-wife team of Renée Taylor
and Joseph Bologna, who were seeking backers for a new romantic

comedy, and the two friends decided to take a shot despite having no theater experience. "We'll learn to do it together," an upbeat Allen told Julian.

School wasn't in session very long; *It Had to Be You* opened May 10, 1981, at the John Golden Theater and ran barely a month. The final debut of the 1980–1981 Tony Award season, the play left *New York Times* theater critic Frank Rich feeling he'd worked one night too many. "I'm afraid the season didn't end with a bang or even a whimper," he wrote, "just an attenuated yawn."

Undeterred, Klein turned next to a play by a heavyweight, the groundbreaking American dramatist Edward Albee, whose most successful and frequently performed plays were *Who's Afraid of Virginia Woolf?* and *The Zoo Story*. But the play Klein produced, *The Man Who Had Three Arms,* might have been the nadir of Albee's career, and it closed after two weeks. The only person who seemed to be getting fat on Klein's theater career was Frank Rich, who had another opportunity to deliver some of his most withering zingers. According to Rich, the play, which was directed by Albee, didn't add up to the sum of its parts; he found it by turns insulting, misogynistic, and a painfully embarrassing spectacle—"a temper tantrum in two acts."

Retreating from the Great White Way, Allen and ABKCO had nothing to show for their troubles except a financial crunch. The company had steady-earning assets in its recordings and music-publishing catalogs but little in the way of new revenue streams. But two angels were about to appear on the horizon: compact discs and Sam Cooke.

As the new vice president of A&R at RCA Records, Gregg Geller had his work cut out for him.

It was the spring of 1984 and Geller, who until recently had been at the far more successful Columbia Records, arrived at a label that, if not moribund, was certainly second tier. Unlike CBS, Columbia Records' owner, which viewed Columbia as a valuable and integral part of the company, the RCA Corporation, a major military and government contractor, was a little embarrassed to be in the record business. Indeed, RCA's corporate executives gave the impression that they were less concerned with the company's profit picture than they were with making sure that the label did not sign anyone too weird and raise eyebrows in Washington. As a result, RCA, which had once vied with Columbia to be the top American recording company, was now a music-industry also-ran. Geller, however, was no corporate hack; he was in it for the music and wanted to change the label's culture and reputation.

Near the top of his to-do list was searching the company's vaults for historic and overlooked material. As Geller was leaving Columbia, another executive, Joe McEwen, had tipped him to a rumor among R&B aficionados about an extraordinary unreleased live album by Sam Cooke that was gathering dust at RCA. While poking around, Geller found the 1962 tapes for a project dubbed *One Night Stand*. When he listened to the tapes, two things were immediately apparent. First, Geller knew why the album had been shelved: at a time when Cooke was achieving pop and crossover success with white listeners, this was something completely antithetical, an R&B show for a black audience in a Miami nightclub. Second, it was an extraordinary performance — incendiary, gripping, and raw. This wasn't the Sam Cooke of "Cupid" and "Everybody Likes to Cha Cha Cha"; this was Sam Cooke sweating and steaming and ripping it up. Geller knew right away it would turn a lot of heads, cast Cooke in a different light, and intrigue a new generation. He had to put it out.

When Geller said as much to his boss, he was told flatly that wouldn't be possible. "There was a laundry list of issues with Allen Klein, who controlled Sam's recordings," said Geller. "And RCA hadn't been able to get anywhere with Klein or put out anything by Sam Cooke since 1970. However, they said if *I* wanted to try and talk with him, please feel free."

Geller was filled with trepidation. He had never dealt with Klein but had heard the stories and rumors about the record-industry robber baron who'd broken up the Beatles, conned the Rolling Stones, and been imprisoned and disgraced for selling promos. But those Cooke tapes were mesmerizing. He took a deep breath and made an appointment to see Klein.

As Gregg was an emissary of RCA, Klein met him coolly. RCA executives didn't know what they were doing and usually got it wrong, and Klein had twenty years' worth of examples to prove it. Clearly, Geller was just the latest in a long line of clueless RCA automatons, and Allen began questioning the nervous executive, first generally and then with increasing specificity, about what he wanted and how he thought it should be done. The interrogation lasted five hours. In the end, Klein agreed to let Geller move forward with a live album.

"I had to prove over and over that I had only altruistic and music reasons for doing this," recalled Geller. But the more he talked to Klein, the more the executive was convinced that Allen was asking the right questions. "I'm sure he had financial concerns as well, but it became clear that his first concern was for the music."

Over the subsequent months, Klein would prove very demanding — and impressive. "Allen's attention to detail was phenomenal — we had to get every jot right," said Geller. "It was endless hours on the phone but you ended up sort of loving the guy. I saw that there is a reason artists gravitate toward him: he loves to do battle. And if he's doing battle for you, you're in great hands. For me, the lesson was 'Don't believe the hype.' He was just from an earlier era in the business."

The resulting album, *Live at the Harlem Square Club, 1963*, was immediately hailed as one of the great live albums and drew comparisons to James Brown's classic album from the same period, *Live at the Apollo*. Just as Geller had hoped, it was a strong seller and sparked a renewed interest in the singer.

Its follow-up, a twenty-eight-song retrospective entitled *Sam Cooke: The Man and His Music*, was a huge worldwide success. In the United Kingdom, where Klein had licensed the song "Wonderful World" to Levi's for an ad campaign, the recording — twenty-six years after its initial release — was reissued as a single and went to number two. In short order, Cooke was selling millions of records throughout Europe.

A shot in the arm for ABKCO, the album seemed the prescription for a reinvigorated and happy relationship between Klein and RCA. That did not turn out to be the case. Cooke's resurrection spurred RCA's foreign affiliates to assemble and release their own albums, despite not having the rights to do so. It wasn't hard for Klein to show

that RCA had violated its agreement, and he wrested back the rights
to release Cooke's recordings. "There was a reason Allen was so difficult for record companies to deal with," said Geller, who left RCA in
1987 and was hired by ABKCO as a producer. "They were frequently
wrong."

A more lasting impact on ABKCO came from CDs. The audio compact disc, co-developed by Philips and Sony and introduced in 1981,
would bring profound changes to the record business. In its first decade, the format ushered in boom times; with a suggested list price of
$15.98, it effectively doubled the price of albums while making vinyl
albums obsolete. Not only were new albums suddenly twice as expensive, but many fans purchased much of their old record collections in
the new format. It was found money for the business, and the major
labels became flush with cash.

For ABKCO, the emergence of CDs held out a great deal of promise
but also a practical problem. With the technology exclusively owned
and tightly held by Philips and Sony, demand far outstripped production capabilities. There were only a handful of manufacturing facilities
worldwide, and record companies had to queue up; an independent
like ABKCO was at the back of the line. It wasn't until late 1986 that
ABKCO was finally able to release its thirteen Rolling Stones albums
on CD, simultaneously with the later albums on Rolling Stones Records, which were then distributed by CBS Records.

For Klein, the coordinated CD program meant the start of a dé-
tente with the Stones. Their last legal tussle, two years earlier, had been
a result of Allen's propensity to drag his heels on royalty payments,
something Allen's lawyer Gideon Cashman believed Klein did just to
annoy Jagger. In 1984, Jagger and Richards had brought a suit to break
their publishing agreement, stating that the company had failed to pay
royalties in a reasonable and timely manner, which constituted material breach. The case was essentially tossed out when the Stones' financial adviser, Prince Rupert Loewenstein, admitted on the stand that he
and Klein frequently made friendly hundred-dollar bets over when the
royalties would be paid. The judge, seeing no reason to treat the situation as a material breach, encouraged both sides to reach a settlement.

"Obviously, if the guy was betting with Allen, it's not a serious thing," said Cashman. "But Allen lost his ability to diddle them as much as he would have liked."

As it had in the past when the Stones' albums were on London, ABKCO continued to handle the manufacturing and sell finished goods to the American record distributor, which at this point was PolyGram. Again, that meant ABKCO's profit margins were unusually high, and the proliferation of CDs lifted ABKCO out of its financial crunch.

"What the fuck are we even doing here?"

It was just before Christmas of 1984 and Allen Klein sat with Michael Kramer in an otherwise empty midtown Manhattan screening room. They'd received an urgent but cryptic call from Paramount Pictures the night before saying it was imperative that Klein come and screen an upcoming film.

Without anyone giving them a word of explanation, the lights went down and the screen lit up. The film, starring Harrison Ford and Kelly McGillis, was entitled *Witness*. Ford played a lawman guarding the only witness to a brutal Mob murder: a young Amish boy. Though the man is an outside and unwelcome presence in the cloistered community, he and the boy's mother, McGillis, are soon attracted to each other. Klein, however, wasn't interested in the plot. "What the hell is going *on* here?" he muttered to Kramer every few minutes. "I don't get why we're here!" An hour into the film, the clouds suddenly parted.

Alone in a barn with the mother, the detective turned on the radio. A sound-alike recording of Sam Cooke's "Wonderful World" was heard in the background. "Oh!" Klein exclaimed, immediately surmising that the producers had neglected to apply for a sync license.

Klein had long complained that film licenses for music were vastly underpriced. But a song playing in the background of the scene was considered incidental use, so it was in Klein's interest as the song's co-publisher to make an easy and reasonable deal — maybe charge the studio a couple thousand dollars — and not force the producers to dub in another song. But when Ford began to sing along with the tune, Klein

sat up in his chair and his eyes got large. Soon the actor was whirl-
ing McGillis around the barn in an illicit embrace, and the strains of
"Wonderful World" became an integral part of the scene. The situation had just changed, and radically: If Klein didn't give permission to
use the music, the song couldn't just be stripped out; the whole scene
would have to be reshot. And clearly, *Witness* was done and about to be
released. He had Paramount by the balls! A wide-eyed Allen turned to
his nephew. "I don't fucking believe this!" According to Kramer, a deal
worth over $200,000 was struck.

As with the five-dollar royalty he'd gotten on the album *The Concert
for Bangladesh,* an extraordinary situation allowed Klein to cut a deal
that, while unique, demonstrated that studios could pay artists significantly more money than they usually did. By the end of the decade,
the popularity of MTV made Hollywood eager to exploit popular music, and licensing and synchronization fees went wild; almost every
record company had a vice president whose sole job was developing
soundtrack opportunities. Films with seven-figure music budgets were
not uncommon. Said Kramer: "The eighties and nineties turned out to
be a good time to be Allen Klein."

In early 1988, Klein's estranged former attorney and crony Marty Machat developed a bad cough that he couldn't shake. A heavy smoker,
Machat was diagnosed with advanced lung cancer and died just a few
weeks later, in March. Allen, who hadn't spoken with Machat since
refusing to include him in his dealings with the Beatles nineteen years
earlier, heard of Machat's passing from Gregg Geller. Klein responded
to the news with a thoughtful, faraway look that Geller read as sad-
ness and introspection. Two days later, when Geller learned that Klein
was now managing Phil Spector — whom Machat had represented — he
wasn't so sure he'd interpreted that look correctly.

If mutual need was the determinant, it was an ideal match. Klein
had become an industry outcast. His only client was the singer/song-
writer Bobby Womack, and his steamroller negotiating skills and en-
cyclopedic knowledge of the music business were largely wasted, applied solely to promoting and exploiting the recordings and publishing

held by ABKCO. He needed a big-ticket, brand-name client — preferably one with problems for him to solve. Spector more than fit the bill; like Klein, the legendary producer had played himself to the industry's margins. His reputation for brilliance remained, but that legacy wasn't enough to erase an equally well-known propensity for paranoid and erratic, sometimes threatening behavior. No one who visited Spector's home knew what to expect: ABKCO's Al Steckler recalled dropping by unannounced with George Harrison — for whom Phil had produced both *All Things Must Pass* and *The Concert for Bangladesh* — and being chased away with a shotgun blast. Spector hadn't worked in years, his last productions having been late-seventies albums by Leonard Cohen and the Ramones that ran counter to fan expectations and received mixed reviews. But he did have business problems that cried out for resolutions.

His biggest difficulty concerned his publishing company, Mother Bertha Music, which held his share of the copyrights on songs he'd written or cowritten. Administration was handled by another publishing company, Trio, which was formed and controlled by the songwriters Jerry Leiber and Mike Stoller, with whom Spector had sometimes cowritten. Trio, in turn, was administrated by a large, global publisher, Warner/Chappell Music. Warner/Chappell collected and paid Trio, which then paid Spector through Mother Bertha. But Spector complained to Klein that he wasn't being paid properly. "Warner was paying his share to Trio and they were not paying him," recalled attorney Don Zakarin, who worked with Klein and handled the Trio dispute. "It was a lot of money."

Bringing a case in federal court, Klein and Spector wanted to break the agreement with Trio, license directly to Warner/Chappell, and then co-administer with Trio. When Zakarin explained to Klein that a win in court could get them only the money they said they were owed and not co-administrative rights, Klein said he wanted to settle the case and seek those rights some other way.

Zakarin thought this a dubious strategy; he couldn't see how they could get more in a settlement than they could through a win. But he was wrong — Klein had recognized that the real deep-pocket target, the one with the most to lose, wasn't Trio but Warner/Chappell. "I think Warner's put pressure on Trio to get this done," Zakarin said. "They were embarrassed and concerned it could blow up into something involving other subpublishers if it were heavily publicized." And it didn't help Warner/Chappell's case when their executive vice president and general counsel Don Biederman made an embarrassing gaffe in depositions.

As was his habit when he took depositions, Klein rented a bungalow at the Beverly Hills Hotel, but he didn't introduce himself to Biederman when he arrived. Biederman recognized Zakarin and a court stenographer but didn't know the two others present, Klein and his English solicitor Peter Howard. Used to peppering his counsel with notes during hearings and depositions, Klein wrote furiously as Biederman answered questions and constantly handed notes to Howard, who read them and passed them to Zakarin. Biederman, assuming Peter Howard was Klein, was at first distracted and then annoyed by the stranger scribbling madly every time he answered a question. Eventually he lost his patience. Jumping up and pointing a finger at Klein, he angrily bellowed, "Okay, who the fuck are you?"

When he was told of his error, an apologetic Biederman slumped back into his chair as if he'd been shot. He approached Klein at the next break and immediately began exploring a settlement. Klein and Spector got the administrative agreement they'd wanted all along. Marveled Zakarin, "I'd never seen that done before, where you got more in a settlement than you would in an outright win."

Klein had another odd win practically fall into his lap courtesy of the British rock band the Verve.

As Allen's constant companion and longtime employee, Iris Keitel didn't have to guess how he would react to a particular proposition or problem. When Jazz Summers, the manager of the British group the Verve, called in early 1997 to say the band wanted to get publishing clearance for a sample, Iris handled the situation. She told Summers that someone from the record company had already phoned and tried to low-ball ABKCO with an offer of 15 percent. "I've told him to fuck

off, Jazz," she said. "We don't like people stealing our music. I've spoken to Allen. We're not going to agree to this."

Indeed, Klein was ultraprotective. ABKCO was happy to support
writers who wanted to collaborate with other artists, but he saw sampling as a dilution of a work's viability and didn't want to encourage
people to use samples and then negotiate retroactively.

That was precisely what the Verve's musicians were trying to do. In
this case, the sample, used in a song entitled "Bitter Sweet Symphony,"
was taken from an instrumental version of the Rolling Stones song
"The Last Time" that had appeared on an album by the Andrew Loog
Oldham Orchestra. The Verve had cleared the rights to sample the
recording from Decca Records, but they hadn't thought about getting
permission for the underlying composition until after the fact. The
irony was that the segment lifted from the Oldham recording didn't
sound a bit like the original Stones song, and the arranger who'd written the riff, David Whitaker, wasn't even listed as a composer. As it
stood, the credits for "Bitter Sweet Symphony" were shared between
Verve vocalist Richard Ashcroft and Mick Jagger and Keith Richards.
But the record couldn't be released without the permission of Jagger
and Richards's publisher, ABKCO Music.

At a loss, Summers let his record company take a whack at it. Ken
Berry, the head of EMI Records, came to New York and called on
Klein. He played Klein the completed Verve album, *Urban Hymns,*
which EMI's Virgin label was betting would be a big hit. And "Bitter
Sweet Symphony" was its obvious lead single. So Allen could appreci-
ate how imperative it was that he grant a license.

"There's no sampling of our music," he said. "We just don't believe
in it."

"Oh, fuck," said the head of EMI Records.

Klein let a day or two pass before calling Berry. He realized EMI
and the band were in a bind, he said, and he was willing to make an
exception to his rule and grant a license — if Ashcroft sold ABKCO his
rights as lyricist and the company became the sole publisher of "Bitter
Sweet Symphony." The bargain was made; Richard Ashcroft was paid a
thousand dollars.

The deal was as unsparing as any in Klein's career; he held all the cards, played them, and raked in the pot. When music photographer Mick Rock happened to call Klein that day to see how he was, it was obvious to him that Allen was enjoying himself. "I was very bad today," he said.

The album did, in fact, become a hit, and the sampled riff in "Bitter Sweet Symphony" was a stadium-ready crowd pleaser that would prove extremely popular for use at sporting events. ABKCO actively exploited the composition, licensing it to be used in commercials around the world for various products, including Nike shoes and Opel automobiles. When the band decided the song was being overexposed and overused, they declined to license the original recording for any more commercials. As the publisher, ABKCO instead commissioned its own recordings for commercial use. To date, "Bitter Sweet Symphony" remains one of ABKCO's best-earning compositions. For Klein, the old lion, it was the chance to linger over one last big kill. For Jagger and Richards, "Bitter Sweet Symphony" produced both a payday and a Grammy nomination for Song of the Year — pretty good, considering they had nothing to do with it and it didn't sound anything like what they'd actually written.*

Spector and Klein were an oddly matched pair, two deposed Napoleons wandering the fringes of the music business as if on a shared Elba. Spector was unpredictable, to say the least; during one visit to his home, Klein and Peter Howard weren't allowed to leave until they convinced Spector they were about to plow the Beverly Hills Hotel limousine through the locked driveway gate. Nonetheless, Spector became one of Klein's frequent companions, socializing with him and Iris and sitting through the couple's fiery arguments over Allen's staunch refusal to divorce Betty.

---

* Such borrowings and elaborations constitute the provenance and history of popular songs. Jagger and Richards's composition almost certainly owes its inspiration — not to mention its chorus — to a traditional gospel song, "This May Be the Last Time," recorded by the Staple Singers in 1955. Fortunately for the Stones, the Staple Singers weren't managed by Allen Klein.

"They used to have some bitter fights, Allen and Iris," Spector said. "She wanted her man and wanted to be married to him. And he was not about to give up his children and wife and that relationship. It made no sense to anyone but Allen, but that was Allen. We would be in the car and he would be driving and arguing with her at the same time. We'd be scared to death that he'd hit a car."

Mostly, however, Klein wanted companionship, someone to climb into the limousine with him at night and drive out to Newark. "He always talked about his childhood," said Spector. "Always. Always talked about growing up in the home. Always talked about his sister. Always talked about the poverty . . . the loneliness . . . the lack of guardianship. As often as he could, as much as he could. He must have told me the story a thousand times if he told it to me once."

Still fighting his lifelong battle against silence and pauses, Klein suffered from not having enough to do. Ever eager to play the host and dictate the agenda, he now became a cross between Uncle Allen and Santa Claus. When Mick Rock had a massive heart attack and required quadruple-bypass surgery, Klein had him moved from a hospital in Staten Island to the care of his own Manhattan cardiologist at Beth Israel and paid the photographer's medical bills. Rock would later joke that the doctors at Beth Israel's cardiac unit used heroic measures to save his life because they were afraid Klein would stop contributing to the hospital if he died, but he told Allen he didn't know how to begin to thank him. Klein waved him off. "You're my ticket to heaven," he said. Klein sent Andrew Oldham to the same doctor and Andrew, when not ruminating on how he'd given away a kingdom to Klein, could be counted on to be Allen's houseguest or traveling companion — on Allen's dime, of course.

Most days at the office, Klein would grab a secretary, head uptown to Zabar's, the Upper West Side gourmet market and temple to all things smoked, pickled, and creamed, and return with several hundred dollars' worth of choice goodies for everyone. Hosted days off — picnics and visits to Klein's Hamptons beach house — became a regular part of the ABKCO culture.

Diagnosed with diabetes at forty, Klein dutifully took his prescribed medications but made no other concessions to the illness in his life-style. His favorite meal remained the Italian at Jimmy Buff's in New Jersey: two deep-fried hot dogs jammed into a giant bun along with a greasy, oozing handful of onions, peppers, and fried potatoes, and he delighted in either wowing or horrifying others with meals at the ram-shackle stand, preferably as the last stop on a narrated tour of Newark covering his old neighborhood playgrounds and the cemetery where his parents and grandparents were buried.

Now in his sixties, the man who once sent out Christmas cards bill-ing himself as the biggest bastard in the valley evinced a softer, gentler Klein.

"There are three phases in the life of many successful businessmen," observed Laurence Myers. "The stages are dishonorable, honorable, and honored. The first phase is when you're struggling and you'll do whatever you have to do and you're as dishonorable as you have to be to establish yourself. And then, when you've got some money, it becomes very important to be known as honorable: 'That man's word is his bond—you don't have to worry about anything.' And in the last stage you want to be honored. If you're in the toy business, you want to be chairman of the Toy Federation; if you're in the music business, you want to be inducted into the Rock and Roll Hall of Fame. Allen's life very much followed that. I was with him in the dishonorable stage. I'm not preaching or disapproving—I learned!"

Some who knew the industry intimately saw little reason for Klein to be ostracized. "I really liked him," said Irving Azoff, who has man-aged dozens of acts since the early seventies, including the Eagles, and who, while head of MCA Records, negotiated with Klein to sign Bobby Womack. "He really cared about his artists. He cared about Bobby and he still cared about Phil Spector long after Phil turned into a joke. Maybe he took too big a piece—I don't know. But in those days, every-body took too big a piece. He didn't strike me as any more mercenary than Ahmet Ertegun or any of the guys from that era."

Indeed, Klein became one of the largest financial supporters of the Rock and Roll Hall of Fame; though a small company, ABKCO bought more tables—at ten thousand dollars apiece—for the hall's annual in-duction dinner at the Waldorf Astoria than most major record companies. His postdinner parties held in Waldorf suite 37A with Spector as cohost but Allen picking up the tab were lavish and legendary blowouts, a must-attend event for both musicians and executives.

Maybe Klein intended his support and high profile to remind the Hall of Fame members that he'd played a key role in modernizing the record business, or maybe he hoped the table packed with friends and clients like Bobby Womack, Lloyd Price, Andrew Oldham, and the family of Sam Cooke demonstrated that he was hardly a pariah, but in any case, he was knocking on a locked door. It wasn't because of his tax conviction; the Rock and Roll Hall of Fame honors musical achievement, music's culture, and music's facilitators, and it hasn't balked at welcoming producers and label presidents who ran dodgy businesses or abused, underpaid, or outright robbed performers. The organization's indifference to an honoree's actions in the wider world is best evidenced by the continued inclusion of Spector, who was inducted into the Hall of Fame in 1989 and remains there today despite his 2009 conviction for murder. But while Klein was certainly a music-industry professional and artists' advocate, he was never a member of the flock — he was the lone wolf terrorizing it. Indeed, he was a constant antagonist who made his money and his contribution to the business by shifting the balance of financial and artistic power away from the labels and toward the creators. Once he started that shift and demonstrated the leverage of the artists, it was only a matter of time before his confrontational tactics (and his ability to charge clients a steep fee) would be undercut by a new class of more conventional managers, attorneys, and financial advisers. "Allen couldn't do anything now," observed Laurence Myers. "Because everyone is aware and advised by people who are aware. There's no deal that could be done only by Allen Klein." Klein became passé, a victim of his own success.

It was no surprise that the business didn't remember Klein warmly, but it was surprising that he seemed to hope it would. He was, after all, the hard-nosed realist who'd dismissed business ethics as a canard and whose calling card was the ability to outthink an opponent and then get under his skin. Doing that well is no prescription for popularity.

Of course, pissing off the two most popular rock stars in the world, Paul McCartney and Mick Jagger, didn't help him, either.

Klein refused to believe Yoko Ono really wished him dead. Even at the moment she spoke so bitterly, he would not accept it. "You'll never lose me as a friend," he recalled telling her. And indeed, the relationship continued. Jann Wenner, a friend of Ono, said it wasn't unusual for him to run into Klein at her apartment.

As always, it was impossible to say whether it was a matter of altruism or self-interest. Klein thought of himself as someone who came through in the clutch — he liked to say he was a foul-weather friend. And he clearly felt a duty to and bond with Ono. At the same time, he never stopped being Allen Klein, business manager and salesman supreme. No matter how much the industry ignored him, he was always on the comeback trail.

The Rolling Stones' early catalog and songs remained far more valuable than anyone had initially imagined, and they proved Allen's greatest tool for relevance. As an administrator, Klein was serious about protecting the integrity of the work, as he had been with Cooke. There was no creaming or discounting of the Stones' music, no eye-rolling licenses for commercial use. "He was so conscious of not diluting their potency," said Kramer.

When he saw a possibility for a worthwhile project, he went after it. As part of an earlier settlement with the band, Klein had acquired the album and video rights to *The Rolling Stones Rock and Roll Circus.* It had been easy for the Stones to give up the rights, since the film didn't actually exist. After they'd decided not to air it on television, editing had never been completed. The original tapes had been scattered all over England and forgotten. But in the 1990s, Klein's daughter Robin, who'd begun what would eventually become her career in 1979 by snagging a job as an editing assistant on the concert film

*No Nukes,* started scouring London for the missing tapes. She found some in the possession of the Who, some in the Stones' warehouse, and much of the rest sitting in Ian Stewart's garage. For a lost performance by Marianne Faithfull, Robin uncovered and substituted a sumptuous crane-shot performance of "Something Better" done for French television. The search and reconstruction of the film took her six years. While only a modest moneymaker, the resurrected *Rock and Roll Circus* would prove both a labor of love and a fascinating document. Though Jagger had reportedly shelved the film over fears that the Who had upstaged the Stones at their own gig, he needn't have worried. The Who's performance in the finally realized film is indeed explosive, and appearances by others, particularly John Lennon and Yoko Ono, Jethro Tull, and Taj Mahal, range from historically interesting to moving. But the Stones, who perform tracks from *Beggars Banquet* and *Let It Bleed,* more than justify their slot at the top of the bill. The film's most extraordinary and revealing performance is by Jagger; watching him seduce and force his will on the audience — singing, crawling, beckoning, *commanding* — you know that there are no accidents of fame.

By the nineties, Klein and the Stones had finally settled into a livable arrangement. Like a divorced couple who've learned to set aside animosity and lingering bitterness when the children need something, they negotiated partnerships and agreements. In 2002, the band toured and marked their fortieth anniversary with a two-CD forty-song collection, *Forty Licks.* The first twenty numbers were culled from the ABKCO-controlled catalog, a deal that required real give-and-take to achieve. The Stones' catalog was ABKCO's lifeblood, and this compilation was just the kind of one-shot alternative to buying the original albums that Klein had always avoided. Yet its value to the band and to their tour — and to the Stones' continuing viability — was obvious. When Allen's son, Jody, suggested a five-year payment formula that approximated what ABKCO expected to lose on catalog sales over that period, everyone found it far-thinking and reasonable. Everyone except Allen, that is, who seemed miffed to have the solution proposed by someone else, even if it was his son.

Having suffered a series of heart attacks of varying severity — one was misdiagnosed as indigestion — Klein was clearly slowing down, relying more on Keitel and Jody in negotiations. In 2003, when Apple Computer was launching its iTunes store, Steve Jobs came to see Klein. Having failed to make a deal with the Beatles, he wanted to debut the store with the music of the Rolling Stones. Klein, the guardian and hoarder of catalogs, had philosophic and economic arguments against unbundling, the selling of individual tracks rather than full albums. But eventually he recognized that downloads, paid or unpaid, were a reality; data from their distributor suggested that hundreds of thousands of Stones tracks were being shared online every day. A year after Jobs's approach, Iris and Jody negotiated a multiyear revenue deal with iTunes, placing the Stones and ABKCO among the handful of traditional artists and record operations who made meaningful money online. But the need for ABKCO to be more than a one-man operation became more pressing in 2004, when Klein, attending the Grammys where ABKCO won an award for the Sam Cooke documentary *Legend,* broke his foot and required surgery. Never the same afterward, he was subsequently diagnosed with Alzheimer's disease.

Peter Brown was a long way from punching a cash register in the Epstein family's Liverpool furniture store.

The former Beatles aide-de-camp and Apple director moved to New York in the early seventies to work for music and film mogul Robert Stigwood, then became a partner in Brown Lloyd James, an international public relations firm that polished the reputations of some of the world's most controversial rulers and dictators. Among its clients were Libya's Muammar Qaddafi, the government of Ecuador, and the wife of Syrian president Bashar al-Assad, and the firm's work has been criticized as "distinctly against the ethical tenets of modern public relations" by the chairwoman of the Public Relations Society of America.

Nonetheless, Brown had adapted well to life in New York. He lived on Central Park West — it had been during a visit to Brown's apartment that John Lennon and Yoko Ono discovered a sublet in the building next door, the Dakota — and liked to lunch at Michael's, the midtown restaurant popular with music, film, and publishing executives. It was here that a dining companion informed Brown that Allen Klein had died.

The news surprised him. Brown had never liked Klein and had taken pains to portray himself as a vigilant soldier protecting the Beatles and their Apple employees from Klein's barbaric onslaught. Still, he was taken aback, and this was the first he'd heard of it. Brown spied attorney Allen Grubman at an adjoining table and was sure he'd know if it was true.

More than anyone else in the music business, Grubman occupied Klein's old spot as the empire-building wildcatter who changed the rules and who was regularly hired by superstars in search of top-of-the-market recording contracts. But unlike Klein, the label antagonist, Grubman wouldn't bite the hand that fed him. His innovation was to *not* fight with the record companies; he always argued for a rich contract, but executives knew Grubman wanted to make a deal, and he rarely advised a client to switch labels. As for his own payday, Grubman, like Klein, recognized his innovations and successes gave him the clout to seek unorthodox and lucrative arrangements with his clients. Rather than set a fee in advance of negotiations, Grubman preferred to talk money after he'd obtained a new contract for the client. Not coincidentally, that was almost always the moment the artist was happiest, and if, as with Klein, the value of the newly secured contract quoted by Grubman was actually a blue-sky number based on extensions, options, and other bonuses that were possible rather than guaranteed and that couldn't be truly assessed for years — well, that was the way the business worked, right?

Turning to Grubman's table, Brown asked, "Did Allen Klein die?"

Grubman shrugged. "I don't think so," he said, and he nodded across the room. "He's sitting over there. But why don't you ask him?"

Later, on his way out, Klein ambled past Brown's table. Dressed in a tracksuit, he nodded a silent greeting, but Brown wasn't sure Klein actually recognized him.

• • •

Allen Klein died July 4, 2009. Yoko and Sean Ono Lennon came to the funeral to pay their respects, offering particular support to Allen's long-term companion, Iris, whom Yoko had come to know well. After decades of being dragged out to the cemetery in Newark by Allen, his friends were surprised to find he was to be interred in a plot in Queens he'd never mentioned.

At a memorial service a few weeks later, Allen's wife, Betty, sat on one side of the room, Iris on the other.

The only former client to attend the service was Andrew Loog Oldham, who spoke emotionally to those who had gathered, saying the Rolling Stones were destined to be successful but wouldn't have been as big without Allen. He recalled their travels together: swimming in Taormina, golfing in New Orleans, playing cards in Paris and tennis everywhere. He called Klein both his father and the elder brother who annoyed and hurt him but was also always a friend. "We knew each other for forty-four years," Andrew said, "and for many of those, he treated me better than I treated myself." Still, in the years to come, Oldham couldn't quite stop referring to his nearly lifelong friend and tormentor as "Allen Crime."

In the year before Klein's death, at least one old partner turned nemesis had been recognized and embraced. Frustrated after decades of ABKCO keeping *The Holy Mountain* and *El Topo* out of circulation, director Alejandro Jodorowsky finally claimed the films were his and released them in Europe. ABKCO responded by suing him in England and France. But it soon became obvious that both sides had grown weary of the feud.

Jodorowsky and Klein, who hadn't spoken in nearly thirty years, agreed to meet informally at the Lanesborough Hotel in London. When Klein opened the door of his suite, he encountered his mirror image: an old Jew with a shock of silver hair. The two men fell into each other's arms.

"I don't know why we're fighting," Klein said.

"Allen, you look so *good!*"

The lawsuits were dropped. ABKCO paid Jodorowsky to remaster the films for video release, and a love fest was the order of the day. Jodorowsky, with a set of beautiful new teeth and a beautiful new wife and still hustling to make his movies, was Allen's kind of guy.

Klein gave him the limo tour of Newark and treated him to dinner at Jimmy Buff's.

# ACKNOWLEDGMENTS

IN 2011, I RECEIVED A CALL from a record executive I had written about, Lyor Cohen. He said Jody Klein, the head of ABKCO Records, wished to meet me. I didn't know Jody, but I certainly recognized ABKCO and understood that he was the son of its founder, the music-business lightning rod Allen Klein.

On meeting me, Jody explained that after his father died, two years earlier, the obituaries in the U.S. and abroad, particularly in the British press, had left him in a quandary. "Some of what was said about him was true," he told me. "And a lot of it wasn't." Since then, he'd been thinking that a more in-depth look at his father's life and career could help sort rumor from fact and illuminate a key period in popular culture and the music business.

His proposal was straightforward: If I was interested in undertaking such a project, he would provide access to personal and corporate records, including correspondence, contracts, and documents from legal and civil cases. There would be no monetary arrangement or quid pro quo; he wasn't looking for a particular result or verdict and would have no editorial control or approval. He just wanted an outsider with a working knowledge of the music business to take a long, hard look at Allen Klein and let the chips fall where they may. When I said the project interested me but that the results might not make him happy, it gave him pause. And then we shook hands.

Jody gave me my own moment of pause when he showed me the skids of documents sitting in a New Jersey warehouse. Allen Klein was obsessive and litigious. He might have been happiest when he was plotting legal strategy, and it didn't seem to matter to him whether he was the plaintiff or the target of someone's ire — it was all good, it was all a challenge; it was like playing tennis without having to change your clothes or get up from your desk. Sifting through the mountains of records, decoding contracts, and extracting Allen Klein's narrative proved to be heavy lifting and I sometimes wondered what I had gotten myself into. But Jody Klein never let me down.

I know Jody loved his father deeply and that reading much of this book cannot be easy. I hope, in the end, that I wrote something that makes that worthwhile.

I also owe a deep debt to Allen's daughter Robin and his wife, Betty, who spoke freely and at length with me — sometimes with difficulty, but always with great candor and affection. I hope they see the person they knew in these pages.

The people at ABKCO made me welcome, but I am especially grateful to Maria Papazahariou and Val Collin, who worked most closely with me and who were particularly helpful with locating documents. Their enthusiasm was an enormous encouragement. I also owe a special thank-you to Michael Kramer, who spoke at length and with great feeling about his uncle Allen and his years at ABKCO. Likewise, I'm indebted to Andrew Loog Oldham, whose own remarkable story is so closely entwined with the one I set out to tell. In speaking about Allen Klein, Andrew seemed torn, and it was a revelation when I realized that he couldn't decide what was worse: talking about him or not talking about him. Thanks also to Bill Flanagan, a great student of music and its business, for sharing his thoughts and advice.

My publisher and editor, Eamon Dolan, surpassed all expectations. Spending years on a book is like swimming in the ocean: not only can't you see the shore, but you cease to believe it exists. Eamon has been a thoughtful, challenging, and patient pilot; I hope he'll let me get him wet again.

Copyeditor Tracy Roe's sharp pencil and sharper mind saved me from more gaffes than I'll confess to committing, and I'm particularly grateful for the enthusiasm she brought to the project. My thanks also to the staff at Eamon Dolan Books and Houghton Mifflin Harcourt: Lori Glazer, Ben Hyman, Stephanie Kim, Rosemary McGuinness, and Ayesha Mirza.

Concurrent with this book, I spent a good deal of time with Irving Azoff and got to know him. His insight into both business and human nature—gleaned over six decades of managing careers, running assorted music and film companies, and making trouble—is nonpareil. Watching Irving work is a little like losing your virginity; it's also a master class at the School That No One Gets to Attend. Though he doesn't know it, he had an indirect but significant impact on how I viewed Allen Klein. I thank him for that—and for his generosity.

In 2014 Jeffrey Ressner, my colleague and friend of more than thirty years, died. We were fellow galley slaves back in the day, then went to *Rolling Stone* together before his long stint at *Time*. Anytime I landed at LAX, you could find me forty-five minutes later in Jeffrey's kitchen. He was an open-minded and attentive reader of words and people; I valued his opinion and admired his goodness. I feel as if Jeffrey's passing has transformed Los Angeles into a ghost town.

A special thanks to Paul Feinman and Adam White for letting me rant.

Tea and Sympathy Department: Paula Batson, Arlene and Barrie Bergman, Lori Berk and Geoffrey Rolat, David and Cathy Booth, Crescenzo and Alicia Capece, Dan Doyle, Rina Echavez, Jim and Pam Eigo, Ruth Fecych, Bill Fuchs, Laurie Jakobsen, Eddie and Nancy Karp, Larry Miller, Barbara Orentzel, John and Patty Shuckle, Al Slutsky, Larry Solters, Sam Sutherland, John Swenson, Will and Julie Tanous, Roy Trakin, Jim Whelan.

Hi, Goodmans.

Thanks always to Chuck Verrill, who said yes.

# NOTES

Unless otherwise noted, all quotes attributed to Allen Klein are taken from approximately fifty hours of previously unpublished conversations with music historian Bill Flanagan conducted between October 2000 and August 2003, which ABKCO recorded, transcribed, and made available to the author. Additional unpublished interviews with others who knew and worked with Klein, conducted by Flanagan and Joe McEwen, are specifically credited throughout the book.

## Prologue: London, August 1969

*page*

xii  *"We've fuckin' had it"*: Jann Wenner, "John Lennon: The *Rolling Stone* Interview," part 1, *Rolling Stone*, December 8, 1970.

*"Don't talk to me about ethics"*: Craig Vetter, "Allen Klein: The *Playboy* Interview," *Playboy*, November 1971.

xiv  *"very much ahead of his time"*: *25X5: The Continuing Adventures of the Rolling Stones*, documentary, directed by Nigel Finch, 1990.

## 1. A Foundling's Tale

3  *"I really loved my grandfather"*: Allen Klein with Bill Flanagan, February 14, 2001.

*"I think she really carried her weight"*: Ibid.

4  *"My sister Esther was working"*: Naomi Henkle, interview with the author, December 5, 2011.

*"It was very strange"*: Allen Klein with Bill Flanagan, January 21, 2001.

7  *"painting behind the radiators and in the closets"*: Ibid., February 14, 2001.

8      *"I'll tell you what I got from my father"*: Ibid., January 24, 2001.

10     *"Who is this guy'"*: Bobby Vinton, interview by Jody Klein, May 14, 2008.

13     *"I was tired and couldn't be bothered"*: Betty Klein, interview with the author, November 10, 2011.

14     *"Allen would have been a great psychologist"*: Alan Steckler, interview with the author, July 24, 2013.

       *"Women were a pushover"*: Leonard Leibman, interview with the author, November 12, 2011.

       *"Klein could recognize a vacuum"*: Harold Seider, interview with the author, December 10, 2012.

## 2. Allen Klein and Company

18     *"In the beginning, it was Don Kirshner"*: Joe Smith, *Off the Record: An Oral History of Popular Music* (New York: Warner, 1988), 128–29.

22     *"Marty knew nothing about economics"*: Eric Kronfeld, interview by Joe McEwen, March 3, 2008.

24     *"We wooed him"*: Betty Klein and Jody Klein, interview with the author, September 25, 2012.

       *"Henry Newfield was a very easygoing guy"*: Joel Silver, interview by Joe McEwen, March 18, 2008.

25     *"We were somewhat friendly"*: Marvin Schlachter, interview with the author, November 2, 2013.

       *"I'd go over the books"*: Vetter, "Allen Klein."

       *"I was signed to ABC/Paramount"*: Lloyd Price, interview with the author, no date.

29     *"The only [underpayment] he found was ten thousand copies"*: Steve Blauner, interview with the author, November 19, 2012.

31     *into production deals with UA:* For an in-depth examination of Hecht-Hill-Lancaster's dealings with United Artists, see Tino Balio, *United Artists: The Company That Changed the Film Industry* (Madison: University of Wisconsin Press), 78–91.

## 3. Sam Cooke

37     *"I said to myself, what the hell is this"*: Mark de la Vina, "Jocko: A Philadelphia Original; His Radio Style Rapped Up Fans," *Philadelphia Daily News,* February 18, 1992.

       *"My economic situation"*: *American Bandstand,* broadcast April 4, 1964.

39     *"Well, what do you think"*: Peter Guralnick, *Dream Boogie: The Triumph of Sam Cooke* (Boston: Little, Brown, 2005), 474.

44     *"Talk about* my *reputation"*: Vetter, "Allen Klein."

50     *"I pray to the Blessed Mother"*: Brian T. Olszewski, "Faith Keeps Fame in Perspective for Bobby Vinton," *Catholic Herald,* May 17, 2012.

52    *"These performers aren't children"*: Vetter, "Allen Klein."

54    *"Allen wanted a new relationship where he was the focus"*: Jerry Brandt, interview with the author, March 3, 2013.

57    *"Allen taught me something"*: Laurence Myers, interview with the author, October 22, 2011.

58    *"There were so many wild rumors"*: Joe McEwen, phone conversation with the author, 2013.

59    *"Allen comes in when your harvest"*: Andrew Loog Oldham, remarks at Allen Klein's memorial service, New York City, July 2009.
      *"He just got it quicker than everybody else"*: Michael Kramer, interview with the author, October 10, 2011.
      *"His whole thing going in was 'I'm Robin Hood'"*: Laurence Myers, interview by Joe McEwen, November 13, 2007.

## 4. The Yiddish Invasion

63    *"I thought they were awful"*: "Life of Brian," Brianepstein.com, accessed December 26, 2014, http://www.brianepstein.com/brian.html.

64    *"He looked to his dad for business advice"*: John Robinson, "Get Back and Other Setbacks," *Guardian,* November 21, 2003.

68    *his own clubs for the insurance*: Eric Burdon, *I Used to Be an Animal, but I'm All Right Now* (London: Faber and Faber, 1986), 41.
      *"I was frontman for a band"*: Nick Hasted, "The Making of the Animals' 'House of the Rising Sun,'" *Uncut,* May 2009.

70    *"It was fun performing"*: John Tobler and Stuart Grundy, "Mickie Most," *The Record Producers* (New York: St. Martin's, 1982).

## 5. "People Keep Asking Me If They're Morons"

78    *"I still can't go by a watch shop"*: Andrew Loog Oldham, interview by Dave Haslam, Liverpool Sound City keynote, May 3, 2013.
      *"We didn't mean shit"*: Allen Klein and Andrew Loog Oldham, interview with Bill Flanagan, December 11, 2002.

79    *"He was smarter and sharper"*: Keith Richards with James Fox, *Life* (Boston: Little, Brown, 2010), 169.

82    *"as attractive as Natalie Wood"*: Andrew Loog Oldham, *Stoned* (London: Secker and Warburg, 2000), 21.

84    *"He taught me how to work"*: Ibid., 144.

86    *"Phil looked more like an act than most acts"*: Ibid., 170.
      *"like Napoleon and Hitler"*: Oldham, interview by Haslam.
      *"There was nothing calculated"*: Oldham, *Stoned,* 172.
      *"Brian gave me the job"*: Oldham, interview by Haslam.

87    *"I heard the whole world screaming"*: Oldham, *Stoned,* 163.

88 *"He was the young, hip youth about town"*: Peter Jones, interview with the author, May 1, 2014.

*"authentic and sexually driven"*: Oldham, *Stoned,* 190.

*"He looked at Jagger as Sylvester looks at Tweetie Pie"*: George Melly, *Revolt into Style: The Pop Arts* (London: Faber and Faber, 2012), Kindle edition.

89 *"he was in awe of what he saw"*: Paul Easton, interview with the author, May 30, 2014.

*"God, the Rolling Stones had so little work"*: Jann Wenner, "Mick Jagger Remembers," *Rolling Stone,* December 14, 1995.

*"He was our age"*: Bill Wyman with Ray Coleman, *Stone Alone: The Story of a Rock 'n' Roll Band* (New York: Penguin, 1990), 184.

91 *"Andrew's music input was minimal"*: Richards and Fox, *Life,* 169.

*"It was nothing to do with what we were doing"*: Ibid., 129–30.

92 *"I honestly don't like Andrew Oldham as a person"*: Bill German, "Boogie with Stu," *Beggars Banquet* 20 (newsletter), March/April 1981.

93 *"The Beatles looked like they were in show business"*: Tim Nudd, "What the Man Who Invented the Rolling Stones Can Teach You About Branding: Image Making by Andrew Loog Oldham," *Adweek,* September 25, 2013.

*"They look like boys"*: Judith Simons, "Rolling Stones Gathering No Moss," *Daily Express,* February 28, 1964.

94 *"hair-combing is rare"*: in "Would You Let Your Sister Go with a Rolling Stone?," Ray Coleman, *Melody Maker,* March 14, 1964.

*"terrible things to the musical scene"*: Maureen Cleave, "The Rolling Stones: This Horrible Lot — Not Quite What They Seem," *Evening Standard,* March 21, 1964.

95 *"There's a theory"*: Wyman and Coleman, *Stone Alone,* 162, 184.

96 *"Brian was loath"*: Oldham, *Stoned,* 288.

*"It was Andrew"*: Wyman and Coleman, *Stone Alone,* 214.

97 *"Once it got to America"*: Robert Greenfield, "Keith Richard [*sic*]: The *Rolling Stone* Interview," *Rolling Stone,* August 19, 1971.

98 Andrew *"slung his fur coat around his shoulders"*: Alexis Petridis, "Straight and Narrow: How Pop Lost Its Gay Edge," *Guardian,* February 28, 2012.

99 *"nothing about music whatsoever"*: German, "Boogie with Stu."

100 *"I think Andrew frustrated my dad"*: Paul Easton, interview with the author, May 30, 2014.

*"Andrew was a lover of speed"*: Richards and Fox, *Life,* 188.

## 6. The King of America

104 *"I never saw a guy so much affected by fame"*: Ibid., 189.

105 *"Don't be so fucking mercenary"*: Wyman and Coleman, *Stone Alone,* 394.

108 *"the best move Oldham made"*: Richards and Fox, *Life,* 178.

*"because of your phenomenal success"*: Two letters written on behalf of Oldham and Easton signed by Andrew Loog Oldham, July 29, 1965.

*"[Klein] raised my royalty rate"*: Marianne Faithfull, interview with the author, March 8, 2012.

109 *"I thought he was crazy to make that deal"*: Michael Kramer, interview with the author, August 7, 2012.

110 *"our Mafia promo man"*: Wyman and Coleman, *Stone Alone*, 421.

111 *"Klein was magnificent"*: Richards and Fox, *Life*, 179.

112 *"The Rolling Stones weren't as big as the Beatles"*: Bobby Vinton, interview by Jody Klein, May 14, 2008.

113 *"You got talent"*: Details of Klein's negotiations on behalf of the Kinks in Ray Davies, *X-Ray* (New York: Viking, 1994), 299–303, 353.

115 *"The whole time"*: Oldham, *Stoned*, 243.

116 *"We shook on it"*: Christina Most, interview with the author, May 18, 2014.

117 *"He had an amazing memory"*: Paul Mozian, interview with the author, February 28, 2013.

*"Flashes would go off in his mind"*: Gideon Cashman, interview by Joe McEwen, January 23, 2008.

*"Allen would get very angry"*: Beverly Winston, interview by Joe McEwen, February 11, 2008.

118 *"He would have you do things a thousand ways"*: Emily Barrata Quinn, interview with the author, September 18, 2013.

*"We never had an argument"*: Clive Davis, interview with the author, April 2, 2014.

119 *"What did I want"*: Donovan Leitch, interview with the author, February 10, 2014.

120 *"He didn't sweat about money"*: Julian Schlossberg, interview with the author, March 19, 2012.

121 *"going out for a cheeseburger"*: Author interview with longtime ABKCO employee who asked to remain anonymous.

## 7. ABKCO

123 What kind of schmuck: Abbey Butler, interview with Joe McEwen, February 14, 2008. Unless otherwise noted, all quotes attributed to Abbey Butler are taken from this interview.

128 *regularly spotlighted them on the show*: For an in-depth examination of Clark's relationship with Cameo-Parkway, see John A. Jackson, *American Bandstand: Dick Clark and the Making of a Rock 'n' Roll Empire* (New York: Oxford University Press, 1997).

132 *"will not meet the applicable listing standards"*: Proxy Statement, Special Meeting of Shareholders of Cameo-Parkway Records Inc., September 16, 1968, 1.

## 8. Rock 'n' Roll Circus

138   "There'd been a big change": Klein and Oldham, interview with Bill Flanagan, December 11, 2002.

140   *"The judge managed to turn me":* Richards and Fox, *Life,* 227.

141   *"I knew that we were in trouble then":* Wenner, "John Lennon," part 1.
    *"I got 'em":* Vetter, "Allen Klein."

142   *"He was probably the largest spender":* Leonard Leibman, interview with the author, November 12, 2011.

143   *"And he did it without fanfare":* Julian Schlossberg, interview with the author, March 19, 2012.

144   *"Suddenly they weren't arriving in the studio with songs":* Klein and Oldham, interview with Bill Flanagan, December 11, 2002.
    *"His box of tricks was exhausted":* Richards and Fox, *Life,* 230.

145   *"to piss Andrew off":* Wenner, "Mick Jagger Remembers."

146   *"I do the minimal amount":* Tatiana Siegel, "Jagger's James Brown," *Billboard,* August 2, 2014.
    *"When it came to numbers":* Walter Yetnikoff with David Ritz, *Howling at the Moon* (New York: Broadway Books, 2004), 137–38.

148   *"He'd show up occasionally":* Anthony DeCurtis, "Review: *Beggars Banquet,*" *Rolling Stone,* June 17, 1997.

149   *"a predator in the field of pop artists":* Wyman and Coleman, *Stone Alone,* 558.

## 9. The Prize

154   *"The amount of money owed by EMI was mountainous":* Peter Brown, interview with the author, February 8, 2012.

155   *"It's a business concerning records, films, and electronics":* John Lennon and Paul McCartney, Apple press conference, May 14, 1968, www.beatlesinterviews.org.

157   *"I wanted Apple to run":* Barry Miles, *Paul McCartney: Many Years from Now* (London: Secker and Warburg, 1997), 479.
    *"We haven't got half the money people think we have":* Ray Coleman, "Interview with John Lennon," *Disc and Music Echo,* January 18, 1969.

158   *"Allen Klein says you are in his way":* Derek Taylor, *As Time Goes By* (San Francisco: Straight Arrow Books, 1973), 143–47. This book is also the source for the meetings and conversations preceding Klein's approach.

159   *"He called me once but I never accepted it":* Jann Wenner, "John Lennon: The *Rolling Stone* Interview," part 2, *Rolling Stone,* February 4, 1971.

163   *"I thought, well, if that's the choice":* Affidavit of George Harrison, James Paul McCartney v. John Ono Lennon, George Harrison, Richard Starkey, and Apple Corps Ltd., case 1970 M. No. 6315 in the High Court of Justice, Chancery Division Group B, February 12, 1971.

*"We were convinced by him"*: Affidavit of Richard Starkey in ibid.

164 *"He was trying to subsume me into what he was doing"*: John Eastman, interview with the author, February 15, 2012.

165 *"Fuck it"*: Wenner, "John Lennon," part 2.

168 *"lie like a trooper"*: John Fielding, "Insight: The Toughest Wheeler-Dealer in the Pop Jungle," *Sunday Times,* April 13, 1969.

170 *"Allen Klein's handwriting"*: Peter Brown and Steven Gaines, *The Love You Make: An Insider's Story of the Beatles* (New York: McGraw-Hill, 1983), 343.

171 *"It's fucking serious to John and Paul"*: Ibid.

172 *"didn't like the way it was going"*: Lew Grade, *Still Dancing* (London: William Collins, 1987), 232.

173 *"Allen Klein is coming over"*: Deposition of Allen Klein, *McCartney v. Lennon, Harrison, Starkey, and Apple Corps Ltd.*

## 10. With the Beatles

179 *"He's only been here three months"*: "The Beatles Besieged," *Time,* May 30, 1969.
*"Yoko told me"*: Vetter, "Allen Klein."

183 *"If you're screwing us"*: Brown and Gaines, *The Love You Make,* 349.

186 *"People were robbing us"*: Wenner, "John Lennon," part 2.

187 *"He wanted to get rid of everybody"*: Tony Bramwell and Rosemary Kingsland, *Magical Mystery Tours: My Life with the Beatles* (New York: St. Martin's, 2005), 325.

188 *"that fat bastard"*: Ibid., 333.
*"Everyone hated him"*: Geoffrey Giuliano, *The Lost Beatles Interviews* (New York: Dutton, 1994), 253.
*"You lay down with pigs and you get up dirty"*: These and all Mansfield quotes from Ken Mansfield, *The White Book* (New York: Thomas Nelson, 2007), www.fabwhitebook.com.

190 *"I got supreme pleasure"*: Brown and Gaines, *The Love You Make,* 350–51.

191 *"The most important piece"*: Chris O'Dell, interview by Marshall Terrill, *Day Trippin',* October 10, 2009.
*"The fact that John was completely convinced"*: Peter Asher, interview by Noel Murray, *A.V. Club,* December 1, 2010.

193 *"Paul and I were too bored"*: Affidavit of John Lennon in *McCartney v. Lennon, Harrison, Starkey, and Apple Corps Ltd.*
*"I thought I would take the letters around"*: Affidavit of Richard Starkey in ibid.

## 11. Mr. Popularity

201 *"grateful to Allen"*: "An Interview with Mick Jagger," *Playback,* August 23, 1970.
*"He felt very aggrieved"*: Prince Rupert Loewenstein, *A Prince Among Stones: That Business with the Rolling Stones and Other Adventures* (London: Bloomsbury, 2013), 85.

203  *"What did he want from us"*: Associated Press, "Jagger Testifies About Feud with Ex-Manager," *Gainesville Sun,* April 17, 1984.

208  *"I still cannot understand why Paul acted as he did"*: Affidavit of George Harrison in *McCartney v. Lennon, Harrison, Starkey, and Apple Corps Ltd.*

*"The reality is we're a partnership"*: George Harrison, interview by Howard Smith, WABC Radio, May 1, 1970.

*"He seemed to think"*: Affidavit of George Harrison in *McCartney v. Lennon, Harrison, Starkey, and Apple Corps Ltd.*

*"Paul is the greatest bass guitar player in the world"*: Affidavit of Richard Starkey in ibid.

211  *"Eastmans-Klein power struggle"*: Affidavit of John Lennon in ibid.

*"Mr. Epstein was not a businessman"*: Statement of Morris Finer in ibid.

212  *"Allen did a lot of things based on principle"*: Don Zakarin, interview by Joe McEwen, December 17, 2007.

215  *"Even a murderer has a great line in his own defense"*: Paul Gambaccini, "Paul McCartney: The *Rolling Stone* Interview," *Rolling Stone,* January 31, 1974.

## 12. Some Time in New York City

222  *"Allen's human"*: Peter McCabe and Robert D. Schoenfeld, "John and Yoko: A Long-Lost Conversation," *Penthouse,* September 1984.

*"There were fundamental levels"*: Dan Richter, interview with the author, September 7, 2013.

224  *"The Beatles were fantastic"*: Paul Taylor, "Art; Yoko Ono's New Bronze Age at the Whitney," *New York Times,* February 5, 1989.

*"Very few women were getting shows"*: "Gary James' Interview with the Former Director of Everson Museum on John and Yoko's 'This Is Not Here' 1971 Exhibit, James Harithas," http://www.classicbands.com/JamesHarithasInterview.html.

225  *"Definitely, the idea was there"*: Sean Kirst, "Imagine: John Lennon, and an Almost-Beatles-Reunion in Syracuse," *Syracuse Post Standard,* December 8, 2005.

228  *"Of course I fucked her"*: Alejandro Jodorowsky, interview with the author, November 1, 2011.

233  *"artistic suicide"*: Stephen Holden, "Some Time in New York City," *Rolling Stone,* July 20, 1972.

## 13. A Sport and a Pastime

240  *attorneys took the case to court*: For an in-depth discussion of the tangled legal history of this case, see Joseph C. Self, "The 'My Sweet Lord' / 'He's So Fine' Plagiarism Suit," *910 Magazine* (1993).

*"Allen so completely misjudged the pulse of Harrison"*: Gideon Cashman, interview by Joe McEwen, January 23, 2008.

*"The thing that really disappoints me"*: George Harrison, interview by Paul Cashmere, 1994, http://www.noise11.com/news/george-harrison-classic-inter view-with-paul-cashmere-20110926.

242 *Harrison never collected*: For a detailed discussion of the relationship between Harrison and O'Brien, see Robert Sellers, *Very Naughty Boys: The Amazing True Story of HandMade Films* (London: Metro, 2004).
*"tireless efforts"*: Roman Kozak, "Apple/Beatles Settlement: ABKCO Gets $5 Mil; Pays $800,000," *Billboard*, January 22, 1977.

243 *"The choice was"*: Simon Harper, "The Final Days of the Beatles: Paul McCartney Recalls His Darkest Hour," *Clash*, October 19, 2010.

246 *"I was never clear"*: Emily Barrata Quinn, interview with the author, September 18, 2013.

247 *"Bennett was a little guy"*: Thomas Engel, interview with the author, November 11, 2012.

248 *"as witless as it is gutless"*: Vincent Canby, "'Greek Tycoon,' Rotogravure Style: Two Jacquelines," *New York Times*, May 12, 1978.

250 *"It took a year out of my life"*: Leonard Leibman, interview with the author, November 12, 2011.
*"I held back no realistic appraisals"*: Gerald Walpin, interview with the author, November 13, 2012.

253 *Allen was fined $5,000 and given two months in jail*: Eric Kronfeld, interview with the author, October 31, 2011.

254 *"He never thought he'd be found guilty"*: Beverly Winston, interview by Joe Mc-Ewen, February 11, 2008.

## 14. No Sympathy for the Devil

258 *"I'm afraid the season didn't end with a bang"*: Frank Rich, "Stage: 'It Had to Be You,' Taylor-Bologna Comedy," *New York Times*, May 11, 1981.
*"a temper tantrum in two acts"*: Frank Rich, "Stage: Drama by Albee, 'Man Who Had 3 Arms,'" *New York Times*, April 6, 1983.

259 *"There was a laundry list"*: Gregg Geller, interview with the author, September 7, 2012.

264 *"Warner was paying his share"*: Don Zakarin, interview by Joe McEwen, December 17, 2007.

266 *"I've told him to fuck off"*: Jazz Summers, *Big Life* (London: Quartet Books, 2013).

267 *"I was very bad today"*: Mick Rock, interview with the author, November 18, 2014.

268 *"They used to have some bitter fights"*: Phil Spector, interview by Bill Flanagan, April 24, 2008.

269 *"I really liked him"*: Irving Azoff, interview with the author, November 17, 2014.

271   *Klein at her apartment:* Jann Wenner, interview with the author, October 2, 2012.

273   *"distinctly against the ethical tenets of modern public relations":* Rosanna M. Fiske, "Letter to the Editor: Against All the Tenets of Modern PR," *Financial Times,* September 1, 2011. For further discussion of Brown Lloyd James's reputation, see Emily Heil, "In the Loop: Ecuador's Embassy Hires PR Firm," *Washington Post,* July 19, 2012.

274   *"Did Allen Klein die":* Peter Brown, interview with the author, February 8, 2012.

# INDEX